To Joan

with my best wishes

Robert [signature]

May 7, 2011

FROM TAJIKISTAN TO THE MOON
(A MEMOIR)

*A Story of Tragedy, Survival and
Triumph of the Human Spirit*

Robert Frimtzis

Copyright © 2008 by Robert Frimtzis

Published by

ECLIPTIC PUBLISHING

P. O. Box 9807
Rancho Santa Fe, CA 92087
bfrim@cox.net

Library of Congress Control Number   2008902890

Printed in the United States of America

Cloth ISBN: 978-0-615-19903-0
Paper ISBN: 978-0-615-20102-3

*This memoir has been written in memory of
my eleven relatives and all the innocent
six million Jews brutally
murdered by the hands of the Nazis
and their sympathizers during World War II.*

Rubin Frimtzis
Sarah Frimtzis
Hannah Fleishman
Zalman Fleishman
Itzhak Fleishman
Freida Rifka Fleishman
Benjamin Iusim
Tuba Iusim
Pesia Iusim
Israel Nulman
Abraham Nulman

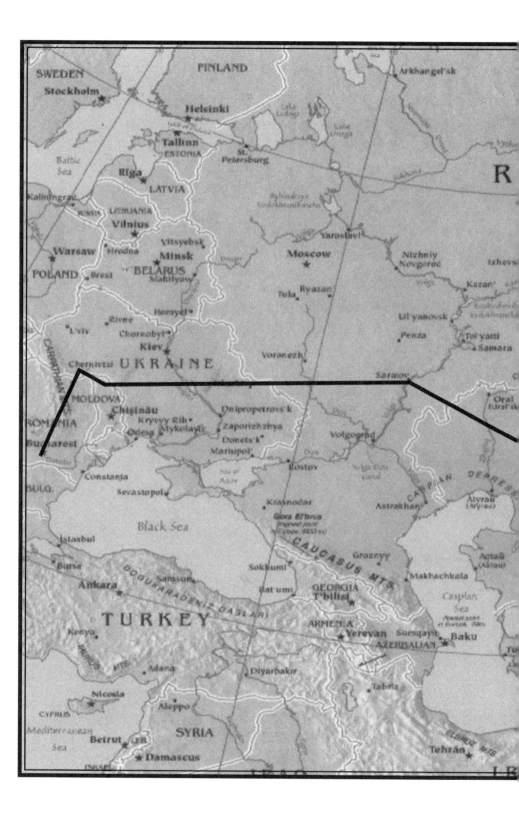

CONTENTS

ACKNOWLEDGEMENTS viii

PREFACE ix

DEDICATION xi

PROLOG xii

Part One: **THE WAR YEARS (1941 – 1945)** 1

Chapter 1   GERMANY INVADES THE SOVIET UNION 3

Chapter 2   OUR ESCAPE – BY FOOT 18

Chapter 3   OUR OWN HORSES AND WAGON 28

Chapter 4   CROSSING THE RIVER DNIEPER 36

Chapter 5   THE TRAINS 40

Chapter 6   TASHKENT 48

Chapter 7   LIFE IN STALINABAD 54

Chapter 8   FIRST FULL-TIME JOB 76

Chapter 9   THE CIVILIAN POPULATION SUFFERS 80

Chapter 10   THINKING OF LEAVING STALINABAD 85

Chapter 11   ENGELS 89

Part Two   **RETURNING HOME (1945)** 97

Chapter 12   RETURN TO BELTZ 99

Chapter 13   DISAPPOINTMENT IN BELTZ 109

Chapter 14   CHERNOVITZ 115

Part Three **THE ROAD TO AMERICA**
             (1946 – 1950) 121
Chapter 15   ROMANIA 123
Chapter 16   HUNGARY 135
Chapter 17   AUSTRIA – Vienna 142
Chapter 18   THE ALPS 147
Chapter 19   ITALY 153
Chapter 20   SWITZERLAND 174
Chapter 21   BARLETTA – The Second Time 186
Chapter 22   VOYAGE TO AMERICA 191

Part Four **LIFE IN AMERICA (1950 -)** 209
Chapter 23   BROOKLYN 211
Chapter 24   THOMAS JEFFERSON HIGH SCHOOL 224
Chapter 25   THE COLLEGE YEARS 231
Chapter 26   ROMANCE 250
Chapter 27   FIRST ENGINEERING JOB 260
Chapter 28   ENGAGEMENT AND WEDDING 264
Chapter 29   COLUMBIA UNIVERSITY 278
Chapter 30   SAN DIEGO 282
Chapter 31   LOS ANGELES 293
Chapter 32   TRIPS TO ISRAEL AND EUROPE 330
Chapter 33   OUR OWN BUSINESS 343
Chapter 34   FINAL THOUGHTS AND
             PERSONAL REFLECTIONS 349

Epilogue   361

ACKNOWLEDGEMENTS

I am grateful to my wife, Annette, for her support and encouragement as I wrote this memoir and for all her help in managing the computer. I thank Jeanne Patterson for her early review of my manuscript and many helpful suggestions. Her writing class served as an inspiration. I'm grateful to Kia and her writer's group for editing and encouragement. A special thank you goes to Laura Taylor who painstakingly edited the manuscript making it the book it is today. I also thank Cheri Pogeler for proofreading the final manuscript.

PREFACE

I have many reasons for writing this book. In addition to fulfilling my solemn promise to my mother, I want to express my gratitude to America for allowing me to come to freedom and for opportunities unequaled anywhere in the world. I am an immigrant, and I support legal immigration. It makes our country great.

I knew for a long time that I would one day write the story of my life. The actual idea took place during the darkest days of World War II. I was ten years old when my mother told me, "Remember, should we survive, you must promise me that you'll write a book about our experiences. You must make sure the world knows what happened to innocent people so it may never be repeated."

My answer to her was always the same, "Yes, Mama, I promise, but first we must survive."

For many years after the war, I did not dare discuss the war years. I was embarrassed and unwilling to reveal my fears, and the subhuman existence we endured and our fight for survival. Besides, I wondered, who would comprehend it? What words could I use to describe our feelings at the time? Since I felt uncomfortable talking about my past, writing a book about it seemed impossible during much of my life. I had higher priorities to concentrate on, getting an education, earning a living and taking care of my family. Only after I retired did I begin to think about fulfilling my solemn promise to my mother. By then, the anger and the fire in my heart had subsided somewhat. I had learned to live with what had happened to my parents and me.

In addition to fulfilling my promises to Mother, I felt a

new obligation to document my life story for the benefit of my children and grandchildren, as well as for the benefit of those who know little of the past. Every survivor's story is different. Future generations should be aware, and hopefully learn from it.

I felt that my story is of historic significance as I am the last of a generation to have lived through the horrific, never to be forgotten events of World War II. I bear testimony to my life as a young boy caught up in the ugly subhuman existence of a war refugee, a displaced person, separated by unseen borders of discrimination and war, who managed to live a full and rewarding life making a difference in the world for generations to come.

Mine is a personal and human story. It presents all aspects of my life, including the good times in America. It is especially gratifying to describe a life that started out hellishly and turned out happy. The transition from bitter to sweet was challenging and it made for an interesting life.

I hope my experience will serve as an example and inspire others whose life is troubled. To them I say, "Don't give up! If I could do it, anybody can in America!"

DEDICATION

I dedicate this book to my mother, Sophie, and to my father, Gregory.

Whenever my dear mother's soul looks over me, and my family, she will know that I kept my promise to write this book.

I credit my father with saving our lives. It was his foresight to leave our bombed out house and the city we lived, and to guide us to safety when there seemed to be none.

PROLOG

A BIT OF HISTORY

LYING 78 miles north and much smaller than the capital city Kishinev, Bălți (pronounced Beltz in Romanian and Moldavian, and Beltsy in Russian) is the largest city in northern Bessarabia, a region defined by the rivers Prut on the west, and Dniester on the east. The two rivers run from north to south, emptying into the Black Sea. West of the River Prut is Romania. East of the River Dniester is Ukraine. Until World War I in 1918, Bessarabia belonged to Czarist Russia, then to Romania until 1940, followed by the Soviet Union until 1941, Romania and Germany until 1944, and then the USSR again. After the collapse of the Soviet Union in 1991, Bessarabia became the major part of the Republic of Moldova.

The earliest chronicles mention Beltz as far back as the 15th Century. It began as a settlement at the confluence of two small rivers, Reut and Reutsel. Early on, various groups controlled the area, including Moldavians, Turks, Crimeans, Poles, and Lithuanians. The Tatars also roamed the area, burning the land.

In 1711, during the Prut campaign, Peter the First of Russia made Beltz a principal base of military supplies for his army. However, as soon as the Russian forces retreated to the River Dniester, the Crimean Tatars attacked the settlement again, plundered it, and set it on fire.

In 1766 Moldavian sovereign Alexander Gicka gave the

lands near the Reut to the mechant brothers Konstantin and Jordaky Panaite. The settlement grew rapidly and became a borough. The first recorded Jewish presence in Beltz was 1779. By 1817, there were 244 Jewish families in residence in the community.

In 1812, Bessarabia joined Russia. Six years later, Beltz became a town and a district center. Its economy and population flourished as trade developed, because Beltz was situated on the trade routes connecting Odessa, Kishinev, Bendery, and Ismail with Soroky, Khotin and Mogilev Podolsky. This geographical position made Beltz a trade center of the North Bessarabian province. The town's importance grew after a railway junction was constructed there in 1894. By 1897, the Jewish population had grown to more than 10,000.

On January 23, 1918, Beltz was occupied by Romania, and Bessarabia fell under Romanian rule for 22 years.

On June 28, 1940, the Red Army crossed the River Dniester and without firing a shot, reoccupied, or as the Russians claimed, "liberated" all of Bessarabia. The Germans and Romanians attacked the Soviet Union on June 22, 1941, and within the first week, destroyed about two-thirds of the city's buildings. By the end of August 1941, nine weeks after the German invasion, fewer than 9,000 of the 32,000 Jews who'd lived in the Beltz district (according to the census of 1930) remained and were deported to concentration camps in Transnistria.

With few remaining Jews, by 1992 the population of Beltz numbered about 600,000, half the population of Kishinev.

PART ONE:

THE WAR YEARS (1941 – 1945)

CHAPTER 1

GERMANY INVADES THE SOVIET UNION

"PROSYPAISIA Buma! *Vstavai* (Wake up, Buma! Get up)!"

From the depths of sleep, I heard Mama and felt her shaking me. Her words barely registered. I slowly opened my eyes. The electric light from the ceiling made me squint. I saw Mama bending over me, her light brown hair falling about her plump, fair face.

"There's an earthquake." Fear shown in her eyes. "We must run outside, hurry!" She yanked me out of bed.

I felt the house shake, heard the wooden floor creak. The sounds of glass and china breaking accompanied the violent movements of the earth.

"Quick!" Mama screamed. "Get out before the house falls on us!"

Papa, Mama, and I stumbled out of the house and onto our street, a main thoroughfare in Beltz, Bessarabia. I saw darting silhouettes of people against the lights emanating from each open door. Neighbors filled the street with noise and commotion.

"Another tremor!" Mama lamented, wringing her hands. Her large nightshirt billowed around her body.

"*Oy, Gevald!* It's shaking again!" cried others in Yiddish, the predominant language of the neighborhood, although I spoke Russian with my parents.

Even though I was on my feet, eyes barely open, I remained disoriented until the second jolt. That tremor brought me to my senses and my heart started pounding. I grew accustomed to the darkness, and I realized that everybody was barefoot, in his or her pajamas, nightgowns, or underwear.

"Are you alright?" asked Grandpa Zeilig as he and Grandma Hannah hurried toward us. "That last shock might have done some damage to our houses."

Mama's parents lived next door, our houses separated by a courtyard. The room fronting the street housed their restaurant. Grandpa, in his seventies with short gray facial hair and large strong hands, towered over Grandma. Her long white hair framed her gentle features. Our neighbors converged in the center of the cobblestone road.

"We must stay away from the houses and electric poles." Papa pulled me by my hand. "They might fall." Barefoot, wearing pajamas, his slim profile, slight belly, and bushy black hair were outlined by the lights of our windows and open front door.

That 1940 summer night in Beltz, a midsized, formerly Romanian city of about 100,000 residents, was warm. Everyone stayed in the street until dawn, fearing another quake or dangerous aftershocks.

I was a nine-year-old husky boy with blue eyes, a freckled face, and light brown curly hair, cut short. Barefoot and wearing shorts, I felt the same fear as everyone else. This was the first earthquake I'd ever experienced. For weeks afterwards, our neighbors talked about it, and how fortunate we were that no one was injured.

One year later, on June 22, 1941, at about 4:00 in the morning, we awakened again to strong earth tremors and muffled rumbling. The memory of the previous summer remained fresh in our minds. Papa, Mama, and I again fled into the street.

As we stood together, we felt another tremor. Once again,

our neighbors noisily vacated their homes on a warm summer night. Clad in their nightclothes, they milled about in the street, fearing more tremors. Many compared the previous year's rumbles to the current shaking. No one seemed overly worried. Nevertheless, we all waited for daylight before returning to our homes.

As night gave way to dawn, we heard new sounds.

Suddenly, I noticed black dots high in the sky. I tugged Papa's arm, pointing upward.

"Look, Papa! I see three airplanes! Do you see them?"

"Oh, yes, I see." He watched the dots overhead. After some consideration, he added, "I hope they are our Soviet planes. If not, we're in big trouble."

The neighbors speculated on the possibility of Soviet Air Force exercises or war engulfing our region. Without warning, a dogfight in the sky above us, machine guns blasting, grabbed my attention. Although the airplanes flew at a lower altitude, we couldn't identify friend or foe. I was thrilled to witness a dogfight, but my excitement turned to fear as I began to realize that Germany must have attacked us.

Visibly shaken, Uncle Tolia, Mama's younger brother, and his wife Sonia, approached us. Aunt Sonia breathed heavily from the exertion of hurrying from their house a block away.

"Hitler attacked us!" declared Uncle Tolia. "We're at war, I have no doubts."

Grandma, her youngest sister Tuba, her husband Benny, and their daughter Pesia, a year my senior, still huddled in the street. Pesia's family lived in the house behind us, sharing our backyard.

"I'm afraid you're right." Papa looked worried.

A tremendous explosion occurred half an hour later. Black smoke billowed into the sky. The Soviet-built military airport, constructed between Beltz and the small town Alexandreny shortly after the Russians arrived in Bessarabia, belched smoke and ash, fouling our air even though far from town.

"Look! Bronia, Uncle Shulim and Aunt Liza are here," I announced to the family.

Uncle Shulim, Mama's oldest brother, limped as he mopped sweat from his shaven head. Overweight, and fair-skinned like all of Mama's family, the neighbors referred to him as Shulim *der Krimmer*, the lame, due to his limping, the result of a child-hood injury. By contrast, Bronia, my age, looked sallow and had black hair like her mother. They lived about a block from us toward Petrogradsky, a rural Christian, mainly Polish suburb.

"That was some explosion. They must have hit the airport," said Uncle Shulim.

"That's what everybody thinks," replied Papa.

Uncle Tolia asked, "What other military targets are in the area?"

"*Calaras cu Schimb,*" answered Papa, referring to the military barracks near the large Jewish hospital in the city where Uncle Zioma, Mama's youngest brother, had done his residency.

The bombs at the airport created panic and pandemonium among the military in Beltz. June 22, 1941 fell on a Sunday. Most military personnel had spent their day off in the city and were caught completely by surprise. Within minutes, Red Army officers, some on foot and others using any means of transporta-tion available – horseback, horse and buggy, and trucks – rushed in the direction of the airport. Some dressed as they ran with their gun belts gripped in their hands.

Soon after, military trucks camouflaged with tree branches and leaves rumbled down our street, a consequence of the bombs that had destroyed the fuel tanks at the airport.

"They must be moving the first fatalities from the airport bombings!" exclaimed Papa.

"What else would they cover with branches?" wondered Uncle Tolia.

"Oh, my God," cried Mama. "Dead people already?"

Grandma Hannah, worried and exhausted, pressed her trem-bling hands together. Cousin Pesia started to cry.

"Don't cry," Aunt Tuba consoled Pesia, hugging and kissing her.

The conversation regarding bodies reminded me of the only dead person I had ever seen. The previous winter Grandpa Zeilig had died after a short bout with stomach problems. The family thought his fear of not being able to pay the Soviet government's high taxes, which they imposed on all so called "capitalists" (in reality, small businesses), had caused his death. He'd owned a small restaurant-tavern and the house he lived in, ours, the one Aunt Tuba and my friend Hersh lived in, and Uncle Shulim's.

After his body had been washed and rinsed with a bucket of water by the *Hevra kaddisha,* undertakers, he'd been placed on the floor with lighted candles following Jewish tradition, as a man watched over him during the night, because the dead must not be abandoned.

I was heartbroken and confused about Grandpa's death, having spent a great deal of time with him every day. I found it hard to believe that he was gone forever. How was it, I wondered, that his soul had left his body? I knew the dead couldn't move, yet I expected him to, and I thought it cruel to put him in the ground. Listening to the talk of dead people, dread coursed through me.

My thoughts then turned to the earliest recollections of Grandpa, when I was five. It was a hot and humid summer afternoon. A cloudburst interrupted my playing in the backyard. The initial heavy raindrops hit and raised the dust off the ground. Instantly the air smelled of dust. Soon it would turn into thick mud, the kind our town Beltz was known for. To get out of the rain I ran through my grandparent's kitchen door and into their house. I then proceeded through the dining room and into the room fronting the street which was my Grandpa Zeilig's restaurant. There I joined him at the open front door watching the heavy rain.

"Grandpa, look at all the *utachki* (little ducks in Russian),"

I said. That is what we called the beads of water lifting off the ground as each raindrop hit the puddles.

"These are really big ducks," replied Grandpa. "We also call them *kachkalach* in Yiddish."

After a while the rain subsided and my attention turned to the calendar. It hung on the wall perpendicular to the front door, the only decoration in the restaurant. The back wall had a door in the center leading to the dining room. Between that door and the wall with the calendar were shelves full of bottles of vodka, various liquors including *tsuica*, a Romanian whiskey, and wines. In front of the floor-to-ceiling shelves stood a bar. Scattered through the room were six square tables and chairs.

"Grandpa, why do you have a calendar in here?"

"To be able to tell the day and month."

"What are the large numbers on top?" I asked.

"That is the year." He walked over to the calendar, pointed and identified each number. "You see a 1, a 9, a 3, and a 5. We are in the year 1935."

From 4:00 that morning until noon, we heard no announcements of any kind on the radio. My friends Benny, Hersh and I, as well as most of our neighbors milled around in the street, listening to rumors and speculations. We knew that we were at war, but we didn't want to believe it. Numbness to the reality of our circumstances overtook us, making us feel like spectators. No one thought about preparations for survival.

At noon we gathered around the radio and listened with fear to Comrade Vyacheslav Mikhailovich Molotov, the Foreign Minister of the Soviet Union, announce that we'd been brutally attacked by Germany. That official announcement brought terror into our hearts. Everyone fell silent, horrified by the reality we now faced.

"No! Not another war after the pogroms of World War I," Grandma said, breaking the silence. "Hitler is a monster. He hates the Jews."

Terrified, I asked Papa, "What are we going to do now?"

Papa, his disturbed emotions evident, rubbed his chin while collecting his thoughts. At last, he addressed us. "We must stay close to the house so we can react quickly if something happens. We need to assemble emergency supplies, food, water, and flashlights. We'll use Grandpa's cellar as a shelter."

"You mean, in case the city is bombed?" I asked, unable to believe what might occur.

"Yes," he said. "We're only about fifty kilometers from the Romanian border, and Romania is allied with Germany. As Grandma said, Hitler's loathing of the Jews is no secret."

Papa's warning brought to mind the times he'd sat at the dinner table, reading the newspaper to Mama and me. His own commentary always followed. He had been greatly concerned about *Kristallnacht* before the Nazis occupied part of Poland and Czechoslovakia. He had shown me the headlines when Denmark and Norway were invaded, followed a month later by France, Holland and the Benelux countries. The *Maginot Line* crumbled and France fell. The latter event had happened shortly before the Red Army marched into Bessarabia and "liberated" us from Romania.

"Grisha, he's too young," Mama often objected. "There is plenty of time for him to find out about the world's problems."

"You're protecting him too much, Sonia. We live in turbulent times and I think Buma should be informed about things affecting all of Europe"

The ensuing conversation interrupted my thoughts.

"What about the nonaggression pact between Germany and the Soviet Union?"

Uncle Tolia paced the room as he spoke. "What about the mighty Red Army? They should be able to slow down the German advance."

"The Germans softened up the targets ahead of sweeping into our territory. The short distance from the Romanian border may not allow the Red Army much time to assemble a meaningful defense." Obviously worried, Papa paused. "I know it is not a pleasant thought, but we ought to choose a meeting place in case our neighborhood is bombed."

"I suggest the Petrogradsky. Past my house, the area is all Christian and sparsely populated. The Germans won't bomb there," Uncle Shulim said. Everyone nodded in agreement before each frightened family returned to their homes.

"Buma, you will help us prepare the shelter," said Papa. "Fetch a pail of water and three loaves of bread, and take them to Grandma's cellar. I'll try to buy salami, cheese, and cold cuts, if I can find them."

"Grisha, I'll assemble blankets, candles, and a flashlight," said Mama. "You should bring down a small table and four chairs from Father's restaurant."

The bakeries and some food stores stayed open only on Monday, the second day after the invasion. The villagers stopped bringing chickens, milk, cheese, fruit, and vegetables into the open market, so the stores closed.

Not only was the attack launched on a Sunday when all Soviet officers were in Beltz on leave, with no one available to take command as the Germans attacked, but most military equipment had been dismantled for cleaning and overhaul prior to that infamous weekend. Years later, we learned that some Red Army divisions from the Ukraine and Belarus had joined the Germans to fight against the Soviets. The Soviets' betrayal by some of their high-ranking, pro-German military officers, who hated the Bolsheviks could be very likely attributed to the Stalin purges, which had wiped out many of the senior officers and some of the most talented people the Soviets possessed.

The events of that morning changed my life forever. The attacks came in increasing frequency for the next several days and nights. The selective bombing targeted the Jewish neighborhoods. All Jewish sections of town went up in flames within three days of the start of the war. Yet the center of town remained intact.

The *Primaria,* our Town Hall, and the *Prefectura,* the Justice Department, two large buildings located on an impressive grassy knoll, surrounded by flowers, and enclosed by a tall wrought iron fence, stood untouched. Those buildings engendered authority, fear, and respect. The *Sobor,* the newest cathedral where as a first grader I went to see our King Carol II during its consecration, was intact. The *Lux* and the *Modern,* the two movie houses in Beltz where I spent hours enjoying Charlie Chaplin and Laurel and Hardy (known to me as *Stan si Bran* in Romanian or *Pat e Patashon* in Russian), were unscathed. *Liceu Comercial* where I had attended one year before the Soviets took over Bessarabia, and *Liceu Ion Creanga,* named after a famous Romanian poet and writer, remained undamaged. *Gymnasias* or *liceus,* were eight-year schools accepting children after completion of a four-year grade school, *scola primara.* Only the Church of St. Nicolas also called the Old Church, located at the edge of the Jewish section, sustained damage to its dome.

A single plane flying unopposed would drop its load and after a quiet period, the destruction would resume. We lived in constant fear, not knowing what to expect as the aerial bombing continued. No Soviet ground fire challenged the German aircraft, nor were there any air battles after the one dogfight I had witnessed on that first Sunday morning.

"A Romanian, someone familiar with the Jewish neighborhoods in Beltz, must be directing the bomb drops," reasoned Mama.

Her logic was credible, because the Romanians hated Jews.

"The Jewish neighborhoods were probably targeted well in advance of the invasion," argued Papa.

Late in the afternoon, I heard the roar of an approaching bomber. German warplanes made a different noise than the Soviet counterparts. Their hum was somewhat rhythmic, a modulated – hum – hum – hum, instead of the constant drone of the Russian planes. I'd quickly learned to recognize that sound of the enemy.

Fear consumed me. When the bombs began to fall in our vicinity, the jeopardy of my predicament overwhelmed me. Confusion and numbness took over. A fire blazed about a block from our house. The surreal image felt like a dream. In that horrific instant, I did not know what to do or where to hide. I froze, becoming paralyzed. My parents emerged from our house. Dumbfounded, they stared at the fire.

"That is really close," Mama wheezed, trying to catch her breath as fear induced her asthma. "It could have hit my brother Tolia's house!"

"*Oy Gotuniu!*" Grandma exclaimed, running out of her house. "We're being bombed!"

"Come quickly!" Papa gripped my arm and jerked me from my shock, "We must run to the Petrogradsky before the bombs drop on us!"

"Run, children!" cried Grandma. "I'll catch up with you!"

I did not question my father. Neighbors, screaming and panicking, accompanied us. As we passed the bakeries and the water kiosk, I turned my head and looked over my shoulder for Grandma, but I could not see her in the crowd. Mama, overweight and asthmatic under stress slowed us down. Panic stricken, her normally light cheeks were fire red, wet from perspiration, and her neatly combed hair, gathered in a bun, disheveled. As soon as we reached the streets of Petrogradsky we paused to catch our breath. Grandma Hannah stumbled up to us shaking, uncomfortably gasping for air like Mama. What's next? I wondered.

"Stay here!" Papa ordered. "I'm going to see what can be salvaged from our house."

"Don't be a hero!" Mama cautioned him, "Take whatever you can, but be safe! Be careful!"

"I will!" He ran back towards our street. "Don't worry!"

The duration for Papa to gather some of our belongings

and then return to us should have taken him about an hour. His absence seemed to last forever.

"What takes him so long?" Mama was worried sick. "Why did I let him go into the bombs and fire? Why did he decide to endanger his life to save a few *shmates,* things?"

"Don't worry, Sonia." Grandma held on to Mama, trying to pacify her. "He knows what he's doing."

She became hysterical by the time I finally spotted Papa. "He's coming!" I shouted. We both ran to him.

"Oh, thank God that I see you!" Mama cried out.

Over his shoulder, Papa carried a smoke-soiled white bed sheet stuffed with clothing and valuables. Behind him, Uncle Benny hauled one of our rugs, while Aunt Tuba held a small bundle. Their daughter Pesia followed in their wake.

"Our home was on fire," Papa, out of breath, struggled to say. "And this was all I was able to save." He dropped his burden. "I managed to get out before the ceiling and roof collapsed. Benny saved some of their things, and he helped carry our carpet." Both men's faces were black from smoke and wet from perspiration.

Papa, of medium height, slim, and fairly fit, looked exhausted. He took out a handkerchief from his pants' pocket and wiped the sweat from his face. It turned wet and black. Uncle Benny, normally a man of few words, said nothing. He looked dazed as he dropped the carpet to the ground, his straight, salt and pepper hair in sharp contrast to his carbon covered face. Aunt Tuba, soundlessly sobbing, held tight to Mama and Pesia, the depth of her anguish over our losses evident, her tear-streaked face contorted as she tried not to cry aloud.

For the first time in my life, I considered Papa a hero, the image reinforced by his comment that the ceiling and roof had caved in during his departure from our home. I felt proud of him. I also felt jolted fully awake from an inconceivable nightmare and I frantically began to question everyone.

"This is all that is left of our house? Where will we sleep?

How will we live? What about tomorrow?" I asked, but no one answered me.

The agony and distress on my usually calm Mama's face as tears streamed from her terrorized eyes prompted me to shut up. I continued my struggle to comprehend the severity and finality of what had happened and was still happening to my family.

Our house and our entire neighborhood burned to the ground on June 25 and 26. To survive, we ran from the inferno surrounding us. That night, we stayed in the sparsely populated outskirts of Petrogradsky. There was no other escape route, nowhere to flee. We watched the falling bombs and the engulfing flames all night long. Not all our neighbors managed to escape. They became the earliest casualties of the war.

That night my mother's youngest brother Uncle Zioma, a physician, remained in town to provide voluntary medical help. His house had not yet been bombed, since it was not in a strictly Jewish neighborhood. Later, he came to check on our family's condition.

"Thank God I found you. I could not believe my own eyes. Your whole neighborhood is up in flames." He wiped dirt from his clean-shaven face. He was tall, his bald spot barely visible under the ash covering him. "I ran through the fire and smoke, praying you had escaped. I hoped I would find you here."

We in turn were relieved that Uncle Zioma was alright and were grateful that he'd found us.

That night, our whole family was together, except for Grandpa Zeilig's brother, Itzik and his wife, Freide Rivke. They were old and lived in a different part of town called Kishineovskaia. We never saw them again. Too old and frail to flee, they became victims of the war.

Gathered around were people just like us, people whose homes had been destroyed, or those who expected their homes to be bombed. The crowd consisted of young and old, men, women and children. Some stared vacantly at the consuming blazes. Others wept.

The smaller children were scared, and cried, although the adults tried to calm them.

Everything seemed unreal to me. I felt small and insignificant. I watched in silent horror as the whole neighborhood I lived in all my life went up in smoke. Our entire block, all that was so familiar, the houses, Grandpa's cellar where we hid, ate delicious pickles and tasted wine from the spigots in the wooden barrels. The backyards where I played, my garden proudly built with my own hands, the mandolin that I never learned to play, were all gone. A horrible nightmare took hold of me, except it was real. I suddenly realized the finality and destruction of everything I knew for the last ten years. It disappeared during one single night.

I also felt confused, because the people I had expected to protect me, my father, mother, our relatives, helpless and heartbroken now, were unable to prevent this cataclysm. They too were devastated and dazed. The future looked bleak, a vast barren landscape. Mama and Grandma were crying. Aunt Tuba, slim with a large scar showing through her straight black hair and another on her hand, stood lifeless, frozen, holding on to Pesia. The *Kazaks* had attacked her with swords during the pogroms in 1917 and left her for dead. Sobbing, I tried to hide my tears. Shell shocked, exhausted, overwhelmed, and shivering, despite the heat, I ached all over. I stood aimlessly staring at the fire, sparks, and smoke until I finally sank down onto the unpaved road and used our sheet-wrapped belongings as a pillow. The expressions on my parents' faces and the lamenting all around me was more than I could endure. Nor could I deal with or understand what we would do tomorrow.

No one slept on that hot, windy, and smoky summer night. A few hundred of us gathered on the dusty, unpaved streets with a few sparse houses. The sky resembled a blazing inferno. The air was hot. Smoke, ashes, and soot blew everywhere. I strained for oxygen, the smoke burning my eyes. Mama wheezed and coughed. The scene was one of utter despair. We were all watching helplessly as the neighborhood disintegrated before our very eyes. At that time, I could not distinguish or identify our individual house from the huge fire from about four blocks away.

The crowd was desolate. Families clustered together, while those separated searched for familiar faces or other family members. Some people wrung their hands or covered their eyes and rocked side to side, questioning what they would do, where they would go, and how they would face an uncertain future.

No one in authority – no Red Army, no fire fighters, no police – appeared to offer shelter, food, or guidance. Although I didn't realize it at the time, we'd become refugees.

Short wave radios were illegal, confiscated by the Soviets after their arrival in Bassarabia, and replaced by a speaker with an on/off and volume control button. Somebody spread the word that a short wave radio tuned to Bucharest had broadcast that *Mihai* (Michael), the King of Romania, was expected to have tea in Kishinev, the capital of Bessarabia, on June 28, the first anniversary of Russia's annexation of Bessarabia. King Michael, the son of King Carol II who had abdicated, was a very young fascist. This news implied that within only two, or at most, three days the Germans would occupy Bessarabia or at least Kishinev. The thought of the frontline coming through and being overrun further terrified everyone.

That fateful night, as we stood in the street, our entire family discussed our next step. My father became the driving force behind the decision to leave the area as soon as possible.

"We cannot stay here in the street, nor can I go into the city and wait for the Nazis. If we are to survive these killers, we must get as far from the front as possible and we must do it quickly."

"How can we just run away?" questioned Uncle Zioma, "Would you if your house was not burned down, Grisha? Let's not panic. The Red Army will hold back the Germans."

Uncles Zioma and Tolia chose to wait and see what would develop in Beltz, and Grandma decided to stay with them.

"We are leaving in the morning." Papa had made up his mind.

Uncles Shulim, Benny and their families decided to accompany us. This turning point signaled the end of our life in Beltz with our extended family. Soon daylight would reveal the full reality of the night's devastation. I shut my eyes tightly, desperate to etch upon my memory our house, each room in it and the neighborhood where I had lived all my life. Sadly, I realized how wonderful life had been only days ago, before the bombs started falling. Only ten years old, I didn't realize that my father's decision to leave Beltz would make the difference between our survival and death.

With my eyes closed, slowly our street appeared in my mind. I consciously memorized every facet of life on our city block, from the homes to the small shops to the families who populated my world. I also promised myself that even the most benign events of daily life would remain etched forever in my mental landscape of childhood. Little did I know that such memories would give me courage in the months and years ahead.

CHAPTER 2

OUR ESCAPE – BY FOOT

THE morning after our neighborhood was bombed and our house reduced to rubble, we left Beltz. Papa and Uncle Shulim hired two drivers with wagons and horses to transport us to Gregory Revenko, a Gentile and a good friend of Grandpa Zeilig's, who lived about 8 kilometers away in the village of Igorovka. Papa, Uncle Shulim and Uncle Benny loaded the wagons and we said our painful goodbyes to those who had chosen to stay in Beltz.

"I hope the Red Army will stop the Germans," said Uncle Zioma with a heavy heart.

"If not," added Uncle Tolia, "we'll try to catch up with you."

From Revenko's, Papa, Mama and I intended to travel to Ataki, where Papa's parents resided. Uncle Shulim's destination was Brichani where Aunt Liza's parents lived.

"*Oi, mine liebe tochter, Got veist tzi meer valin ziech noch ein mol zeien* – God knows if we'll ever see each other again," Grandma Hannah cried bitterly, clutching at Mama. "God should watch over you and give you peace."

As she spoke, I realized that she didn't expect to see us again.

"*Vein nisht, Mome, lo meer hoffen az mir valin noch zein tzuzamen gich*. Don't cry Mama, let's hope we'll soon be together," my Mama replied, tears streaming down her face.

"Let them go, Mother," Uncle Zioma finally interrupted. "We'll see them soon. Ataki is only a short distance away."

We climbed into the wagons and the horses pulled out slowly. Mama continued to weep, her tears making me sob. Our departure felt even more heart wrenching than the painful experience of watching the inferno of our burning homes. In the stark morning light, the desolate unpaved street where we had spent the frightening night hiding revealed a sinister sight. Smoldering skeletons of houses and chimneys stood like ghostly sentries in the once thriving neighborhood. Only death and an eerie silence remained. A chunk of the city was missing and with it a chunk of everyone's heart. Separating from our family with an unknown future magnified the tragedy. From the back of our wagon, I watched my hometown slowly disappear from sight, not knowing if I would ever see my relatives and friends again.

We soon reached the massive stone Old Bridge, also known as the Turkish Bridge, whose arches spanned the River Reut. The Turks had built it during their occupation of Beltz. The *Asmansky Zavod*, a large sugar factory, and a spirits distillery were located on the banks of the river.

We passed through the section of town called Slobazia, which included the Large Railroad Station, *Gara Mare*. Beltz was an important commercial center and a major hub with two railroad stations.

Crossing the bridge brought back memories of my childhood. The river froze each winter and people cut blocks of ice in order to sell them in the summer. In spring, as the ice started to melt, the river would swell. Large chunks of ice clogged the arches, threatening to damage the bridge as the river flooded the adjacent low-lying fields. Every spring, people who lived in small shacks along the river often were stranded on their rooftops as the land flooded. Men in small rowboats tried to rescue them. Watching these rescue attempts was a springtime ritual I'd witnessed with Mama and Grandpa Zeilig. Now, I wondered if I would ever see the Old Bridge again.

When we arrived at Revenko's, he quickly ushered us inside and sent the wagons away so that his neighbors would not realize that he was harboring Jews. Unknown to us, it was a preview of things to come. Revenko offered one of his men to take us with a horse and wagon to the small town of Ataki, which was located on the western side of River Dniester, northeast of Beltz. That was the furthest east one could travel in Bessarabia, because the Dniester separated Bessarabia from Ukraine. Papa's parents, Grandpa Rubin and Grandma Sarah, lived there. Papa wanted to check on them and persuade them to flee further east with us.

Revenko also provided a man with a horse and wagon to take Uncle Shulim and his family to Brichani. Not having anywhere else to go, Uncle Benny and Aunt Tuba chose a village in which they had once lived. They believed that the villagers, who were mainly Gentiles, would protect them. All the villages were predominantly Russian Orthodox Christian, because earlier laws had not permitted Jews to own or cultivate land.

In retrospect, Mama expressed her belief that Uncle Benny's family should have been included in our journey. The only reason they went their own way was because, neither we, nor Shulim asked them to travel with our families. Mama felt that had either family asked, Uncle Benny's family would have joined them. Of course, hindsight is always perfect. Who could have known they'd be slaughtered in that village? Who knew that our path was a better choice? We could have just as easily perished. Mama lived with her regret and guilt for the rest of her life.

Before we left, Papa asked Revenko to store our heavier possessions until we could return for them. Papa knew we needed to travel unencumbered and he sensed that we would not return soon.

"You'll need food for the road." Mrs. Revenko handed us two loaves of bread, cheese, hardboiled eggs and apples.

"God bless you," cried Mama, hugging Gregory's wife. "We thank you for your hospitality and the food."

The sky turned black on the way to Ataki, and a hard rain fell. Sitting in the wagon, my mind wandered to earlier train trips to Ataki and our visits with Papa's parents. I loved to travel by train. The Large Railroad Station in Beltz, to distinguish it from the Small Railroad Station or Pominteni, had a fair size platform that allowed me to watch the trains with their powerful locomotive engines, the noisy puffs of smoke shooting out of the stacks, and steam hissing around the wheels, as they roared into the station. The bars attached to the wheels moved horizontally back and forth, as the wheels turned. I was intrigued and didn't understand their purpose.

Every time the train stopped, the engineer descended holding a can with a spout and oiled what seemed like the joints between the wheels and those horizontal bars. I was excited whenever I saw the station chief, who wore a black uniform with gold buttons and an official hat with a red velvet top and a black shining visor. He seemed to come out onto the platform just before the train approached the station and always held in his hand a circular sign with a concentric circle painted on it.

When the railroad cars doors closed, I watched him raise the circular sign and blow a whistle. The train would start moving, pick up speed, and depart. This well-orchestrated process seemed magical, and it always mesmerized me. I thought that he had so much power. He could start and stop a train. I was puzzled to see the rails and ties move up and down as the wheels rode over them. It amazed me to see the train going around a curve. Perhaps that was the early curiosity of a future engineer.

Grandpa and Grandma Frimtzis, *Dedushka* Riven (Rubin) and *Babushka* Sura (Sarah) lived in a small apartment in Ataki.

I will never forget the colorful geraniums spilling from the flowerboxes on their windowsills.

Ataki, on the western shore of the River Dniester, was the border with Ukraine, the Soviet Union. Across the river from Ataki on the eastern shore, I could see Moghilev Podolsky, a larger city, where Papa's family came from.

Life in Ataki was very quiet compared to Beltz. It was not as hot, and with sandy terrain, it had no dust or mud. Our entertainment there consisted of going to a park or to the railroad station to meet the train and see who arrived into town.

Dedushka Riven, with a white beard and a meticulous appearance, was a frail looking man who spent most of his time reading Hebrew religious books. Since Papa was their only child, he always supported them financially.

"*Dedushka*, how come you always sit and read a book?" I inquired.

"Reading is very important and interesting. I learn a lot from the books. Don't you learn from the books you are assigned to read in school?"

"Yes, but I go to school to learn. *Deduskas* don't go to school."

"No one is too old to learn."

"But *Deushka*, you always read the same Hebrew prayer book."

"No matter how many times I read the *Talmud*, I always learn something new," Grandpa replied.

Grandpa Riven traveled to America as a young man, but he decided that America was not for him. Who can imagine what would have happened if he had stayed there? I certainly would have not existed.

Being soaked to my bones from the penetrating rain brought me back to reality. It must have been the 26th or 27th of June. When we finally arrived, we found my grandparents' house locked and neighbors informed us that a day earlier they crossed the Dniester to Moghilev Podolsky. For extra money,

Papa convinced our driver to take us across to Mogilev. Despite an extensive search, we didn't find them.

The day we were in Moghilev the sky stayed dark and torrential rain fell. By then we, and our belongings, were thoroughly drenched. The dismal weather did nothing to help our downtrodden spirits.

"First we lose our home," Mama lamented, "then we abandon our family in Beltz. Now we've lost Papa's parents, too!"

The driver had to return to Igorovka. We desperately wandered around the stormy town, no idea where to go next. Having traveled so far, we couldn't escape the reality that our journey east and away from the advancing German army had to continue. The pressing concern was how far and how long we could walk.

"Zachary, Basia," Mama said, "what are you doing here?"

While Papa examined a local map at the City Hall and pondered our next destination, Mama had noticed Zachary Volinsky, his wife Basia, and their two sons as they pulled up in a nice wagon drawn by two fine horses. They too had lived in Beltz, several blocks from our house and closer to the Turkish Bridge. Volinsky had owned a feed store. He was well versed in horses, carriages, and wagons.

"As you can see, we escaped with very little from our burning house," answered Zachary while Mama and Basia hugged and wept like long lost relatives finally reunited. "We intend to travel east."

"We're also heading east, but we have no transportation."

Zachary and Papa shook hands. "Let's travel together. You read the map and find the shortest route for us. You can put your belongings in my wagon."

"Zachary, that's a very kind offer," Papa thanked him. "I greatly appreciate it, but I intend to find the safest and not necessarily the shortest route."

Volinsky agreed and the men, once again, shook hands.

"To a safe journey!" Papa declared.

"Na dobryi poot!" repeated Zachary.

Papa laid out the beginnings of an eastward route from village to village avoiding towns, railroads, and stations. His reasoning was to minimize the probability of being bombed, and shot at by enemy warplanes. Main roads and arteries, used by the military would no doubt make them congested, in addition to being major targets of German attacks.

We began our escape and assumed the status of refugees, walking from early morning until past nightfall each day. Volinsky would then leave the road and find a camping spot for the night. He and his sons cared for the horses, while the rest of us huddled close to one another. We slept on the ground under the open sky or beneath a tree, if one was available close to the wagon.

At the beginning, Volinsky allowed Mama and sometimes me to ride in the wagon for short intervals. However, Basia, an obese woman who claimed she could not walk would give us an ugly stare every time we wanted to climb into the wagon. We walked most of the time. At the end of our second week with Volinsky, he told Papa to seek some other means of transporting our belongings. We were not the only people on the road. There were vast numbers of refugees, perhaps extending for miles, with wagons, pushcarts, or on foot.

German warplanes often appeared out of nowhere. The first sight or sound of a plane resulted in instant panic and chaos. Instinct and self-preservation ruled everyone. I would freeze for a split second, then, an adrenaline rush would double my heart rate. Without thinking, we scattered in all directions, hiding under bushes, trees, in cornfields, and under wagons.

"Hide, Buma, hide!" my parents would scream while trying to conceal themselves.

"Hide, Mama, Papa!" I simultaneously shouted at them.

Mothers grabbed infants and ran, or dropped to the ground

covering them for protection. Small children shrieked in fear as they ran, their parents chasing them and calling their names.

The engine noise of the airplanes increased as they descended, deafening, as they flew low overhead and fired at people. Long bursts from machine guns punctuated the air around me as bullets riddled everything nearby. I ran for shelter, hunched with bent head. I dove to the ground, covering my face in my arms and my head with my hands, aware that I couldn't protect myself from being shot. My heart raced so violently, it felt on the verge of jumping out of my chest. The pounding of my heartbeat seemed to compete with, and often modulated the noise of the attack: the droning of the engines, the flying bullets, and the terrified screams of people fleeing. Instinctively, I covered my ears in attempts to drown out the horrible reality, but I never succeeded in silencing the rapid rhythmic banging of my own heart in my eardrums.

The planes often made a second pass. The horses spooked and ran, jeopardizing anyone hidden beneath the wagons. Panic and weeping continued well after the aircraft disappeared. Casualties were common and indiscriminate and more nerve wracking than words can truly ever express.

After thanking God for having saved us, we prayed for Him to keep watch over us. No one ever fully calmed down, the brain unable to forget. At night, I relived the attacks and our attempts to survive. When I managed to sleep, I would awaken in a cold sweat, my body and mind exhausted from nightmares in which I had been shot. Our entire existence became a surreal landscape of loss and the determination to survive, regardless of the peril we still faced.

None of us could have imagined how quickly our whole life would change. Within one week, we had lost our home, our relatives, our friends, our comfort, and our dignity. We had regressed from a civilized to a subhuman existence. We lived and slept on dusty, unpaved rural side roads and in fields. We ate whenever we found nourishment for our exhausted bodies.

Running for our lives was our sole activity. We feared being overrun by the German army, being wounded or killed by the warplanes. Even the local Ukrainian peasants, many of whom were involved in pogroms, hated Jews and eagerly awaited the arrival of the Nazis, to be free to kill us with impunity. We lived in constant fear and total uncertainty of what dangers the next hour, let alone the next day, would bring. Each night we felt grateful to have survived another day.

We stole whatever fruits and vegetables we could find from unattended fields. Need overrode guilt, although the thefts nagged at me. Our hunger bordered on starvation. We were beyond dirty. When it rained, as it often did, our clothes were plastered to our bodies. In the heat of the day, sweat and dust coated us. Our bodies smelled, at times unrecognizable as human. I wore short pants and sandals at the beginning of our journey. Later I walked barefoot to save my shoes. My feet and legs were black with dirt and dust by the end of each day.

Whenever we encountered a stream or other water sources, we attempted to bathe without soap. We learned to do whatever necessary and possible to merely survive. Our will to survive surpassed everything else. Instinct superseded decorum. Like all other living creatures, self-preservation dominated our actions and thoughts.

Time had no meaning to us. We trudged along like zombies on bumpy dirt roads. The longer we walked, the further the fields seemed to stretch. At night and regardless of weather, we slept wherever possible on the ground. By having to beg and barter our remaining possessions for any food from villagers, who despised us, we abandoned our city-bred dignity.

At night, lying on the hard cold ground unable to fall asleep, I developed a private mantra, reminding myself, I have to survive. I will not die. I'm too young to have my life end. I haven't lived yet. Before long, I couldn't tell if I was thinking or if I had been dreaming.

"I dreamt we made it," I would tell Mama in the mornings, "that we will survive. It must be a good sign."

"Let's hope," my worried and exhausted Mama would respond. "It is good."

We felt better for a while, but reality quickly set in as we faced another grueling day.

I longed for basic rules I had hated just weeks ago, such as Papa's insistence on the civility of having clean hands, tidy clothes, impeccable table manners, excessive study time, and his usual strict discipline. Of course, none of these things concerned Papa now. I had realized how fortunate I had been then. Subsisting as we were now, I yearned for his restrictions, and wondered if I would ever again have a chance to live like a civilized human being, with normal standards, which I had taken for granted and even complained about. Now, as we hid and fled, our old lifestyle felt far removed and unattainable.

CHAPTER 3

OUR OWN HORSES
AND WAGON

A S fast as we fled the advancing German army, it took all our strength and courage to stay one step ahead of them. Often news would reach us that the last village we had passed through had been overrun a day or two after we left. Papa often checked at the administration building of a larger village to determine the location of the front lines and to adjust our escape route accordingly. We barely avoided capture by the Germans, as they were moving east as quickly as we were.

"How come you're running away instead of joining the Red Army?" one village administrator guilefully asked my father. "Don't you know that there is a mobilization in effect?"

Terrible fright enveloped Mama and I. We feared Papa would be taken away from us. Then what would we do? What would happen to us?

"My family and I have already suffered the bombing and destruction of our home and town," explained Papa. "I believe I am entitled to evacuate my family to join our only known surviving relative, who is expecting us in Stalinabad, Tajikistan. After that, I will certainly join the army, fight the Nazi invaders, and defend our motherland." He provided the administrators with our Aunt Sheiva's address in Stalinabad. Sheiva was Grandma Hannah's sister. "We are on foot, carrying our meager belongings saved from our bombed-out home," he added. "We use what little we still own to trade for food when we can."

"How long do you think we'll survive?" Mama interrupted, tears streaming down her face. "My young son and I are exhausted and starving. I can barely move."

"Could you spare a horse and wagon from your *kolhoz* (a collective farm)? You'll save three lives," Papa suggested. "We'll return them to another *kolhoz* when we can catch a train."

Somehow, Papa's assurances that he planned to join the army and Mama's pleading convinced the administrators to give us a wagon and horses. With no private property to speak of in the Soviet Union, the two horses and wagon belonged to the collective farm, which was Soviet government property.

"I bet you don't even know that your wagon has wooden axels," Zachary Volinsky made fun when Papa returned triumphantly with them. He pointed at the wagon which sides resembled two ladders positioned horizontally. "What a bargain you got. These are used primarily for lugging straw, and look at the horses. They are in terrible shape and ready to drop dead."

Papa did not answer. It didn't take an expert to see the horses were emaciated. I doubt Papa knew the wagon had wooden axels. We were very happy because from then on we were able to ride instead of walking constantly. We covered greater distances each day. More importantly, our physical conditions improved. Our bodies no longer fatigued, aching from the painful journey and carrying our belongings.

Papa and I named the horses Katia and Vania. Katia bit and kicked at every opportunity. Handling the horses daily with my father, I was bitten once and bucked off several times. We drove slowly on the unpaved, bumpy roads to preserve the horses' energy. Whenever possible, we stopped at rivers, streams, or ponds to wash the horses and ourselves. I was always the first to jump in the river when we found one.

"Be careful! It might be deep," Mama would call after me as she carried our filthy clothes to the water. "You can't swim. Don't get hurt, Buma!"

I splashed, jumped, and played until thoroughly chilled in the refreshingly cool waters. I forgot our plight as refugees, our hunger and fear, and our attempt to outrun the invading German army. I felt, however briefly, like a boy again. I savored these brief respites from the overwhelming agonies that had consumed every waking moment of each strenuous day.

We traveled slowly from village to village, stopping to update our map or to buy or obtain by other means whatever food we could. Some villagers cooperated by trading food for whatever we might have of interest or use to them. Others neither spoke to or traded with us.

For several weeks after the start of the war, most people did not believe the German armies would advance as swiftly as they did. Consequently, most villagers did not dare show their true feelings toward us out of fear of the Soviet authorities. Most people remained civil and willing to barter our clothing, pieces of silver, or even jewelry for eggs, milk, vegetables, fruit, and bread that they had available. However, they made no secret of their disdain for the masses of Jews fleeing through their villages. The anti-Jewish sentiment escalated with every mile gained by the German army. Most Ukrainians welcomed the Germans with open arms, perceiving them as saviors from the harsh Soviet regime.

After several days of absolutely nothing to eat, Papa traded the only suit he'd managed to save for a loaf of bread.

"It is altogether nice of me to trade with you, since you're Jews," a woman informed us. "After the Germans come, you will be in no position to trade anything at all."

Her rhetoric only emphasized the prevailing attitude of the region, serving as additional proof that we were hated by those capable of hating for no reason other than we were Jews. The unvarnished prejudice further depressed us. Starving us was their preference. There was little humanity or simple decency. Yes, anti-Semitism was that strong in Ukraine.

The villagers' attitude reminded me of earlier days when Grandpa Zeilig had many villagers as friends and customers. Although the Romanian Iron Guard and Cuza openly espoused anti-Semitism, that sentiment was not evident in the local villages. Grandpa dealt with the villagers in friendship and with mutual respect.

Our treatment by the Ukrainian villagers was inhumane and cruel. I found it inconceivable and it depressed me to realize that someone I had never known or harmed despised me enough to want me to starve to death. This was long before I had any knowledge of the treatment of Jews in the Nazi run extermination camps. The intense hatred and treatment of one group of people toward another that I'd witnessed and endured at such a young age left a permanent scar on my character during my formative years. Decades passed before I overcame my cynicism and bitterness toward the human race.

We traveled day after day. The days turned into weeks, and the weeks into months. Each day presented new challenges over and above the pain of hunger, the fear of being hunted, and the omnipresence of death. From the beginning of the war, the long caravans of refugees diminished to a point where, at times, ours was the only wagon on the road.

Even though we rarely admired the scenery, I could not help occasionally noticing the picturesque countryside. In spite of our situation and living conditions, we still possessed the human emotion of appreciation.

"Isn't that a beautiful village?" I would point out. "It's just like in a story book."

"I always knew the Ukraine had breathtaking land," Papa would reply, then add, "too bad the people are not very kind. They'd rather lead a pogrom than live peacefully."

The whitewashed houses had straw roofs and picket or

other fences made of unfinished wood. Some houses had colorful sunflowers while others sat in the middle of orchards. Acres of sprawling vegetable gardens surrounded a few houses, which may have belonged to a well-to-do *kolhoz*.

I thought of my vegetable garden I started at the age of about seven. I grew scallions, corn, garlic, dill, and parsley, a couple of sunflowers, radishes, and cucumbers. I made trenches so one could walk without stepping on the growing things. I spent a lot of time planting, watering, and weeding, and I missed the simplicity of those days.

"Today we are eating the veggies from Buma's garden."

Mama's announcement at the dinner table always made me proud. The garden also helped me in my botany class in grade school. It gave me familiarity of the shapes of various leaves, which I could easily identify. At that age, I felt like it was a wonder and somewhat of a miracle that a vegetable grew out of a seed and that I made that happen.

Other villages looked poor and rundown. The houses were not kept up and hadn't been painted in years. Most households had chickens running in the yards. Some had pigs and sheep. When we passed a large *kolhoz*, I noticed several large barns with horses or cows, and lots of acreage. Cattle grazed in the fields. If we slept near a village, the crowing roosters awakened me at dawn. Most of the time we tried to sleep in open fields, away from a village, fearing that the local villagers might try to harm or kill us at night. Being on guard against the constant threat of death wore on me and altered every perception I possessed about the world.

At night, we pulled the wagon off the road, un-harnessed the horses, and let them graze near the wagon while we slept. One starless, very dark, and humid evening my parents fell asleep in the wagon as I guided the horses. I pulled the wagon off the road, tied up the horses as we did every night, and lay down on the ground on a somewhat elevated mound. It felt cooler than trying to squeeze in next to my parents on the wagon on that hot night.

"Wake up! Wake up!" My Mother's wild scream startled me at sunrise. "My God! Look where you're sleeping."

I opened my eyes and as the fog of my sleep lifted, I realized in horror where I was. My body felt anesthetized. For an instant, I could not move a muscle. I was lying on a newly dug grave. I leaped up and ran to the wagon. We were in a graveyard adjacent to the dirt road. It took some time for my heartbeat to return to normal, and I relived the scene several times in my dreams.

Frequently, the road we traveled passed through a village. Most of the homes we saw were far apart. The terrain varied, although it was mostly flat. Occasionally we encountered gentle hills. When we did, we had to get out and coax the horses to move forward. Often we pushed the wagon to aid the horses.

Many fields covered with wheat undulated in the breezes and created waves of various shades of gold, especially before sunset. We also passed vast fields of corn. I liberated several, and we ate them raw. Eventually, we passed fields with farmers harvesting wheat. Further, into our journey we saw miles and miles of haystacks of gathered wheat spread before us. We also passed fields of watermelons and cantaloupes.

We were a part of a small caravan of several horse drawn wagons. As we were passing a watermelon field a German warplane suddenly appeared and started blasting at us with its machineguns.

At the first sight of the plane, instant fear set in. It seemed like my mind and reasoning process stopped. My survival instinct, quite honed by then, automatically took over. I was barely aware of my actions. We jumped out of our wagon. It took Mama longer. I heard her screams punctuated by the machinegun fire.

"Run! Run, Buma!" she ordered. "Don't wait for me!"

Papa and I fled into the watermelons as bullets whizzed by our heads, pelting melons and earth as we scattered. Hunched and head down in response to the zipping bullets, my heart pounded in my ears, deafening me. I don't want to die, was the only thought in my head. Blinded by terror I tripped on a watermelon. I lay there as the terrifying sound of the plane diminished. The pilot completed his pass at us and flew away.

I realized that I was wet and sticky. Frantically I ran my hands over my damp body as I clambered to stand up. Was I shot? My heart almost stopped. I didn't feel pain anywhere. I finished running my hands over the wet areas of my chest and belly and was relieved to find the red stickiness was not blood, only watermelon juice.

"We're alright!" my parents yelled at me.

I looked up to find them waving at me from another part of the field. "You're alright?"

"Yes, I am!" I waved back, grinning, and a little drunk at the thought of being alive.

Some people hadn't been so fortunate and were hit. Two lay dead a few yards from Papa.

"No! God, no! Why? Why them? What did they do to deserve that?" A few people sat on the ground next to the dead, crying hysterically, raising their fists to the sky, while others gathered around them.

"Buma, don't come this way!" ordered Papa, as he stopped to join the crowd. "Go mind the horses!"

Fortunately, the horses had pulled the wagon off the road into the fields of the watermelons and stopped.

These attacks were random and a daily threat to us as we traveled. Many people picked up watermelons, some broken and a few whole. While it had been a horrifying experience and two people had lost their lives, we ended the day filling our empty bellies with sweet watermelons.

That night, I could not fall asleep, my thoughts on the

two who'd died. It could have been Papa, Mama or me. I'm glad that Papa prevented me from seeing the dead bodies. Who decides who shall live and who shall die? God? If it is, I thank You for sparing our lives, but it's still not right. A ten-year-old should not think of death, nor should the innocent be killed.

CHAPTER 4

CROSSING THE RIVER DNIEPER

I T became increasingly more difficult to obtain food, and we faced imminent starvation. We constantly feared being overrun by the enemy, although the front lines were further behind us. Stories circulated that the Germans were dropping paratroopers behind the front lines. The weather grew steadily colder. We knew our days of travel by horse and wagon were numbered and that soon we must abandon this means of transportation.

"We must cross a river before we can catch a train," Papa decided. "The bridges spanning the rivers are key targets and will all soon be destroyed."

"But we may starve," Mama worried, "or our horses will drop dead before we reach a river safe enough to cross."

Each day we were hungrier than the day before. Our bodies and minds suffered from the cumulative effect of near starvation. At the start of our escape, I was overweight and Mama obese by today's standards. I believe that the extra weight we carried contributed to our survival.

The horses, emaciated and ready to drop, hindered our travel as our circumstances turned desperate. Our situation actually looked bleaker than before. We began to question if we would survive the escape. How far could we travel by foot once the horses and wagon had to be abandoned?

The back axel of the wagon broke when we hit a pothole and a rock on the road. We lost more than a day trying to fix it with pieces of wood and wire, all the while aware that the wagon would soon fail us permanently.

"We will reach the river," insisted Papa, "even if we have to crawl the last bit. I will not get on a train only to be bombed and killed, and that is final!"

"I admire your spirit and determination. Now if you could only keep us from starving," Mama replied.

During the darkest hours, the human mind wages an inner battle between despair and hope. The longer the terrible times continue the more despair triumphs over hope. We refused to give up. Every night when I went to sleep, I repeated my mantra: I can't just die! I have not lived yet! It's not right! Not like this! We lived from hour to hour, and day to day. Each night I said to myself, "Don't give up! You see, we made it one more day."

At that time in 1941, I didn't know the name of the river that signaled our transition to train travel. Now, I believe we'd reached the River Dnieper, which empties into the Black Sea. As the crow flies, the distance between Beltz and the Dnieper is approximately 350 miles. Avoiding towns and railroad stations as we traveled the back roads from one small village to the other most probably tripled the distance we traveled.

We journeyed on foot and by wagon for nearly three months.

Papa, who read the maps to establish our route, said that we traveled at least a thousand miles before boarding the train. He wanted to get as far east as possible to increase our distance from the battlefront, prior to risking train travel.

When we reached the river, we didn't search for a bridge, because we feared being caught in a bombing raid if we attempted to cross it. Instead, we located an encampment at the river's edge, which served as a docking area for large rafts used to transport people across the river. At least a thousand refugees were gathered there, and this village-sized population seemed to invite an attack by German aircraft.

The riverbank terrain consisted of sand dunes, reeds, bamboo, and other high grasses. After we registered our names in a queue to cross the river, we made camp. Like everyone else, we slept on the cold ground at night. Boredom soon hallmarked each day. I explored the area, always hungry and cold. The deprivation we endured made me think of food all the time. Thoughts of the overabundance of food I'd been forced to consume between the ages of six and nine filled my mind and exacerbated the hunger gnawing at my empty belly. Fat translated into health and prosperity in those days.

Vivid memories replete with daily doses of 100 grams of butter, ten teaspoons of sour cream, and fat-marbled meats flooded my conscious and unconscious thoughts to the point of madness. Even the daily dose of cod liver oil, a winter staple, held an odd appeal, despite my loathing of the stuff. I hated the taste of it, and had to eat a piece of tangerine or orange immediately after, to prevent gagging. That fat diet was fully supported by my Uncle Zioma, the physician. No longer could my former classmates tease me, calling me *balena,* which meant whale in Romanian.

The weather had turned wet and windy, and we were unbelievably cold because we had no warm clothes. Families grouped close to one another on a blanket to keep warm. One night I got up to look for a bush with no one in the immediate vicinity so I could relieve myself. I couldn't find my way back in the starless dark night. Lost, I walked around and searched for my parents. Every grouping looked like the next. I did not panic, but I became pretty upset and angry with myself. I kept thinking, how stupid to get lost and not find where Mama and Papa are sleeping. I'm not a child. What's wrong with me? It took hours until dawn before we found each other.

We spent nearly two weeks awaiting our turn to embark aboard a primitive raft made of tree trunks tied together. Guided by four men, each of the two floats transported approximately twenty-five passengers across the river two times each day. The float, flimsy and unsafe, heightened the danger of the crossing. Horrified, we prayed that no German planes would attack us as we navigated the river.

CHAPTER 5

THE TRAINS

W E walked for two days before we reached the nearest railroad stop, a non-descript waypoint, not even a station. Glad to be rid of the horses, my excitement grew at the prospect of traveling by train. I anticipated arriving in Stalinabad with a degree of promptness that our journey thus far had lacked. Three months of dragging my exhausted, starving body across a thousand miles of terrain, and then sleeping each night exposed to the elements, gave rise to thoughts of comfort. Little did I realize the jeopardy of train travel or the new perils we would encounter.

As we had bartered for food, our baggage became lighter and easier to carry. With our remaining belongings distributed into two bundles and a valise, we each carried one. We waited for an eastbound train not far from the railroad tracks, but far enough to avoid being bombed, or strafed by German Luftwaffe pilots.

"How long must we wait?" I asked, impatient after a few day of waiting for a train to slow down or stop. "Are there even trains running on these tracks?"

"Stop fidgeting!" Papa managed to control his temper. "We've made it so far, we'll get a train. Don't worry."

Not long after, I heard the sound that renewed my hope. "I hear a train coming. Let's go!"

We ran toward the train stop, although the trains frequently didn't stop at all. Often they hardly slowed down. Many trains were fully loaded with military equipment and Russian soldiers. Freight train or passenger train, if it didn't stop, we returned to our hiding place some distance from the tracks and resumed our wait for the sound of another approaching train.

One afternoon in September, not long after my eleventh birthday, a train finally slowed enough for us to board it. A few men extended their hands though the partially open door of the freight car and assisted us as we scrambled inside. The car, filled with refugees, some sitting, others stretched out on the floor, made space quite sparse. Several people shifted in unison, albeit reluctantly, to allow us to sit down. Most of the passengers kept quiet and to themselves, everyone appearing as hungry and emaciated as we were. A few small children cried from hunger, and their parents tried to pacify them with bits of food.

Even though train travel proved to be less strenuous than on foot or with the horse and wagon, we encountered new problems. As Papa feared, the trains and railroad tracks were often bombed and strafed. We felt under constant attack or the threat of it. German warplanes fired on our moving train. All the while, we prayed for a reprieve. When the engineer feared that the bombs might destroy the tracks, he stopped the train. We jumped out and scattered as the planes continued to strafe the area. Twice, the bombs hit the tracks and repairs forced us to wait several days. The noise of exploding bombs was more deafening than machinegun fire and caused panic among the refugees. Men and women screamed and cursed the Germans, while children cried loudly.

After the planes departed, a stampede ensued as everyone sought to return to the train. We all shouted, *"Derji paravoz! Ne otkhodi! Ne uiezjai! Ne ostavliai menia* (Hold the train! Don't leave! Wait for me! Wait for me)!" as the train rolled away without signaling its departure by blowing the horn. The engineer didn't seem to care when people were left behind and stranded without their possessions. Often I had to run to catch the train as it pulled away at a fast clip. Mama would have conniption fits every time that happened.

It is very hard to do justice in describing what people do instinctively when motivated by fear to save their lives. As we traveled by freight car, the first sound of an exploding bomb and flying bullets caused me to become irrational. My heart pounded mercilessly. I didn't know what to do. I felt trapped. I had to get out but couldn't with the train moving fast and the doors shut as the crowd squeezed. My fear amplified by the panic around me. I glanced at my horrified and confused parents.

People near the sliding doors on both sides of the car tried to open them, while others pushed and shoved making it impossible to slide the doors open.

"*Otkroy dver* (Open the door)!" panic-stricken voices yelled.

"*Ne otkroy dvery* (Don't open the doors)!" others screamed. "We'll all fall out!"

At the same time, people irrationally covered their heads with their hands, as if to protect themselves, and so did I. The crying and screaming continued with increased force and tempo.

When the train finally began to slow down, the crowd somehow slid open the doors. People held on, others were pushed out, and a few jumped. Eventually I jumped out. Driven by my adrenaline and barely aware, my legs carried me away from the train. I looked at the airplane and back, to see where my parents were. They were getting out of the train. I dropped to the ground and covered my head with my hands. The bullets made whistling sounds as they flew by. My lungs strained for air. Helplessly scared and trembling, I prayed for it to be over. I have no idea how long the strafing lasted. During what seemed an eternity, I feared that the next bullet would have my name written on it.

As soon as the planes left, relief washed over me. Oxygen

filled my lungs as I inhaled deeply. The burning fright started to subside as I picked myself off the ground. Frantic, the immediate need to get back to the train hit me. I looked for my parents and yelled in all the commotion and noise around me, "Mama, Papa!" as I continued to run to the train and glimpsed at them doing the same.

I don't believe that the trains were prime targets. The airplanes simply happened to see them and decided to shoot, making a couple of passes before continuing on their way. The bombing and strafing occurred often at the beginning of our train journeys. Each time, I was just as unprepared and scared as the first time, hoping this would be the last time I'd be a target. How many lives did I have anyhow?

Our trains had the lowest priority. When we encountered trains transporting military or other strategic materials, our train stopped and waited, sometimes more than one hour to allow the other train clear passage.

We disembarked and changed trains frequently. Our objective was to travel as far east as possible to distance ourselves from the battlefront. The deeper into Russian territory we traveled, the fewer aircraft we encountered. A constant lack of food only served to heighten our fear and anxiety.

Hunger became the one common denominator throughout the war years. When our train stopped at a station, mainly to wait for another to pass, people quickly formed a line desperate to get hot water because we had nothing else to consume. I would jump out of the train and join the line, hoping for hot or even boiling water. Each station had a faucet, sometimes two, with hot running water. People ran clutching a teakettle, a pot, or a tin cup or two, looking for the faucet. Queues formed, with each one desperate for the only source of hot liquid in our diet. Often the train left without any warning. I would forgo the hot water if I hadn't reached my turn at the faucet yet, and race back to the train.

I often walked along the tracks, hoping to collect scraps

of food from the discarded garbage. I found bits of spoiled food, dried, moldy, or sometimes soggy bread, and pieces of rotten fruit. Papa scoured the ground for cigarette butts. On rare occasions, he bought food, but at such a high premium he couldn't do it often.

It pained me to see Papa, once so meticulous about his appearance, with manicured fingernails, wearing a suit and tie and so faithful to proper etiquette, reduced to foraging along railroad tracks for pieces of spoiled, dirty food and cigarette butts.

I know it deeply wounded Papa to go against the ingrained moral and ethical code of his life, the same codes he'd taught me and by which our household ran. The mores of civilized society ceased to apply in the face of starvation and deprivation during war. Papa temporarily lost his sense of decorum. Obviously dismayed by the war's impact on him, he avoided direct eye contact, an indication, I sensed, of his humiliation. Implicit was my understanding that we would never discuss his embarrassment once life returned to normal. Now as an adult, I am amazed I grasped the impact of our situation. Our daily existence matured me well beyond my eleven years.

We were refugees, not normal passengers on a train. We jumped on any train that traveled east. They were all crowded. Schedules no longer existed, so we were without tickets and seats and had no specific destination. Most of the time, we traveled on freight trains, open platforms, or in cattle cars. No freight or any other trains were dispatched to accommodate refugees. We simply took advantage of any trains heading east. Nobody on the trains was responsible for the well-being of the refugees. Sometimes we managed to catch a passenger train. We boarded and detrained for any of several reasons, for example, if the easterly direction changed, there were too many stops, if the stops were overly long, or if another train appeared to be heading east.

One particular night, our train slowed for a station. It was very dark outside, the stations blacked out, as lights would only attract enemy air attacks. As the train stopped, Papa assisted Mama off the train while I waited with our possessions for my turn to get off. As soon as I handed down the valise, the train started to move again. We realized our mistake. We weren't at the station. Standing below the open door and its last step, my parents couldn't climb back on board. Papa might have made it, but Mama would be left behind. I wanted to throw down our other packages and join them, but Papa's voice stopped me.

"Don't!" Papa shouted. "Stay on the train! We'll meet you at the next station!"

The train gained speed quickly. I stood alone with our two packages by the door as my parents were left behind.

"Oh, my God!" Panicked, I couldn't catch my breath. "What do I do now? I'm alone in the middle of the night on a train going nowhere. Oh, my God! Will I ever see Mama and Papa again?"

Luckily, I noticed that the train was slowing down again. When it stopped, I realized I'd reached the real station, and it wasn't too far from where my parents had descended.

I entered the dark station by myself, carrying our possessions. In a strange place with hundreds of people, I knew no one. I moved onto the platform and sat down on the packages, trying to make sure they wouldn't be stolen. Then I waited, more frightened and worried than I'd ever been in my entire life.

The wildest thoughts went through my mind.

What if my parents never found me? Where would I go? What would I do? I had no money or food. Could people see in my face how scared I was?

I knew that our ultimate destination was Stalinabad in Tajikistan, where we supposedly had an aunt I'd never met. I tried to figure out what to do. Think Buma! I told myself. Calm down and think. I would sell some items for food, and lessen my burden to only one package. I'd continue going east until I reached Stalinabad. How would I do this, a boy alone? What if someone hurt me, or took away my package? How would I get food?

Stop, Buma! I finally ordered myself. Stop with the questions and calm down!

When the platform cleared a little, I approached a uniformed railroad worker and with tears in my eyes told him what had happened.

"Don't be afraid, son," he tried to reassure me. "Just wait here. Your parents are a short distance away and they will be here soon."

I was still quaked with fear, despite his words. He hadn't calmed me down. I sat on the packages in the dark and worried. I couldn't sleep a wink all night long. My anxiety became apparent to some of the people around me, and a few tried to calm me.

"Don't worry, son," said a woman seated on the floor nearby, her back against the wall. "I'll keep an eye on you."

I tried to assess the woman's character by her modest appearance. Heavy set, a shawl partially covered her graying blond hair. I thought she might be about 50. She smiled when she looked at me, and her eyes seemed kind.

Dawn finally arrived. The rising sun warmed the chilly night air, but still no sign of my parents. When I had to go to the bathroom, I tried to carry the two packages with me.

"Put them here next to mine," the woman sitting next to the wall said. "I'll watch them, nobody will take them. Don't worry, take your time." She noticed my reluctance and motioned with her hand. "Go, you can trust me!"

While in the bathroom, I'd wondered. Had I made the right decision, or would she be gone when I'd returned. Had I made my first and biggest mistake? I'd wished that I wouldn't be embarrassed or worried about other people's feelings.

Concerned and feeling uncomfortable that she might think I didn't trust her, I returned quickly.

Upon my return, a big load lifted from my chest when I saw the woman's familiar smiling face. I'd realized that I needed to be more trusting because not all people were bad.

While I waited, I kept my gaze fixed on the clock above the station platform. Time seemed to stand still. Somehow, the night passed into morning, and the morning stretched into noon. My exhausted parents finally appeared, having walked through the night and the whole morning along the tracks, carrying the old broken down valise.

"Mama! Mama!" I ran to meet her, more relieved that I would ever be able to express.

She embraced and kissed me, crying hysterically. Some of the people on the platform surrounded us, delighted by our reunion. Although I had only been apart from my parents for fourteen hours, it felt like an eternity.

"We told him you'd be along soon," a man said to my parents.

Papa thanked them for their kindness. Strangers patted me on the back, as if to say, "See, we told you not to worry."

"I thought we'd never see you again." Mama sobbed as she continued to hug me.

She did not let go of me for a long time. "We'll never separate again, ever. I promise."

CHAPTER 6

TASHKENT

OUR ultimate objective was to reach Stalinabad, the capital of the Republic of Tajikistan. Years later, after Stalin's downfall, the city was renamed Dushambe. Mama and Papa chose Stalinabad because they believed Aunt Sheiva, one of Grandma Hannah's sisters, still lived there. Nobody had corresponded with Aunt Sheiva for many years, and we weren't sure if she was alive.

Mama had told me that after the Russian Revolution, the Soviets had exiled Aunt Sheiva and her husband to Tajikistan, a distant, undesirable region. Aunt Sheiva's husband had owned an oil press prior to the Revolution, which was the reason for their exile. According to the communist doctrine, the Soviet government considered him "an undesirable capitalist and exploiter of the working class."

Regardless of Aunt Sheiva, we still would have headed to Central Asia, perhaps Uzbekistan, Kazakhstan, Tajikistan, or Kirghizistan. Central Asia and Siberia quickly became the only areas in the Soviet Union considered safe for refugees during World War II. The Germans had occupied all of Ukraine and Belarus before the Red Army stopped them at Moscow and Leningrad. Tajikistan, located at the most southeastern corner of the Soviet Union, bordered China to the east and Afghanistan to the south. For the Nazis to reach Tajikistan, the Soviet Union would have had to lose the war. In that event, our destiny would have been death at their hands.

Some nights when I could not fall asleep, I tried to imagine Tajikistan. I had no idea what to expect, other than the possibility of very hot weather. As far as the people residing there, I guessed that they might be like the characters from a "Thousand and One Nights" fairy tales.

After about a month of train travel, in early October we reached Tashkent, the capital of the Republic of Uzbekistan. Tashkent, a large, two thousand year old city with a population of close to two million had belonged to Imperial Russia since 1865. The train station, huge, old, and mid-eastern in architecture, contained Arabic arches, columns, and colorful mosaic tile work.

Station officials ordered us to vacate the platform and move onto the street. Outside the station sprawled a huge plaza with a trolley terminal. Thousands of refugees and their belongings inhabited the plaza under the open sky. At first, I registered only a rainbow of colors and the cacophony of sounds. The scene was not pretty. Old and young alike were packed into the large open area, some on blankets spread atop the cobblestones, others on the bare stones, with little room to pass and no privacy at all. Most waited for some sort of housing assignment, which was in short supply. Each week, the refugees endured being sprayed with DDT, a white powder disinfectant primarily meant to rid them of lice. We waited among those who intended to travel further east.

Papa registered us with the authorities at the station, indicating our need for a train to Stalinabad. He learned that as soon as a train was available and it was our turn in line, we would hear the announcement. The temperature was rather warm, even for that time of the year. During our wait, we received a small piece of bread and a modest portion of soup each day. We accepted the daily rations with gratitude, meager as they were. Still hungry, we knew we wouldn't starve. We supplemented our handouts with whatever food we could purchase in the open market.

Asia, the first continent beyond Europe that I'd ever seen, felt like an adventure into the unknown. Excited, I explored as much as Mama would allow. This new and strange part of the world and its unique architecture contrasted sharply with Beltz. The Uzbeks, Tajiks and other Asians clad in their colorful native clothing intrigued me. Instead of bread, they ate *lepioshkas,* a flat bread resembling pizza, but without cheese and toppings. To me they appeared so strange, but very interesting. They spoke a variety of guttural-sounding languages, and they seemed to resent the invading hordes of refugees. I was truly a foreigner in an environment where people spoke unknown languages. Yet I had experienced that feeling since the age of five, when I realized that most children in our neighborhood spoke Yiddish and I spoke only Russian.

As a small child, Papa had not permitted me to learn Yiddish or to play with the neighborhood children who spoke the language. He proclaimed it the language of common individuals, which frustrated me.

"Russian is the language of the upper class," he'd lectured, "and the language of those with a good upbringing."

His rationale, at least from a child's perspective, simply eliminated a group of potential playmates.

Later, I realized that I was somewhat of an oddball in other respects. I was among the few children overweight, dressed cleanly (inappropriately for playing in the dust), and above all, didn't speak their language. I spent my childhood in the company of my friend Benny, my cousins Bronia and Pesia, and the neighbor's boy, Hersh. Both Pesia and Hersh lived in the house sharing our backyard. With the exception of Bronia, the others spoke very little Russian. Papa forbade me to play with Hersh, because he was older and spent time with older and wilder boys. Pesia, one year older, had started kindergarten while I was not yet eligible. After weeks of throwing tantrums, my parents had obtained special permission to register me early. The only language taught in kindergarten was Romanian, which I couldn't speak. The first sentence taught in kindergarten was "*Dati'm voie to ies afara* (Allow me to go out to the bathroom)." When I had to go, I couldn't remember the sentence. I had stood up with a raised hand and embarrassed, ran out of the classroom ashamed to come back.

Little did I realize at the age of five that my life as a frustrated foreigner was just beginning. Regardless of one's age being a foreigner translates into being an outsider with no common language, an inability to prove one's capabilities and intelligence, and battling for every opportunity that most people take for granted.

The railroad plaza in Tashkent reminded me that for the second time in my young life I was a foreigner and it engendered feelings of uncertainty and insecurity.

After living on the street outside the Tashkent railroad station for over a week, we finally boarded a passenger train to Stalinabad. Not surprisingly, our conversation turned to Aunt Sheiva.

"Do you believe Aunt Sheiva is still living in Stalinabad?" I asked.

"Let's hope she is alive and well," Mama answered.

"Is she expecting us?"

"I don't know if she received my letters," Mama admitted. "If she got at least one, she would know to expect us."

"What will we do if she isn't there?" I worried. "We don't know anybody in Stalinabad. Where would we live?"

"Buma," Papa said in an effort to calm me, "we will not worry until the need arises."

"I wish we were there already," I continued. "I wonder what it will be like."

"Relax. It won't be long now," Mama assured me.

The train ride reminded me of my first and only trip to Slanic Moldova, a resort.

During the years before the war, Mama was obese and suffered from asthma. Beltz, hot and dusty in the summer

months, prompted her to spend four weeks each summer in
a sanitarium in order to ease her respiratory problems. She
traveled by train to a resort in the mountains for fresh air,
the mineral waters, and inhalation therapy. A professor in Iasi
prescribed the inhalation treatment and medicated cigarettes.
Her brother, Zioma the physician, supported her treatment.
Imagine a physician prescribing medicated cigarettes to an
asthmatic in the twenty-first century.

Since Beltz did not have a university, people had to travel
to Iasi or Chişinău (Kishinev in Russian) to see a professor or a
specialist in case of serious illness. Both cities were much larger
than Beltz and easily reached by train. Uncle Zioma graduated
from the Iasi University Medical School in Romania proper,
southwest of Beltz. Kishinev, the capital city of Bessarabia was
less than 80 miles south of us.

The popular resorts at the time were Campulung, Vatra
Dornei, and Slanic Moldova, all three in Romania. The first
two resorts were located in the Carpathian Mountains, southwest of Chernovitz.

"Buma, would you like to accompany me to Slanic
Moldova?" Mama asked, surprising me.

"It sounds great. We'd go by train?" I asked, very excited.

"Of course, we would take the train, and you'll keep me
company for a whole month."

Mama rented a cottage for four weeks. Nearly every morning
we shopped at a beautiful and clean open-air market full of
nicely arranged fresh fruit, vegetables, and colorful flowers.
She bought a large baguette, a small spring chicken, vegetables,
yogurt, sour cream, butter, and fruit, especially sweet strawber-
ries and cherries. Then we returned to the cottage, where she
cooked the chicken and prepared the rest of the food. Mama
bought food daily because we had no refrigeration.

In the afternoon, we went to the park where there were lots
of flowers, shade trees, and a few fountains. The mountain air
was as fresh and cool as she had promised. What a difference

from the dusty summer months in Beltz. The place seemed unreal, like in a fairy tale.

The inhalation room was close to the park. Usually, I hung out on the sanitarium grounds while Mama took her inhalations. She entered a large metallic cylindrical tank. It had a window and a door shut tight. Inside she'd sit for an hour and breathe deeply.

The park contained several natural springs, where the mineral water flowed freely. We forced ourselves to drink mineral water daily. To reduce the foul smell and bad taste, we drank it using a straw made of glass. Like most visitors, we each carried our own cup and glass straw.

This was my first vacation ever. I must have been about six or seven, and I enjoyed it tremendously. The year was 1936 or 1937.

CHAPTER 7

LIFE IN STALINABAD

W E reached Stalinabad at the end of October or the beginning of November 1941, four months after our escape from Beltz. We thought that, regardless of how things turned out in Stalinabad, we had come to the end of our running. The railroad station and the city itself were much smaller than Tashkent and surrounded by a bleak-looking mountain range.

The three of us, shabbily dressed and each carrying a package, boarded and changed buses several times until the last driver gave us directions to Aunt Sheiva's. From the bus stop, we walked a block on a paved street. Then the paved street gave way to several unpaved streets before we found her address.

I was shocked and disappointed at the sight of the mud huts called *kibitka*. I'd never seen endless rows of clay roofs before. I did not expect to see that kind of a neighborhood in the middle of a modern capital city of a Soviet Republic. As an eleven year old, I was able to reach the roofline with my outstretched arm. Each house had a small door and windows. The walls, the roofs, and as I found out later, the floors inside, were all made of mud, clay. Unpaved dirt streets were the norm in the neighborhood.

While I was glad to have reached a place to live, the shock of seeing the huts made me think of our home in Beltz. Until four months ago, we'd lived in a middle class part of the city where the inhabitants were mainly small storekeepers and business people. Even though many houses, including Grandpa Zeilig's and ours, didn't have electricity until 1938, and none had indoor plumbing, the collection of mud huts we were about to call our new neighborhood stunned us all.

The non-uniformly paved sidewalks bordering our cobblestone main thoroughfare in Beltz seemed far more civilized compared to *Samarkandskaia Ulitsa*, with no sidewalks or paving of any kind, where Aunt Sheiva lived at Number 58. In her seventies, with white hair and a slim body, she seemed full of energy. Because she had received one letter out of the many Mama had sent from various places during our exodus, she expected us and welcomed us with enthusiasm. Mama had been a young girl during their last encounter.

Her home, which became our residence, consisted of two small rooms. Mama and I slept in a single bed placed against the left wall just beyond the entryway. A hanging curtain separated the two rooms. A small table and a couple of chairs and a hand-operated old sewing machine completed the furnishings of this room. Aunt Sheiva's bedroom contained her bed, a nightstand, an armchair, and a few small tables. The primitive dwelling lacked running water, electricity, or a bathroom.

All the furniture was old and worn. Beams of tree branches with twigs in the ceiling supported the mud roof. Each year, before the winter rains began, we recovered the roof and the floor with a mixture of clay and manure. A little shack attached to the right side of the hut housed Aunt Sheiva's goat, Katia, who provided minimal daily milk.

Although humble and often awkward, Aunt Sheiva's home provided an improvement over sleeping in fields, trains, or on the ground as we had during the previous four months. At last, we weren't living in fear of flying bullets and falling bombs. We'd stopped running. Now, we'd try to live a normal life. Mama needed to earn money, and I wanted to go back to school.

Papa immediately reported to the Red Army, because his mobilization papers waited for him at Aunt Sheiva's house. Papa had used her address as our evacuation destination when he'd obtained horses and a wagon in the Ukraine. At first, Papa was stationed in the vicinity of Stalinabad and he visited us occasionally. He wore his Red Army military uniform. Once he shipped out, we communicated by mail. Prior to his departure, he managed to bring us a small wooden crate filled with hard candies. Aunt Sheiva instructed Mama to separate the candy into small packages. Then they went to the black market to sell a few packages at a time. Mama's inventory soon sold out, providing us with a bit of money on which to survive.

Mama registered me at the local school located only two blocks from Aunt Sheiva's home. The school year was already in session. I enrolled in the sixth grade, a grade higher than I finished in Beltz. I looked rather different from most of the other students, my hair completely cut to the scalp to stay clean, and my European clothing rather shabby. While I spoke Russian well, I did not know all the dirty words or local slang. According to my upbringing, only thugs and hoodlums used such language. I felt uncomfortable with the students, who stared at me and made snide anti-Semitic remarks.

The first week in school, during a lunch break several boys from my class attacked me, calling me *"Jid!"* a derogatory name for Jew. They pushed me around, jumped on me, and beat me badly. After some adults broke up the fight, I could barely get up. When the boys on top of me dispersed, one boy remained on the ground beneath me. I had attempted to punch him as hard as I could, since I couldn't defend myself from the others. I was barely conscious, exhausted, and in pain. Fueled only by adrenaline, and unsteady on my feet, I did not return to class. Instead, I dragged myself home. There, I realized that I was bloody, with a black eye, scratches on my face, a cut lip, bruised ribs, back, knees, and elbows. I had never taken such a beating in my life, yet my ego hurt most due to the unfairness of it. How could this happen in the Soviet Union? I was a free citizen, not a prisoner under Nazi occupation.

Several days passed while I recuperated. I didn't return to school for a week. My experience with corporal punishment, which occurred only if I broke school rules, hadn't prepared me for this assault.

In grade school, maintaining strict discipline was part of the teacher's function. To discipline the students, the teachers inflicted physical punishment upon them. While there were standards for teaching and evaluating a student's knowledge and accomplishments, no such standard existed for punishment. Each teacher had his favorite method.

The punishment varied from a pinch on the cheek, pulling the ear, slapping the face, hitting the open palm with a ruler, or having the student stand in a corner in front of the classroom. Another favorite punishment was to have the student kneel, or worse yet, kneel on loose kernels of corn. The latter was rather painful, because the corn kernels quickly dug into the knees.

In *liceu*, grades five through twelve, a special person called *petagog* (pedagogue) maintained student discipline. Teachers reported to him any student who misbehaved in the classroom. He then disciplined him. He focused on the younger students, not daring to discipline the older ones, because they were physically as large, and sometimes taller than he.

He was thin and of medium stature, with straight light blond hair that always fell in his face, and covered his ice-cold blue eyes.

"Behemoth! Have you no sense?" was his favorite question as he pinched the victim's cheek, let go of it, and followed up immediately with a slap.

Whenever we saw him in the school corridor, we avoided him. He made a lasting impression on me. I truly believe that the *petagog* was a sadist. His facial expression proclaimed his pleasure at inflicting pain on others who could not defend themselves.

After the beating I received, I felt relief that the teachers in the Soviet school system could not physically harm me. When I returned to school, the teacher sent me to the principal's office.

"Tell me, Buma Frimtzis," the principal looked me in the eye, "did you start the fight?"

"No," I replied.

"Who did then?"

"I don't know." I refused to be a snitch, because I didn't want another beating.

"You mean to tell me you didn't recognize the boys who beat you up?"

"I'm too new in school," I said convincingly. "I don't know anybody."

"I don't believe you. You'd better get to know the other boys," she said sternly. "If this happens again, you won't have the same excuse."

I learned to smoke, curse, and integrate myself into the student body within a few weeks. I behaved like one of the boys, a hooligan. Some of the boys called me the "dirty --- Jew," or they insulted me by calling me *Abrasha* (Abraham) and asking whether I have a *Sarachka* (Sarah). The Russians derogatorily called Jews *Abrasha* and *Sarachka*.

Soon after I began school, Mama found a job in a bacteriological pharmaceutical laboratory, the Sanbak Institute. It stood for Institute for Sanitation and Bacteriology. She wore a white lab coat and worked as a *sanitarka*, a lab assistant. Mama had never been employed a day in her life because, for a female, in the prewar days in Bessarabia it was considered socially inappropriate. Only the very poor widows worked. As long as there was an able-bodied husband, the wife in a poor family stayed home, for to work was admitting poverty. Besides, there were no opportunities for women.

A female local government representative visited us at Aunt Sheiva's home a few months after our arrival in Stalinabad.

She informed my mother's aunt that the housing shortage for refugees necessitated the addition of another person to our household. Aunt Sheiva, upset and tearful, failed to convince the government official that we needed to be able to house another relative who would soon arrive. She even showed the government official letters from her niece, Raya, hospitalized due to shrapnel wounds. Neither the letters nor Aunt Sheiva's pleading moved the woman. They brought in Gitta Davidovna, a female refugee in her mid-forties from Babruisk in Byelorussia. We moved our bed into Aunt Sheiva's room and Gita Davidovna placed her bed where ours had been. Aunt Sheiva did not receive rental or any other compensation for the new tenant. Those were the Soviet Union rules.

Bronia and her parents, Liza and Shulim, arrived shortly after Gitta Davidovna moved in with us. They too spent a few months with us. I honestly don't know how we all squeezed into those two small rooms.

To divert our attention from constant hunger and the terrible living conditions, Bronia and I reminisced about our life in Beltz and the games we'd played as children.

"Remember Buma, the incident with the horse?"

I smiled and, for a brief moment, we were seven or eight years old and playing in our backyard, which was full of local villager's horses and wagons. Bronia wanted to leave the yard but she couldn't because a horse blocked her path, the remaining narrow space covered with horse manure.

"The horse is in my way," she said as she turned to me.

"Just kick him, and he'll move," I said, picking up a small branch and offering it to her.

"You do it! You're a boy, and I'm afraid."

I poked the horse in its rear with the end of the branch, and he promptly kicked me in the stomach.

"Mama Sonia! Mama Sonia!" Bronia shouted as she ran to find my mother. "Buma fell asleep!"

Mama immediately surmised I was in trouble. She came

running and found me passed out on the ground in the manure.

I obviously survived that episode. I never poked a horse in the rear again.

"Do you remember your white doves?" Bronia asked next, "and what we did to the cat?"

"I'll never forget," I replied. "It was pretty terrible."

Papa came home one day, smiling and carrying a covered birdcage.

I jumped up and asked, "Is that for me?"

"Only if you promise to take good care of what's inside," he replied.

"I will, I will! What is it?" I answered excitedly.

He removed the cover to reveal a pair of perfectly white small doves.

"I promise to take care of them!" I vowed in my excitement.

He put the cage on the table, then handed me a packet of seeds. I loved playing with them, and I felt equal to the older neighborhood boys who also had pet doves. I proudly displayed the doves to Benny, Bronia and Pesia.

About a week later, I discovered the empty cage. Fear and anger overcame me as I realized I'd left the cage unlocked. I quickly summoned Bronia and Benny, and we searched for the doves. We found them dead and partially eaten soon after. Despite my sadness, my real concern was Papa. How would I face him? What could I say to him? I'd failed to keep my promise to take care of them. What do I do next? I wondered, thinking of a stray neighborhood cat that often prowled in our backyard.

Benny, Bronia, Hersh, and I gathered in our backyard.

"Do we all agree that the cat killed my doves?" I asked.

"Yes!" they shouted in unison.

"What are we going to do about it?" Hersh, the oldest of

the group asked. Without waiting for an answer, he raised his fist and yelled, "We'll punish that killer cat!"

"Everyone who thinks the cat should be punished put your hand on top of mine!" Hersh extended out his hand.

One by one, we each placed a hand on top of his.

"We must hang the cat. That is the verdict!" Hersh proclaimed.

We basically agreed to punish the cat, not necessarily hang it. However, after voting Bronia, Benny and I felt guilty and uncomfortable. Yet we did not want to look like sissies in front of Hersh.

"You're not going to back out now, are you?" he asked as he noticed our skittishness.

We caught the cat, but she escaped us and fled. Other than Hersh, we felt relief that our attempted feline execution had failed. Mama coached me on what to say to Papa when he arrived at home.

"Papa, the doves have escaped, and the cat killed them. It's all my fault, and I am very sorry. I broke my promise to you. I tried to take good care of them but I must have forgotten to lock the little door after I fed them." With fear in my eyes, head bowed and trembling voice, I pleaded my case as soon as Papa stepped through the threshold.

Papa silently pondered my whimpered confession. "As long as you are sorry and realize that you broke your promise to me, I will not punish you this time. The loss of your doves is your punishment."

To this day, I regret our cruel plan for that stray cat.

Shortly after Bronia's family arrived in Stalinabad, they discovered that their relatives had survived and settled in a *kolhoz* in Sultanabad, Anderjanskaia Oblast, in Uzbekistan. The cramped living quarters and pervasive hunger we were experiencing prompted them to join their relatives. The *kolhoz* grew various crops and raised cattle. Their existence in the *kolhoz* wouldn't be easy, but at least they wouldn't starve.

Within a few months, Aunt Sheiva's niece, Raya (Rachel) Grosman, arrived. She was a young metallurgical engineer from Zaporojie, a mining town in Donbas, destroyed and occupied by the Germans. Donbas, a concatenation of the River Don and basin, contained Ukraine's major mining and metallurgy industry. Germany intended to destroy those important Soviet resources and subjected the area to heavy bombardment.

During the shelling, Raya suffered several shrapnel wounds in both her legs and walked with some difficulty. Nevertheless, she found employment in Stalinabad until the end of the war. Five people now occupied four beds in that tiny hut.

When the goat Katia gave birth, we named her offspring Borka. Aunt Sheiva kept him inside, tied to the bed Mama and I shared. The little goat died after only a few months, a victim of lice infestation. His skin crawled with them. I was the source of the lice and I felt guilt-ridden and embarrassed for causing Borka's demise. Although Aunt Sheiva didn't accuse me, I couldn't look in her eyes. I never forgot that incident. Such things did not happen to people, I thought, only sub-humans living in caves.

The mud hut lacked a bathroom. We washed outside in the summer. In winter, we used a pan of water when privacy was possible. Soap was very expensive, and there was no coal or wood for the stove to heat the water. We had used manure mixed with straw dried in the sun on the roof to fuel the stove. Our poor diet and the lack of necessary vitamins contributed to our lice infestation. No matter how hard we tried to rid ourselves of the lice, we lost the battle, just like everyone else.

The Soviet government issued monthly bread ration cards to buy 600 grams of bread daily for a worker, and 400 grams for a dependent, sold by government bakeries for pennies, *kopeks,* a very low price indeed. However, you had to stand daily in long queues, pushing and shoving in the unruly crowd to obtain your allotted share.

The black bread was sour tasting and nearly raw, resembling

a chunk of dark brown clay brick. Under normal prewar conditions, we never consumed 400 grams a day, because we had other food, and 400 grams represented a large piece of bread.

Due to the lack of food, everyone was emaciated as the war years unfolded. Mama lost a great deal of weight. Consequently, she no longer suffered from asthma. I was so skeletal the school doctors decided I needed a month in a sanitarium. They believed I might contract tuberculosis. That summer for a month, I lived in a dorm in a rural setting. Even though we had more food, it was still not enough. Sleeping on a cot was an improvement to sharing a single bed with Mama, but I felt guilty that I could not share my food with her. A blonde nurse and overseer in her mid-thirties sat some evenings on my cot, and she encouraged me to recount the horrors of my escape. She seemed sympathetic and kind. I felt despondent, a lonely Jewish boy among all Christians. I could not fall asleep and wept silently as I recalled our home, the bombs, the bullets, the pervasive hunger, and our questionable future. I'd wake up in the morning exhausted. With the exception of the extra bit of food, the month in the sanitarium didn't improve my mental state.

I also missed Papa. He wasn't here to guide and protect me as he had from the Iron Guard and Cuza before the Soviets entered Bessarabia. These Fascist organizations attempted to intimidate and eventually destroy the Jewish population in all of Romania, including Bessarabia. From 1937 to 1939, anti-Semitism was rampant, and the Beltzer Jewish community had felt threatened.

At the time, Papa met with other men in our community to discuss and plan our defense in case of a pogrom. He carried a pistol and a heavy steel walking cane for self-defense. During a dozen nights, Papa and other men took turns patrolling the streets of our neighborhood.

"How was your vacation?" Mama inquired as she hugged me and smiled. "Did you have more food?"

"I had a good time," I lied, "and enough to eat." I didn't want her to know I'd been lonely, and still hungry.

"I did not turn in your bread ration card for the month you were gone." Mama's expression turned defiant, "I just couldn't give up 400 grams of bread for a month."

"Will you go to jail?" I asked, alarmed.

"Only if I'm caught," she answered.

I knew that she risked going to jail for five to ten years if someone reported her to the authorities. Such was the abject state of affairs in the USSR during the war years. She risked jail over our hunger. She took my daily bread, cut it into two or three slices, put it on the roof to dry, some distance from the drying manure and straw mixture used for fuel. It dried into hard black boards, instead of toast. That served to supplement our diet when I returned. We soaked it in water to make it palatable and not break our teeth. Lacking tea and sugar, Mama drank hot water with salt. She preferred that to drinking just hot water.

We obtained extra food by whatever means possible. Sometimes, at school I received milk in the morning. At the end of each workday, Mama came home from work with an aluminum pot of soup, which sold for *kopeks* in her work cafeteria. The soup rarely contained a few paltry vegetables but no meat. Mostly it looked and tasted like warm colored water.

Mama carried the soup pot in a string bag. Everyone possessed a similar knitted cotton bag, which folded to stow in a pocket. They were called *"avoshka"* or "the perhaps bag," or "the perhaps I'll get lucky bag." People hoped to pass a store selling something so they'd be lucky enough to carry home the purchased items in the *avoshka*.

That summer, I found a part-time job sewing soles onto shoes. The father of a boy I knew from school, a long time resident of Stalinabad, made shoes in their home. I was given a precut upper skin pulled tightly over a wooden shoe form to which a leather sole was temporarily nailed. I sewed the soles to the uppers after my employer demonstrated the technique of using two curved needles simultaneously. He paid me for each pair I completed. At twelve, I was proud that I could earn money to help Mama.

I discovered that my employer was also Jewish. In general, the Soviet Jew was a Jew in name only, somebody to be hated, and without knowledge of Judaism, the holidays, customs, Yiddish, or Hebrew. The USSR considered Jewish a nationality, not a religion. Soviet citizens had lived under the Communist regime in an atheistic society since 1918.

There were beautiful churches, built during the reign of the Czars, but the Soviets used them as museums. Religious worship was forbidden. Because of anti-Semitism, those of Jewish origin did not openly admit it. The old people knew how to pray, but failed to teach the younger generation. There were no synagogues or temples. Those that existed were abandoned, destroyed, or in disrepair. With no prayer books, Torahs, or rabbis, the only option was to abandon religion. While a Soviet Jew held little meaning in a religious sense, discrimination remained in full bloom against anyone with a Jewish name.

Even before the Soviets entered Beltz our family hadn't been highly religious. At the age of seven, my parents, prodded by Grandpa Zeilig, hired a rabbi to teach me *dovenen* (prayers in Hebrew). The poorer and traditional families were also old fashioned and sent their children to a *cheider*, a Jewish religious school. Papa, more progressive and less religious, objected to my going to *cheider*.

Most of the rabbis who taught me were old with white beards and mustaches yellowed around the mouth from smoking. They smelled of cigarette smoke. The rabbi came twice a week for an hour each time. He sat next to me at the dining room table and aimed his homemade pointer (made from a toothbrush handle) at a letter or a word in the prayer book, *Siddur*. I read the word, and he corrected me if I pronounced it incorrectly. Prior to the rabbi's arrival I would hide. Mama searched for me at Grandpa's house and in the yard. I once climbed into the attic of Pesia's house to avoid my lesson. To get into the attic I scrambled onto the attic floor. I didn't notice a chunk of glass from a broken seltzer bottle lying there. I cut my knee badly, probably hitting an artery, because blood gushed from the injury. Mama found me after I cried out in pain.

We went immediately to the pharmacy across the street for help. The pharmacist applied pressure to the cut, washed it with hydrogen peroxide, and bandaged it.

"I hope you learned a lesson and you'll be more careful next time," said the pharmacist.

To this day, I have a scar on my left knee. After that episode, I stopped hiding from the rabbi's lessons.

My grandparents and parents belonged to the Beltz Large Synagogue. The voluminous, ornate building displayed frescos of the twelve tribes on the walls. The ceiling was in the form of a dome and painted with blue sky, white cloud puffs, and angels. Each year we purchased the same seats and attended on *Rosh Hashanah* and *Yom Kippur*. During the High Holidays, the rabbi and the cantor wore white coats, *kittel*, and fancy tall white silk hats. The cantor, accompanied by a choir of five or six young boys, chanted beautifully.

I sat between Grandpa and Papa. Mama and Grandma sat upstairs in the balcony with the rest of the women. I knew that I belonged to the Levy tribe, because my father was a Levy. When members of the *Kohanim* (the priestly tribe) performed their blessing, Grandpa held my head down so I could not watch them. My curiosity always got the best of me, however.

Every year between *Rosh Hashanah* and *Yom Kippur*, Grandpa Zeilig purchased a small white rooster for me and a small white chicken for Bronia to *shlugen kapuras,* to make a sacrifice. I sat with Grandpa at his dining room table with a *siddur* and *shlugged kapuras.* I held the little rooster by his tied legs, and under Grandpa's supervision, I recited from the *siddur* a prayer while circling the rooster over my head several times. The rooster was my *kapurah*. Then I went with Grandpa to the *shokhet* a few doors from our house and had him slaughter the rooster. The same day Mama cooked the rooster, and we ate my *kapurah* for dinner.

About that time of the year, we also went to the River Reut. Standing on the Turkish Bridge, we emptied our pockets (crumbs, etc.) into the river. The ritual, called *tashlikh*, implied that we disposed of our sins. During the High Holidays, we prayed for forgiveness for our sins for the past year, and for a good and happy new year. *Tashlikh* reminded us of our obligation.

On *Simchas Torah*, there was a large procession through the streets, and people carried several *Torahs*. Each youngster, myself included, carried a paper flag with a red apple on top and a candle on top of it. *Klezmer* played, and there was a lot of noise and dancing in the streets. The Gentiles referred to this holiday as the "Jewish Crazy Day."

During the eight nights of *Chanukah*, we kindled the *Menorah* lights each night. The synagogue owned a beautiful menorah. At home, we made our own *menorah* out of potatoes. Mama and Grandma each cut four large raw potatoes in half, lengthwise, hollowed a large part of each half, to make room for oil and a cotton flint. I participated by saying the *brokhah*, the blessing prior to kindling the light. On *Chanukah*, we also played with a *dreidle*, a four-sided top marked by a Hebrew letter on each side. Mama and Grandma prepared potato *latkes*, pancakes, which we enjoyed eating. The most awaited prize of the holiday was *Chanukah gelt*, *Chanukah* money. Sometimes I received new clothing for the occasion.

In preparation for *Pesach*, Passover, my Grandma Hannah gave the house a thorough cleaning. The intent was to get rid of *chometz*, bread, and cereal products in the house, before Passover. We put breadcrumbs around the oven and on the table. Next, we used a goose wing instead of a brush, to collect all the breadcrumbs and disposed of them. The result of the exercise was a house cleansed of *chometz* and *kosher* for *Passover*. I also helped Mama go through the same ritual in our home. During the Romanian regime, we purchased readymade *matzo*. After the Soviets arrival, eating *matzo* was forbidden or at best frowned upon therefore readymade *matzo* was not available. Grandpa went to a special baker out of our neighborhood to order matzo for the whole family. To avoid breaking the baked *matzo*, he carefully placed it in white bed-sheets with the corners tied together and brought it home in a horse drawn wagon.

We celebrated *Passover* as a reminder of the freedom of the Jews' freedom from slavery in Egypt. Because they had to depart their homes in a hurry, they could not wait for the dough to rise. Therefore, we eat *matzo*, or unleavened bread. During the *Seder*, I asked the *Feer Kashes*, the Four Questions, because I was the youngest boy at the table. The adults answered the questions. As a girl, Bronia didn't study prayers.

Grandpa took me with him to synagogue on the Sabbath though Papa didn't approve. Mama kept our house *kosher*. She bought meats from a *kosher* butcher and chickens slaughtered by a *shokhet*. Before cooking the meat or chicken, she washed it well, let it stay in rock salt for some time, and thoroughly washed it again, thus making it kosher and ready for cooking. She used two sets of dishes during the year and different sets for *Pesach*.

On Fridays, Mama always prepared a standard Sabbath dinner consisting of fish, chicken soup, and chicken. She also always lighted and blessed the Sabbath candles. We lived in a predominantly Jewish neighborhood and followed the Jewish rituals even though we were not considered strictly religious.

Life in the Soviet Union remained extremely difficult. There was very little food and those whose jobs dealt with food stole to sell it on the black market. For example, if a man worked in a bakery, he could sell a loaf of bread for about 170-200 rubles, whereas the same bread rationed and sold in the government run bakery sold for a few *kopeks*, a fraction of a ruble. Those who worked in a kitchen, a grocery, or a slaughterhouse stole food items at work and sold them for an inflated price. Everything was in high demand, independent of price, because the population continued to go hungry.

Similarly, if any kind of merchandise, such as shoes or clothing items, infrequently arrived in a store, a large queue formed. Within a short time, the sales person announced, "It's all gone." Meanwhile the store employees bought the balance of the merchandise at the government offered price and resold it on the black market for 100 or even 1000 times the government set price.

Stealing and reselling at a huge profit created a vast black market. Trading on the black market for a profit was forbidden, the police could jail the *speculant*. However, the authorities rarely enforced the law. The black market was a necessity to feed and clothe the population. It also encouraged theft, as it provided an outlet for stolen goods. Anyone with money could purchase most necessities on the black market.

People caught stealing received stiff jail sentences. In fact, there was a Russian saying, *"ty ne grajdanin esli ne sidel"* or "you're not a citizen unless you spent time in jail." A high percentage of the population served prison time. Five to ten years was a rather common sentence. Yet the long imprisonments didn't deter the starving Soviet population because stealing was necessary for survival. Those stealing did very well for themselves, but they lived in constant fear of being caught and jailed.

The Soviet economy was constantly in trouble due to centralized planning by the Moscow bureaucrats. Working people did not own any shares in the economy therefore had no incentive to produce. During the war, the economy turned into a complete shambles. Despite the terrible shortage of all goods such as food, clothing, paper, wood, and heating oil, these items occasionally sold cheaply in stores. People referred to the items as "given" instead of sold. The general population used the word "got" instead of "bought," and the word "give" instead of "sell." To illustrate this Russian colloquialism, the question, "What are they giving?" is *Chto dayut?* The question, "What are they selling?" in Russian is *Chto prodayut?*

When people saw a line in front of a store they'd run quickly and ask those in front of them, "*Chto dayut?*" Sometimes the people knew what the store was selling. In many instances, they did not. Most people remained in line anyway. It did not matter what the store was selling. The population, in dire need used anything and everything available at cheap prices. If they did not need an item, they bought it to sell on the black market at a good profit. A very lucky day, and the reason many carried their *avoshka*, lucky bag.

A joke circulated about a woman who entered a store after standing in line for a long time. She asked the clerk, "Do you have toilet paper for sale?"

"No," the clerk promptly replied, "today we do have sand paper."

"Good, I'll take it," the woman answered happily.

In winter, it rained endlessly. Our unpaved streets became very muddy. We had no choice but to walk in it. Many of the natives, Tajiks, Uzbeks, and others used an *ishak*, donkey, to navigate those muddy streets. I walked barefoot, because I either did not have shoes or I wanted to save my torn shoes. Wearing my torn shoes wouldn't protect my feet from the water and mud. The cold mud froze my feet. The first winter the school provided me with a pair of new shoes, which I wore for less than one week before they fell apart. Merchandise rarely sold in government stores was cheap, made with inferior materials, with cardboard often used in place of leather.

I also received a winter jacket. Both the outside and the

lining of the jacket were made of the same thin cotton material. Sandwiched between was a thick layer of white cotton. The entire jacket quilted like a bed comforter was very popular and called a *fufaika*. Mine was several sizes too large.

Within a few days, the sleeve ends of my *fufaika* had burn holes, from my smoking cigarettes. I tried to hide the cigarette by keeping the lit end in the palm of my hand and by pulling my hand into the sleeve. Many times, I smelled cotton burning as the sleeve smoldered. Since all young boys smoked, most of their sleeve ends also had burn marks. We made our cigarettes out of chopped tobacco stems, called *machorka,* rolled in pieces of old newspaper. The smell emitted from the rolled *machorka* hardly resembled cigarette smoke. It also felt rough in my throat and made me cough. I smoked to fit in, to be like everybody else in the hope for less discrimination. I wanted acceptance as an adolescent. Many of my older classmates also smoked hashish, which was readily available from the native population.

The natives in Stalinabad, like in Tashkent, were Muslims. They wore turbans and colorful skull caps which they called in Uzbek or Tajik *tibiteika*. The designs and embroideries on the *tibiteikas* represented their various nationalities. For example, the Uzbeks wore a black *tibiteika* in the shape of a square with four folds. Each quadrant contained a white embroidered challis design. Many natives, particularly the younger generation, did not wear turbans, but only *tibiteikas*. They also wore three quarter baggy white Muslim pants, pointy slippers on their bare feet, and a collection of layered striped robes. The higher the temperature outside, the more robes they wore. They claimed that multiple robes kept the heat and the sun out. They reminded me of the characters in the "Thousand and One Nights" tales. With their Mongolian facial shapes and colorful attire, they also resembled the ancient people depicted in Hebrew religious books. Since then, I've seen similarly attired characters in the movie The Ten Commandments.

Most of the older natives wore beards and did not speak Russian. They spoke only Tajik, Uzbek, Tatar, or Kazakh languages. They loaded up their donkeys and, at times, rode them bareback with their legs dangling nearly to the ground. To get the donkeys to move they used a little stick, the length of about two pencils, with a point at one end. They poked the pointed edge at the donkey's neck or backside. Sometimes they walked with big wooden canes, like in Biblical times.

Often, the segregated white population made fun of the primitive and uneducated natives. They also called them derogatory names. The younger natives formed gangs, and they fought with the white gangs. Some of these fights resulted in bloodshed, followed by revenge and more bloodshed. Many natives somehow avoided the draft into the Red Army.

Summers in Central Asia were extremely hot, with no rain for eight or nine months. A large tree, about four times taller than the huts, grew between our house and the next-door neighbor's at the right of us. In the summer, that *tootovnik* tree bore white berries, resembling white boysenberries, with a denser consistency and different taste. Early in the morning, the next-door neighbor boy, Vasiatka, who was my age, and I climbed the tree and ate as many berries as we could. We were barefoot and wore only shorts. We did not eat them for pleasure. Because we were both so hungry, we often ate unripe berries. We became nauseated from eating these berries, but out of necessity they became part of our diet.

One summer, I developed excruciating stomach pains, and I experienced nausea, severe diarrhea, and rapid weight loss. While going to the bathroom I saw a white tape-like appendage protruding from my rectum. It hurt inside my guts to pull on it. I cleaned up, ran into the house, and with scissors cut it off. Mama took me to a doctor who determined that I had a rather large tapeworm, *soliteor*. He prescribed laxatives and other medication to get rid of it. This traumatic experience was painful and embarrassing. I suffered for a couple of weeks before the problem went away.

The summer heat made it unbearable to sleep indoors. Having no backyards, Vasiatka and I slept on blankets spread on the ground in front of our houses. Many people slept outside. We kept a couple of sticks with us when we slept outside for protection. Boys from our school had threatened to beat me up because I was a " *Jid*." Vasiatka acted as my protector.

"They won't attack you," he said, "as long as you're with a Gentile boy and there are two of us."

During the summer, most of the locals walked around barefoot, primarily due to lack of shoes. This was particularly true for youngsters, boys and girls alike. The ground was very hot, but after some time the soles of our feet became calloused.

While walking barefoot, I stepped on a piece of a broken, rusty shovel and cut my left foot rather badly. Sanitation being what it was and with our poor diet, my immune system failed to provide me with adequate protection. My foot became infected and I ended up on a crutch. The infection lasted the whole summer. I was in much pain, uncomfortable and clumsy using a crutch. I still have a scar on my left foot as a reminder of my time in Stalinabad. Skin cancers in my older age are another lasting "gift" from Stalinabad where I walked barely clothed and unprotected in the hot Asian summer sun.

The city of Stalinabad was in a valley surrounded by large foreboding granite looking mountains. To the south Tajikistan borders with Afghanistan, north is Kyrgyzstan, northwest is Uzbekistan, and east is China. The River Dushanbinka ran near the city.

In the summer, we went to the river. However, it was treacherous and too cold for swimming. It felt like melted ice. My friends and I swam in a nearby manmade lake that was much warmer than the river. Sometimes we managed to go out on the lake in a small rowboat. One time the boys threw me out of the boat in the middle of the lake. They knew I could not swim, so they kept the boat near me, but not close enough for me to reach it. That was my swimming lesson, and no instructions were necessary. Sink or swim. My so-called friends were wild, but I had to keep up with them to avoid ridicule and harassment as a Jew.

In spite of the adversities and hunger, we had fun. Being young boys, we needed our games and playtime. Even when hunger pangs made me think of food, I tried to distract myself with other things.

In school, I met a boy named Misha. He and his family were refugees from somewhere in Byelorussia, now known as the Republic of Belarus. He had an older sister of about nineteen. His father was a cobbler, a *sapojnik*. In the Soviet Union, a *sapojnik* was a trade held in very low esteem. For example, when the film broke in a movie theater, a frequent occurrence, the public would scream *sapojniki*, an insult expressed to the movie operator. It implied he did not know what he was doing, a *sapojnik*. Instead of just repairing shoes, Misha's father made boots and sold them on the black market for a lot of money. Their family lived comfortably, and they never went hungry.

Misha was tall, myopic and had to wear glasses. Despite being three years older, we became good friends. Before we left Stalinabad, he had a love affair with a girl who lived next door. They were both about seventeen years old. Rita and her mother did not mind having Misha sleep in their house. Rita's father, like many, had been killed in action. Her mother's permissive attitude and opinion that life is short, a direct result of high war casualties, allowed Rita to live for the present. The neighbors said Rita's mother was looking for a man, and she lived vicariously through her daughter's love affair. Misha's parents did not seem to mind his behavior, either.

Oh, how I envied Misha. Of course, I was too shy to admit it. During my childhood, I'd never heard the word "sex" uttered in our home. I did wish, however, that a girl like Rita would want to have sex with me, but without anyone ever discovering the truth. I'm not sure I was even physically able to have sex, despite the inspiration provided by Misha. He told me several times how great their sex was and I couldn't stop thinking how wonderful it would be to have a naked girl in bed. It is amazing I had those thoughts even though I was hungry. My desire for sex, even at an early age, and my desire for additional food were not mutually exclusive. I knew that if Papa were home instead in the Red Army fighting the war, he would have forbidden my friendship with Misha.

CHAPTER 8

FIRST FULL-TIME JOB

H UNGER and lice were our constant companions during the years in Stalinabad. We barely survived on Mama's meager earnings. She inquired about employment for me at the Sanbak Institute, but my age proved an impediment. After some time she persuaded the electrical technician there to take me on as his apprentice, even though I was only twelve and a half. In 1943, I dropped out of the seventh grade to work full time. I didn't regret leaving school, since it would allow me to help improve the quality of our life.

The electrical shop occupied a fifteen by twenty-five foot room in a maintenance building located at the far end of the yard. With an entry door and a large window at the front, the room contained closets, two large workbenches, a couple of tall stools and a table against the far wall. All kinds of wires hung on the walls, and various tools, equipment, and motors lay all over the place. The disorganized room made it hard to find any item.

My boss Sergey Semionovich, also a refugee from Sochi, a resort town on the Black Sea, was talented and well versed in all aspects of electrical work. Tall and slim, with graying blond hair, he wore rimless glasses. He possessed the aura of an important man, looking more like a diplomat than a technician. How he could appear so neat and yet maintain a sloppy workshop baffled me. During working hours, he wore a blue technician's coat. Unbeknownst to me, he was also an avowed anti-Semite.

"I'm a busy, impatient man," he told me on my first day. "I'm not paid to be a teacher. When I want you to do something, I'll tell you. Don't expect me to waste my time teaching. Watch me and stay out of my way. For your sake you'd better be a quick learner."

"I'll do my best," I promised.

"Start by straightening out this mess," he ordered. "Hang up things so we can find them easier."

"I will, right away."

"How did it go?" Mama anxiously asked on the way home from the Sanbak Institute later that day.

"He gave me quite a reception." I recounted our conversation.

"Buma, no matter how much we need your job, you can quit. We can find other work for you."

"No way, Mama!" I answered angrily. "I'll show him I can take anything he throws at me. Besides, we need my job. Who knows if the next one would be better? I have no skills, so I'll have to learn wherever I go."

Sergey Semionovich was cold but not an entirely bad person. I enjoyed working for him, watching him, and learning about electricity. When he gave me an assignment I didn't know how to do I asked for help and he would show me. A month later, he began implying that I'd stolen items from his shop. Every time he couldn't find a piece of wire or a misplaced tool, he looked accusingly at me.

"Did you take it?" he would demand.

"No, Sergey Semionovich," I replied, "but I'll look for it."

Most of the time I'd find the item; a few times, I couldn't. He may have already used the materials and forgotten. At first, I found it very hard to live with his accusations. The second time this happened, I came unglued.

"I'm not a thief, Sergey Semionovich." Tears welling in my

eyes, I could hardly speak. "I'm working to earn my money honestly."

"I didn't say you stole." He glared at me, incriminatingly. "But the item is gone. We are the only two people in the shop."

"Maybe you've used it up."

"Perhaps," he grumbled.

He never accused me again, but I worried constantly that he might find an excuse to fire me. In addition to working there, I started building hot plates to sell. I learned this skill by watching Sergey Semionovich. They were fairly easy to construct, although I had to build them from scratch.

I built the body in the form of a short cylinder, then a round surface that held the heater element out of a piece of sheet metal. Next, I wound the wire element into a spiral, and installed the spiral on ceramic isolators attached to the circular plate, connected a twisted pair of wires and a plug, and *voila*, a hotplate. With the money from the sale of a hotplate, Mama and I bought food to supplement our allotted diet.

Close to the shop was a large wooden outhouse, divided lengthwise to separate the women's section from the men's. Below the outhouse roof was an opening between the sections. The opening was high, providing adequate privacy. Mama used that opening to pass me carrots. Infrequently, the institute received a shipment of carrots to feed the rabbits they kept for experiments. Whenever Mama could, she stole one or two.

For a long time I developed sties on my eyelids. It reached a point that my eyelids were constantly red, swollen, and in pain. In addition to being painful, I was embarrassed by their unsightly appearance. A doctor explained the sties were caused by a lack of vitamins and other nutrients. After I'd suffered for months, Mama's female coworkers suggested I should drink malt and hops, substances used to make beer. The Institute made that malt. My mother's coworkers had her call me every time they had saved some, and I would find an excuse to go drink a cup or two of malt. It was extremely bitter and foul tasting, but I drank it whenever they had offered it to me. In addition to curing the sties on my eyelids, the liquid was a nutrient rich supplement.

After six months as an electrician's apprentice, I decided to install electricity in Aunt Sheiva's house. It was quite an undertaking. Sergey Semionovich told me where to buy wire, isolators, switches, and other equipment, and I was on my way. The electrical wires were carried on the surface of the walls on little ceramic isolators. I also installed the switches and outlets above the wall surface. I decided on the placement of the devices in each room, installed a light fixture in the middle of the ceiling, a switch next to the door, and an outlet on a wall. Then I screwed the ceramic isolators into the walls to form straight lines at ninety-degree angles. Next, I twisted individual insulated wires and slipped them over the isolators on the walls for support.

I knew how to connect the appropriate circuitry for each device. After I'd finished the interior installation, I climbed up the electric pole beside the house, connected and pulled two wires from the line to the two large isolators, which I'd installed on the roof's edge. I did not have permits or a license to hook up and install electricity. I didn't know if I needed them. I doubt that I had installed a watt-hour meter to measure the consumption, nor do I think we ever paid for the electricity, or if it was free because it belonged to the state. My effort was successful and we had light, a hotplate for cooking, and an electric heater, which vastly improved our standard of living. Lavishly praised, I felt like a hero in our house. Such praise went to my head at the age of thirteen.

I ended up working as an electrician's helper until we left Stalinabad in August 1944. Sergey Semionovich never became my friend. He was my boss, but he also never accused me of theft again. When we left, he told me that I had done a good job and he would miss me.

CHAPTER 9

THE CIVILIAN
POPULATION SUFFERS

I T is hard for anyone, especially an American fortunate not to have seen or experienced privation, to comprehend the catastrophic losses perpetrated on the population of the Soviet Union during the war. The ravages of WWII were unimaginable. Of course, I was unaware of the Holocaust at the time. The Holocaust is beyond any comparison. The victims of the Holocaust were under German occupation, shipped to concentration camps for the sole purpose of their complete eradication, by the most inhumane methods of annihilation since the Dark Ages.

Not under Nazi occupation, as a young boy living in Stalinabad I witnessed the most deplorable living conditions often defying explanation. I was one of the Soviet inhabitants, a very young citizen of the USSR and not some third world country. A huge country much larger than the United States, with a moderately educated population, a sizable army and weaponry. The country that eventually defeated mighty Nazi Germany, of course with help of the Allies but only after the country had almost been decimated. Our living conditions as refugees were sub-standard in the extreme. The constant defamation of being labeled "a f--- dirty Jew" matured me quickly. I had frequent discussions with Mama about our struggle, but we remained grateful to the Soviet Union for being our asylum. It saved our lives.

The male population was nearly obliterated. In addition to hunger and the lack of daily living necessities, I hardly ever encountered a young man of military age within a year after the start of the war. Women, children, old timers, and some natives like Tajiks, Uzbeks and others were the only people I saw on the streets. No military personnel were seen, especially in Stalinabad, a city far removed from any battle or front lines.

Each household was without husband, father, sons, or brothers. As the war continued, many families learned that their men were either dead or missing in action. The lucky ones often returned without a limb or had suffered other serious injuries. The neighbor women on both sides of our house and across the street received notices that their husbands were killed. My friend Vasiatka found out that he lost his father. Three out of four households suffered death. Just like all the other children in the neighborhood and in the whole Soviet Union, I spent the darkest of the war years without a father.

Russian women became desperate as they led their families and tried to provide food when it was beyond scarce. They had to be mother and father, disciplining their children to keep them from straying. Most did not succeed. The despondent children refused to accept their mothers' rules and lacked the interest to pursue a trade or contemplate a future. A high percentage dropped out of school, or while in school, joined gangs, became thieves, and used drugs. Many youngsters on our street quit school and didn't seek employment. They carried knives and displayed tattoos.

A pretty, blonde sixteen-year old girl, who lived across the street from us, became a prostitute. Her mother, unable to stop her, enjoyed the fruits of her daughter's labor. Each evening, unsavory characters gathered. The neighbors complained about the loud noise. Within a year, she lost the luster of youth. She had tattoos on both arms, and who knows where else. The gossip in the street was that she'd contracted syphilis.

The war and the consequent absence of fathers and older brothers in families created one or more lost generations. Of course, there were some children with missing fathers or brothers, who were exceptions, but they swam upstream to succeed.

Bulletins posted on major street corners, at kiosks, and in parks provided daily updates of the war. On our way home from work Mama and I stopped to read the bulletins on the gates of the central park. Early in the war, the news was grim. The Red Army retreated daily. I read the discouraging news, painfully frightened about our fate if the German advance continued.

"When will the Red Army stop the Germans?" I asked Mama.

"I hope it is soon," she replied without conviction.

We both worried about Papa, who served in the Red Army. We surmised the notices softened the actual truth so not to further discourage the Soviet population. They always praised the heroism of the Red Army with descriptions of the severe destruction and losses inflicted on the enemy before our army abandoned a town or village.

As we found out later, this war was responsible for the annihilation of about six million Jews, including eleven of our extended family, and an estimated twenty-seven million Soviets, both military and civilians. It is hard to imagine a country losing that many people. Those enormous numbers who perished were human beings, not just statistics. Each person had a face, a life, a family, loved ones, hopes, and plans for the future. Now, they were consigned – millions of men, women, and children – to history.

My personal war began on June 22, 1941, when my hometown was bombed and Germany invaded the USSR. The date of the invasion and the sights of Beltz's destruction remain etched into my brain forever. Romania, Italy, Finland, Hungary, and Slovakia also joined the invasion.

Although defense preparations were in force, the Soviet Union was caught by complete surprise. By the end of 1941, the Germans took Belarus and most of Ukraine. They surrounded Leningrad, which is now St. Petersburg. The siege lasted 900 days, and the resulting famine caused countless deaths, but the Germans never took Leningrad.

On November 27, 1941, the Germans reached the outskirts of Moscow. However, they encountered stiff resistance and retreated. Stalin's order and the Soviet will to fight for their capital city, combined with the Russian winter, stopped the German offensive.

"The Battle of all Battles" for Stalingrad was the severest of the war. It was also one of the bloodiest battles in human history. Stalin praised the heroism of the Red Army in radio speeches. "We will never give up Stalingrad!" He ordered, his broadcasts heard by the entire population. The Red Army had to hold Stalingrad at all costs.

The battle of Stalingrad began on June 28, 1942 and lasted more than seven months. On February 2, 1943, it finally resulted in a Soviet victory, and it was the decisive battle of the war. The invincible German might was broken. The Soviets lost an estimated 1,100,000 soldiers and 100,000 civilians while the Axis lost 500,000 soldiers, half of them Germans and the other half their allies.

There were frequent announcements saying the Allies were supposed to open a second front to help us militarily. We were all aware of the material help USSR received from America, including new American GMC trucks and Jeeps.

"When are the Allies going to open the second front?" people often asked each other in the streets. "Are they waiting for us to bleed to death?"

We could not understand why the Allies dragged their feet

during the siege of Stalingrad when the Soviets had tremendous daily casualties and the outcome was uncertain.

As the Soviet army started liberating their own lands in a westward advance, they discovered the total destruction of towns and villages, as well as the savage atrocities committed against Russian women and children. The newspapers and daily notices were full of lament on the subject. Hatred of Germans reached its peak.

I will never forget that war as long as I shall live. It left an imprint on my entire being. Everything that has happened to my family and to me since June 22, 1941 has been influenced by the events that began on that fateful June day.

CHAPTER 10

THINKING OF LEAVING STALINABAD

PAPA wrote us frequently soon after the Red Army transferred him out of Stalinabad. He could not describe his location although he assured us that he was well. The postmark on his letters provided no clue. As time passed, we received fewer letters. During one worrisome period, we stopped receiving any mail from him. We prayed for his safety. At the same time, we feared that something horrible had happened to him. However, Mama and I never voiced our concerns, as if speaking of them might cause them to occur. Often at night, I lay thinking about Papa and why we hadn't heard from him.

After a long emotionally stressful wait, we finally received a letter from Papa, now recovering in a military hospital. During the battle of Stalingrad Papa became a near casualty when bombings buried him in rubble and earth. His hearing and nervous system became impaired. Had his fellow soldiers not rescued him he would have suffocated.

At the end of many months of recuperation, Papa received orders for a desk job with the Red Army in Engels, a small town near the city of Saratov on the River Volga. This happened in September 1943 at the time of my thirteenth birthday. We corresponded frequently, and he assured us that he was getting better as time passed.

The town was named after Friedrich Engels (1820-1895), a German political philosopher who developed communist theory together with Karl Marx. I can still see his face on placards superimposed with those of Marx, Lenin, and Stalin. These four took the place of God in the USSR.

The Soviet victory at Stalingrad reversed the fortunes of the war. The German advance stopped. While fierce battles still raged and casualties mounted, the Germans were in retreat. Daily radio announcements and written communiqués informed us of the Red Army victories, their advances, and the liberation of Soviet territory previously controlled by the Germans.

We began to think about returning home to Beltz, but the word "home" sounded hollow to us. Our house and community had been destroyed. The alternative, spending the rest of my life in a backward Asian city and living in a mud hut, held little appeal.

Then it finally happened. On March 26, 1944, three years after our exile, the Red Army liberated Beltz. Mama and I were ecstatic. Our joy however turned to worry over the fate of our loved ones left behind in Beltz on that sad morning. We wondered if any of them were still alive.

Mama immediately wrote to Bronia's family, now living in Uzbekistan. With Beltz no longer in Nazi hands, we wanted to discuss with them a plan to go home.

I followed up Mama's letter with my own letter to Bronia on April 3, 1944. I praised the heroic Red Army for liberating our land, and recommended our return to Beltz as soon as possible. Some fifty years later, Bronia visited me in Los Angeles. She'd kept the letters for sentimental reasons, hoping some day, should we live and see each other again, she could give them to me as a memento of our survival. I was pleasantly shocked to see my yellow aged letter dated April 3, 1944 in Stalinabad. Since we had no envelopes, I formed the letter into a triangle, a standard practice at the time, and sent it by mail.

Soon after the liberation of Beltz, Papa asked us to join him in Engels. Mama immediately responded that we would. We did not know what to expect, but we welcomed this reunion with Papa. We all hoped it was an interim stop on our way home to Beltz.

We said our goodbyes and thanked Aunt Sheiva for welcoming us into her life and her home. Without her, we would have had no destination or hope to reaching it. Our separation from Aunt Sheiva, Raya, and our other friends was bittersweet. Although sad to leave them, we looked forward to being with Papa and eventually returning to Beltz.

Oh, how long we waited for the day we would leave our temporary evacuation quarters. We dreamed about that blessed day when we would go home, but not without realistic expectations and hopes. Before the Soviet victory in Stalingrad, when the Red Army was constantly retreating, I did not dare think that we would ever leave Stalinabad. I was afraid of negative thoughts about the war's outcome, because there was no way out for us. We had no alternate plan. For us it was the end of the road and life itself.

A couple of months before leaving Stalinabad we received the news that the Allies had invaded Normandy on June 6, 1944, another long awaited event. There was jubilation in the streets when we heard that the invasion, or the Second Front as we called it, had finally occurred. For the first time we believed the war might be over soon, but the heavy fighting and severe Allies' casualties sobered us and reminded us of the losses we too had suffered.

The Red Army continued its advance into Western Europe, and we followed the progress on both fronts, learning of the heavy bombardment of German cities. To deny my delight that the Germans were given a taste of what they had done to us would be disingenuous. Pictures of thousands upon thousands of captured German prisoners of war marching in endless lines under the surveillance of Red Army soldiers with drawn guns appeared in newsreels and the Soviet press. The once brave and mighty German Panzer divisions, which had caused horrific death and destruction and threatened to conquer the world, now appeared a downtrodden lot. To keep from freezing, they wrapped blankets over their military coats and rags over their heads and feet. Revenge felt ever so sweet.

This German reversal of fortunes hastened our departure from Stalinabad. We'd lived in Stalinabad for two years and nine months, from November 1941 to August 1944. My memories of Stalinabad aren't all negative. Even though I was hungry most of the time, I enjoyed the friends I made. I learned from the school of life, and I'd matured beyond my actual age. Although I never asked for that kind of an education, seeing that I received it, I was grateful.

Our trip from Stalinabad to Engels took two weeks by train. The trains, extremely crowded with frequent stops, felt like they stood still most of the time. With the exception of a few days aboard freight cars, we traveled primarily in passenger cars. The usual lack of food pursued us. Even though we were experienced railroad travelers and were excited about our reunion with Papa, the trip seemed like it would never end.

CHAPTER 11

ENGELS

OUR reunion with Papa entailed tears, embraces, and kisses.

"I'm so happy to see you alive and in one piece," cried Mama, tears running down her face. "You'll never know how much we've prayed for this moment."

"It's so good to see you both. Buma, you look so grown up," Papa looked proudly at me. "And you, Sonia, are so skinny. Are you both alright?"

"We're fine and very happy." Mama and Papa kissed and embraced for a long time.

"I thought of you often, and I wondered if I'd live to ever see you both again. The incessant firepower during the many months of the Stalingrad siege was indescribable. It was hell on earth. Then came the last blast – it buried me. For a brief instant I thought – that's it – goodbye! Everything went black – I could not breathe."

"Oh, Grisha, how much you suffered, and we knew nothing about it." Mama held on to him. "We were just hungry all the time and Buma became a young man without you."

I felt a spark of resentment that he hadn't been with us. He'll never know how tough it was to grow up without a father. I had to stand alone with no moral support or advice when called "dirty Jew," beaten up at school and often threatened. It was ironic I thought. He was there to discipline me but not to protect me. I forgave him because I loved him. The previous three years had been the fault of Hitler and the Nazis and not Papa. I prayed that being together as a family would improve our life.

We described in some detail our life in Stalinabad.

"I'm truly sorry," he said sympathetically. "You had it much worse than me. At least, I wasn't hungry."

"What about your hospital stay, Papa?" I asked. "Were you in a lot of pain?"

"Not really, just a long recuperation period."

This was the first time I had ever seen Papa sporting a goatee. Mama and I could not get used to it. He wore his military uniform and looked fit. He lived on a military base, which permitted civilian dependents.

We arrived in Engels in early September 1944. Already cold, it did not take long for the snows to settle in for good. After all, we were in the center of Russia near the Volga River, and winter had begun. The military cleared the snow daily, making paths between houses, barracks, and the main road. We walked on paths surrounded by towering walls of snow five or six feet above us, giving it a maze-like feeling.

The permanent snow on the ground reminded me of Beltz when I was six or seven. I had known many villagers who frequented Grandpa Zeilig's restaurant. One elderly man, short and stocky, had only thumbs on both hands. Grandpa had told me that the man was caught in a bad blizzard during which his fingers froze and had to be amputated. I recall one cold winter morning. Heavy snowflakes were falling, enveloping the town in a white blanket. The old man with the missing fingers and his two sons had arrived in a sled drawn by a *troika*, three gray horses. I'd heard the small bells attached to the harnesses ringing as the sled pulled into our yard. The men must have left the nearby village before dawn to arrive in town early in the morning. Steam rose from the frost-covered, overheated horses. The men stepped into the fresh snow, then loosened and covered the horses with wool blankets. They shook some of the snow off their clothes and feet and entered the restaurant.

Icicles hung from the gray mustache and thick eyebrows of the old man. His sons were taller and clean-shaven. Each wore a heavy sheepskin coat, and a lambskin *kutchma*, drawn over the ears. The coat had the animal hair on the inside, whereas the *kutchma*, a cone shaped hat, had the animal hair on the outside.

At the bar Grandpa served each of them a six-ounce heavy octagonal glass of vodka as soon as they walked into the restaurant. Before downing it, they took the peppershaker and poured black pepper into the vodka. Then they all took off their *kutchmas* and coats, and remained in lambskin vests over peasant shirts. The old man wore lambskin pants, whereas the sons were clothed in heavy woolen, grayish-beige pants. Their legs were wrapped in wool bindings up to the knees. The *opinci*, (goatskins sewn in the shape of rowboats) on their feet were tied to their legs with leather straps. Inside the *opinci*, the villagers donned woolen socks, rags, and sometimes straw, characteristic of Moldavian and Romanian footwear.

In Engels, I wished I had their warm clothes and *valenky*, instead of the *opinci*. *Valenky*, lightweight, knee-high boots made of heavy-gauge, stiff felt, were worn in Russia, where winters were very cold and dry.

The three men sat down for breakfast with food they had brought from home. They opened two towels containing black peasant bread and *salo*, a thick slab of white pork fat attached to the pigskin. Each cut the *salo* into bite size cubes with a pocketknife, using it instead of a fork. Their breakfast consisted of black bread and *salo*, with shots of vodka and black pepper.

To earn money, Mama baked potato knishes to sell at the railroad station about a kilometer from our barracks. She wrapped them in several towels to keep them warm and walked to the station in the cold and snow. She stayed outdoors until she sold all of them. Every so often, she returned nearly frozen with one or two unsold knishes, and we'd feast on them.

I found a job as an electrician's helper at a nearby ceramics factory. My responsibilities consisted of maintaining the electrical equipment under the supervision of another electrician. My counterpart for maintaining the mechanical equipment, primarily the boiler room, was about a year older. Without much work to do, we sat in the boiler room to stay warm during those frigid winter days.

One heavy snowstorm brought down several electric lines. Sent to help with repairs I climbed up the poles to pull up downed wires, wearing heavy rubber gloves and special climbing hooks on my shoes. Soviet climbing hooks were completely different from those used in the United States. They resembled sickles with sharp points at the foot and the end of the semicircle. I would encircle the post with the semicircle, place the front end against the pole, and slide my foot downward until the sharp points sank into the wooden post.

After climbing the pole, I received an electric shock, which sent me slipping all the way down to the ground. I wasn't injured, except for splinters that penetrated the heavy rubber gloves as I tried to hold on. The front of my *fufaika* also tore. My hands soon healed.

We lived in a single room in a large, long one-story building. We had minimal furnishings and a bathroom. The large room stayed very cold despite an iron stove.

I do not recall any social activities in the small town of Engels. My memories are of the cold and the constant efforts to warm ourselves.

We discovered a new wooden electric pole in the snow outside our building, left there to replace an older pole. One evening, we dragged it to our door with the assistance of my friend the mechanic. Without a saw, we chopped chunks from the pole with an axe, using the pieces sparingly to cook our meals, but it only lasted for about a week. We knew we could have received a ten-year jail sentence if we'd been caught stealing and destroying government property.

My parents and I had frequent discussions about returning to our Beltz. Finally, we decided that Mama and I would make the trip and Papa would join us as soon as the army discharged him from service. Mama bought flour on the black market to bake flat breads for the next train journey. The flour was very rough, containing large amounts of bran and something resembling pieces of straw.

About the same time, Papa accidentally encountered a young Jewish female refugee in the local market. He mentioned that he was from Beltz, and she told him she shared a room at a *kolhoz* with a young woman from Ataki. The young woman from Ataki turned out to be Lena, the girlfriend of father's cousin, Lazar. The *kolhoz* was located twenty-five kilometers from Engels.

Soon after, Lena visited us. I was never sure how she made her way to our apartment, perhaps by the kindness of someone driving to Engels or on foot. We told her that we had received permission from the government to travel to Beltz.

"Could I travel with you?" she inquired.

"Of course," Mama replied. "It would be much safer to travel together."

I told her, "It would be more fun."

"Thank you. I've postponed my return to Ataki because I feared traveling alone. A single woman on such a long journey would be inviting trouble."

Several weeks later Lena walked twenty-five kilometers in the cold snow with a bundle of possessions on her back until she arrived in Engels. Frozen and exhausted, she removed her knitted hat and gloves. We helped her warm up by rubbing her hands and feet. She stayed with us, in the same room, until we departed for Beltz. At the time, Lazar was in the Red Army. Mama had already baked a large amount of flat breads and stored them in a bag. Finally, the three of us departed by train for Beltz and Ataki.

During the war and German occupation, many families were destroyed and others uprooted and scattered all over Europe and Asia. We had no means to determine if our relatives had survived and, if so, where they now resided. As soon as the surviving refugees returned to the liberated cities, they posted their addresses and other notices at the postal office, city hall, and at other gathering places. They also listed names of members of their families whose whereabouts were unknown. People searching for missing relatives went daily to peruse the notices in the hope of finding a family member or friend. Those not in town wrote to the post offices or city halls.

Prior to our departure, we learned that Uncle Zioma had not survived. However, Uncle Tolia and his wife Sonia had returned to Beltz. Mama and Uncle Tolia communicated by mail, and he supplied the documents requesting permission for us to travel to Beltz. Tolia wrote that they had returned to Beltz within days of its liberation and managed to find a single room. He also informed us of the town's destruction, and that at least fifty percent of the buildings were in various degrees of disrepair. With so many refugees returning, rooms in town were nearly impossible to find. Uncle Tolia had managed to get his old job back at the spirits factory in the capacity of head distiller. Mama wrote to Uncle Tolia of our departure date, sometime in February 1945. We had lived in Engels for about six months. I was fourteen and a half years old.

Our trip by train back to Beltz, hallmarked by frigid weather, took a long time. February weather in Mother Russia is brutal. We began our journey in a passenger train, but we made numerous changes; most of the time we traveled in unheated freight cars, freezing and uncomfortable.

The breads Mama baked became hard, went stale, and later turned green. Yet, they were our principal sustenance. We pared off the mold and ate what remained.

The long journey gave me time to think about Beltz and our life there. I knew the city had been partially destroyed, but I didn't want to dwell on that harsh reality. I recalled Beltz as it had been before the bombs and destruction. During the nights, I lay awake and reminisced about the happy pre-war days. My nostalgia grew a life of its own as I relived the memories of my unscarred childhood.

As a child not yet five years old, my blue eyes and long straw-colored curls resembled Shirley Temple's childish appearance. During my first haircut at the age of five, Mama collected and saved my shorn curls in an envelope. A photo of me in a blue sailor outfit, with curls running down my forehead, ears and neck stood on the nightstand in our bedroom.

Grandpa Zeilig influenced my childhood. Because he had only two grandchildren, Bronia and me, he showed us a lot of love and affection. I spent a great deal of time with him, accompanying him to the open market and to Synagogue on Friday evenings. Mama seemed to be his favorite, probably because she was his only daughter.

Grandpa Zelig rose early each morning to open his restaurant. He bought two fresh bagels for me and Bronia, and delivered them to us while they were still hot. The bagels in Beltz looked like a soft untwisted pretzel. We ate our bagels with butter. Grandpa also gave us our daily coin, a Romanian *leu*. Sometimes, we tried to cheat our grandma by asking her, *"Bubbe*, would you give us our daily *leu?"*

"Didn't Grandpa give you your *leu*, today?" she would ask, knowing Grandpa's routine.

"No!" we shouted in unison. Thus, we managed to double our daily take, unless she verified our claim of nonpayment with Grandpa. In that case, we asked, "Don't you believe us?" Even though she knew what we were up to, she usually gave it to us.

Armed with that coin in our hand, we'd run across the street to Benditovich's grocery and purchase two candies, or popcorn. We also bought sunflower seeds from one of the two old Gentile women who sat on our street corner. Those seeds were sold by the glass, freshly roasted, and in the shells. Other vendors who walked the streets sold hot corn-on-the-cob and pickled apples. The ethnicity and origin of the people living in our neighborhood was such that the street vendors chanted *heise papshoies,* hot corns in Yiddish, and *machonye yabloky,* pickled apples in Russian. The vendors did not chant in Romanian, the official language, even though Beltz was under Romanian rule. At times, we spent our daily *leu* with those vendors.

Our journey finally concluded as the train arrived in Beltz after a few long cold weeks. We were home again.

PART TWO

RETURNING
HOME (1945)

CHAPTER 12

RETURN TO BELTZ

A T the end of February 1945, almost a year after the liberation of Beltz, we finally returned home. The sky was gray, the air chilly, and a light rain fell. The roads, muddy with many slippery frozen areas, reminded me of Beltz's reputation as the mud capital of Bessarabia. We searched the Big Railroad Station for Uncle Tolia who worked nearby and checked daily if we had arrived. We hadn't found him so Mama and I waited.

Soon after, I saw Uncle Tolia, immediately recognizing him despite his fatigue and much older appearance. His shoulders drooped and he carried his head lower than I remembered. Thinner, what remained of his hair was now gray. He looked like a man who had lived through hell. With muddy army boots and khaki bindings over his legs, he reminded me of the Romanian soldiers I had seen.

Our reunion was very emotional as Uncle Tolia, Mama, and I held one another and wept for a long time. Finally, Uncle Tolia told us of Zioma's death in Bershad, a concentration camp in Transnistria, on the other side of the River Dnester in Ukraine. He continued with a description of Grandma Hannah's final moments during a forced march of Jews, rounded up as prisoners and driven eastward by the German army. A neighbor who'd survived the march, had watched Grandma Hannah lag behind and collapse from exhaustion. A German soldier had hit her a couple of times with the butt of his rifle, leaving her for dead on the road like the abandoned corpse of a stray dog.

"Those were times for innocent Jews to die. Dead Jews lying in the streets were more common than stray dogs," said Uncle Tolia, bitterly.

In lieu of a taxi Uncle Tolia had arranged for a driver with a horse drawn wagon to transport us to his lodgings. As soon as we settled in the wagon, Tolia explained that he'd prepared a bed for us in the foyer outside his room. On our way to his single small room, we drove down one ruined street after another, crossing the Old Bridge and proceeding down what was King Carol II, renamed by the Soviets to Lenina, to where our home had once stood at Number 57.

An eerie feeling and depression settled over me as I studied the uneven terrain on each side of the road where once had stood homes and businesses. A sharp right turn in the road signaled our street corner. Tolia asked the driver to slow down the wagon, allowing us to search for the site of our home. We counted four such mounds from the street corner and stopped the horses. We descended from the wagon with tear-filled eyes, still unsure if we were in the right place. Shivering, we held on to each other as we looked at the empty space around us and assessed the graveyard of our street. The first sight of the war's complete destruction of the life we once lived made me feel gut-punched.

"They were only houses," Mama lamented, "but what about the people who lived there? They are gone forever!"

Learning of the fate of our now dead loved ones made the loss of our house seem relatively unimportant.

Tolia and Sonia lived with several other families in what used to be a private house. Upon entering the foyer, we discovered that it served as the only access to each room. In one corner of the foyer stood a metallic stove used for cooking. The bed shoved against the wall between the entry door and the stove would be our new "home."

We stored our bundles under the bed. It was clear that Mama and I must start looking for a place of our own. It was worse than at Aunt Sheiva's, living in a foyer with no furniture, where families from four separate rooms had to walk past our bed as well as to use the stove for cooking.

That first night, lying in bed with Mama in the foyer, I couldn't fall asleep. With nostalgia, I recalled our life in Beltz. I visualized the interior of our home and Grandpa Zeilig's, the beautiful Turkish rugs hanging on the walls of the living room and bedroom, and less costly rugs scattered across the rough-finished wooden floors.

Both houses had five rooms with similar interior layouts, a large dining room, a master bedroom, a kitchen, a living room, and a room adjacent to the master bedroom. Grandpa had used his living room to house the restaurant. Walking into each house was akin to walking in a train; there were no hall-ways. One passed through each room consecutively to reach the last room.

The dining room, considered the primary room, hosted most activities. One of the dining room walls served as the fireplace. Two feet above the floor, the wall contained a rectan-gular opening covered by a metallic door that measured twelve to eighteen inches on each side. Wood or sunflower shells fed through the opening sustained the fire. The entire wall heated up and warmed the room. We stood with our backs to the wall to warm ourselves.

We entered each house through its kitchen door by way of the side yard separating Grandpa's and our houses, using our front entry into the living room only when we had special company.

Electricity had been installed in 1938 but neither of the houses had a bathroom. We had to use the outhouse in our backyard, making it especially difficult to access in heavy snow or sleet and not much fun to trek through the mud when it rained.

We bathed in a large tin tub, which was not comfortable, but we were used to it. On special occasions, Papa took me to the Turkish bath in town, a large old building, its floors and walls covered in white ceramic tile, wet and steamy with a musty smell. In addition to the bathtubs, there was a large steam room where men on wooden benches sweated profusely. When Bronia's father installed a tin tub in his house with a primus fitted beneath it to heat the water, we went there to bathe. The walk home in frigid temperatures after a hot bath wasn't pleasant.

Each house had a cellar with exterior entrances. Our cellar was often flooded so we used Grandpa Zeilig's for food storage. Grandpa stored barrels of wine, pickled cucumbers, tomatoes, and watermelon in his cellar, and sold these items in addition to food in his restaurant.

Bronia, Pesia and I would sneak into Grandpa's cellar, gorge on the delicious pickles, tomatoes, and watermelon straight out of the barrel. Once when I was tasting wine out of the barrel using the wooden spout, I spilled some. Afraid that Grandpa would notice it I quickly wiped it.

The final room in Grandpa Zeilig's house was Isrul's (Israel), Mama's oldest brother. Prior to the revolution of 1918, he fled to Ukraine to escape the draft. He spent time in Balta with relatives, and in Odessa. After the revolution, he decided it was safe to return to Beltz by train. At the time, the trains overflowed with military and civilians. Some people rode atop the railroad cars.

Isrul's body was found next to the railroad tracks near a small railroad station. Grandpa traveled there, identified his body, and brought him home for burial. The railroad official speculated that perhaps he'd fallen off the roof of the train. My grandparents believed that someone had pushed him from the train. A gentle person, he must have stood out like a sore thumb among the revolutionaries and soldiers. His death, a terrible tragedy for our family, devastated my grandparents.

That was right after World War I. Surely nobody expected World War II and its unimaginable consequences.

Although Isrul had been dead for many years, my grandparents left his room as it was when he lived in it. In addition to works of Tolstoy, Pushkin, Dostoyevsky, Zola, and others, a large clock with a motionless pendulum hung on the wall. Trying to find out why it had stopped, I stood on a chair, opened the ornate clock's glass door, inserted the key, and attempted to wind it. Not understanding what made the pendulum move, I decided to unhook and remove it and hit it several times with a hammer. Grandpa Zeilig passed near the room, heard the hammering noise, and caught me red handed at the scene of the crime with the hammer in my hand and the pendulum destroyed.

"Why did you do that?" he shouted angrily.

"*Dedushka*, I wanted to fix the clock. You know it didn't work, it was broken."

"So now it works?"

"I am sorry, *Dedushka*," I knew what was coming.

"I'll give you something to be sorry about." As he uttered these words, he grabbed me, put me face down over his arm, and spanked me on my behind. That was the only time, ever, my grandpa hit me. I must have been seven years old.

In view of my current situation, reminiscing about my living conditions before the war made me more despondent. Instead of being happy to have finally returned to Beltz, Mama and I felt depressed as we faced the death of our loved ones, the sight of what had once been our home, and our appalling temporary living quarters.

"Is this why we came home?" Mama sobbed. "Is this why we survived, to live like this?"

We spent the rest of that day grieving while Tolia described the horrors they'd survived in Bershad, where Jews from Bessarabia and other regions had been interned. The Bershad *lager* (concentration camp in German), had been established to starve, beat, intimidate, and execute Jews rounded up by the Nazis. Uncle Zioma's daily life was somewhat better than the rest of those in the *lager* because he was a physician. He'd been able to obtain more food, which he shared with the family. Tolia told us that Zioma also helped the inmates of Bershad, just as he'd helped everyone before the war.

They endured the concentration camp for three years. Just three weeks before Bershad's liberation by the Red Army, the Romanians and Germans who ran the camp rounded up three hundred Jews, marched them out of town, and made them dig a large ditch. Then they shot the people, dumped their bodies in the ditch, and covered it with earth. After the execution, the people in the Bershad *lager* were informed that the Germans had found a list naming those who'd been executed as having made donations to the partisans, the guerilla fighters who fought the Nazis. Internees approached to donate to the partisans would do so, with their last possessions. By conducting raids and fighting the Germans, they provided hope to the camp internees, who prayed that the day of their liberation would come sooner because of the partisan activities.

After the liberation of Bershad, the mass grave was unearthed and individual burials took place for those murdered in cold blood. Uncle Zioma had been at the very bottom of the ditch, the only murder victim found completely naked with the exception of his socks. Witnesses said the Nazis had persecuted and ridiculed him prior to shooting him. Uncle Tolia suffered psychologically for the rest of his life over Zioma's death. He had headaches, insomnia, and bad dreams, including daydreams or visions of his brother Zioma.

Uncle Zioma's death hit me hard. His life had been intertwined with my family as I'd grown up in Beltz. I recalled the visits Mama and I had made to the Jewish hospital where he'd lived in a single room during his residency. Later when he had a successful practice, he'd bought a two-story home in a nice section of town. I loved his Telefunken short wave radio, and was impressed with his telephone, both rare in Beltz.

"May God bless your son, the doctor." A man approached Grandpa Zeilig as we walked in the street. "He saved my wife's life and never charged us a *leu*." The man then turned to me and said, "I hope you'll be a doctor like your uncle."

Embarrassed, I didn't know what to say as Uncle Zioma had often been thanked and praised for his good deeds.

Everything had changed. Mama and I now lived in a foyer with no privacy at all, the Beltz I'd known had been destroyed, and Uncle Zioma was dead. There was hope for me, but none for those taken from us and brutally murdered.

Tuba, Benny and their daughter, Pesia, had gone to hide in a village where they had lived years earlier. They thought that because the villagers knew them, they would be safe there. Tolia explained that the villagers had murdered all three of them in the center of the village. Pesia's death especially pained me. She was only one year older than I, and certainly hadn't harmed anyone. Mama wept, regretting that she hadn't asked them to come with us instead of allowing them to go their own way alone. At the time we'd fled, no one had known which path would lead to survival and which path to death.

We experienced survivor's guilt in the face of so many family members who'd perished while we'd survived. My complaints about lice and hunger seemed trivial.

Tolia often expressed his guilt for surviving Bershad while Zioma was murdered.

"Zioma certainly deserved to survive. Being a physician, he saved many lives. He would have continued to save others. I should have died, not Zioma, who helped feed our family. Without him we all would have perished," Tolia lamented. "I have no reason to live, no great merits."

It broke my heart to listen to him weep and to regret his own survival.

Uncle Itzik, Grandpa Zeilig's brother, and his wife Aunt

Freida Rivka Fleishman, died in Beltz because they were too old to run. Later, we learned that my other uncle, Israel Nulman, Grandma Hannah's brother, and his son, Avrum, only a few years older than me, were murdered in Iasi, Romania. Somehow, his wife Basia survived and immigrated to Israel. My father's parents, Rubin and Sarah Frimtzis also perished somewhere in Ukraine.

Eleven people in our family lost their lives under terrible conditions during the war. That number does not include the losses of Bronia's mother Liza's family. With the exception of Zioma, exhumed and buried in a proper grave, we never discovered the remains of the others.

Uncle Tolia's wish to have died in Uncle Zioma's place is similar to the guilt of many Nazi extermination camps survivors. They question if they are more deserving of survival than those murdered. Some felt the reason they survived was because those who were murdered must have taken their place, and for that reason alone, they must have been more deserving of life, which reinforced their guilt. Other survivors believed that because they survived, they must have done something wrong. Perhaps they had stolen someone's food, found a warm space to avoid freezing to death, or successfully hidden when the Nazis rounded up people for the showers. Consequently, someone innocent had filled the quota and died as a result.

An extreme example was Primo Levy, an Italian Jewish chemist sent to Auschwitz. He survived. After his liberation, he bore witness to the atrocities committed at Auschwitz through his extensive writings. He became so guilt-ridden for surviving that he eventually took his own life.

I find it impossible to comprehend that being Jewish was the sole basis for the Nazi-designed Holocaust, and justified the savagery orchestrated by Adolph Hitler and the hierarchy of the Third Reich.

Since the Stone Age, humanity has advanced and progressed in every conceivable field. We have learned about medicine to improve our health and prolong our lives. We have devised and invented technologies that allow us to improve our living conditions. We have explored our solar system, and we've developed literature, music, art, and philosophy to satisfy our curiosity and expend our mental capacity. I personally aided in the endeavor that transported a man to the moon. We have written laws to guide us in a civilized manner, to provide us safety, and to protect us and our property. Yet some people displayed a level of cruelty and savagery more pronounced during World War II than ever seen or experienced since the Dark Ages. They either demonstrated a complete disregard for human life or worse yet, created laws to justify their inhuman behavior. While some people tried to prevent the Holocaust, most of the world stood and watched as it unfolded.

The Jewish tragedy brings to mind the world's indifference to other races and inaction in other parts of the globe. As a result, I developed a cynical attitude. I am well aware of those who worked hard and in many instances endangered their own lives to help the oppressed. Called "Righteous," their names are inscribed on honor rolls in Israel because of their efforts to save Jewish lives during the Holocaust. Unfortunately, they were a small minority.

As I consider the events of the war, I also realize the parallels of life and death. At times, there is little separation between the two. In the case of our family, my father's decision to leave Beltz early allowed us to escape capture. Those few days made the difference between living and dying. Are such events simply a matter of chance, or preordained?

As a child, I learned of a Higher Being who watches over us. I would like to believe that there is a God, but I must ask, "How could He allow such calamity to befall people whose only sin was being Jewish?" This is a significant question, but there seems no adequate answer.

I had also known of a covenant between God and Abraham, and that Jews were the chosen people. In the story, *"Tevia*

Der Milchiker" by Shalom Aleichem, made into the musical "Fiddler on the Roof," Tevia complains to God, to paraphrase, "I know we are the chosen people, so why don't You choose somebody else for a change?"

Throughout the centuries and even millennia, across the globe Jews have been persecuted and killed. This wholesale slaughter began before Christianity and continued with the Catholic Church, followed by the crusades, the inquisitions, the expulsions, the ghettos, and the forced conversions.

All those events I considered as part of the painful history of the Jewish people. Then came the Third Reich and Hitler, who intended to wipe out the Jews from the face of the earth. They almost succeeded.

James Carroll, author of the New York Times Bestseller book *"Constantine's Sword – The Church and the Jews,"* and Winner of the National Book Award eloquently and painstakingly traces the history of the Church's guilt directly and by neglect for the past two millennia. He includes a chronology, beginning with the Middle Bronze Age (circa 2800 – 2200 B.C.E.) and an exhausting list of references. I found it painful to read, but at the same time, I felt encouraged, and I admired the author's candor and honest stance, which was based on endless research and literary proof. I only wish there were more Catholics like him, for the world would certainly be a more just and tolerant place to live. I also wish I had the power to change the hatred in the world, but it would take the combined will of all people, not a single individual. During World War II, Hitler began the Holocaust, but the will of the German people made it happen.

CHAPTER 13

DISAPPOINTMENT
IN Beltz

BELTZ had changed beyond recognition. Aside from the park and City Hall, I recognized little of the city. For the second time in my life, for completely different reasons I was a stranger in my hometown.

We had no idea where to look for a place to live. It became painfully clear to us that we could not remain in Beltz. In many ways, I wished we had never returned home.

While we were refugees in Stalinabad, it was natural to want to return to my childhood home. I'm sure everybody feels a certain deep-rooted nostalgia regarding one's hometown. I certainly did. One is full of childhood memories, especially if they were good. One looks forward to revisiting the neighborhood, the school, the ballpark, the store where one bought candy, or the ice cream parlor, the church or synagogue, the friends, and the special places to relive those memories. One longs for "the good old days."

A few weeks after our return to Beltz a mass grave was discovered in town. It created utter hysteria in town. The bodies had decomposed beyond recognition. It took days for each corpse to be examined for identification and reburied in an individual grave.

Shock paralyzed and devastated all the returning Jewish survivors. No one seemed able to resume a normal life. Good humor faded, replaced by a collective anguish. People asked one another, "How long will we keep finding dead Jews? When will the murder of the innocent stop?"

Most Jews in town went to the mass grave and recited the prayers for the dead, *"El Malley Rachamim,"* and *"Kaddish."* No one knew the identity of the bodies. Perhaps they were missing relatives, perhaps not. Most prayed, seeking some form of closure for those lost or missing. The stench of death lingered, as did the mourning for the dead.

Mama and I searched for weeks for a place to live. Mama finally found a room for us in a two room dilapidated house. We shared the house with another woman and her young son. We occupied the front room, which meant that the woman and her boy walked through our room to reach their quarters. This modest living arrangement became our home. Papa remained in the Red Army.

Uncle Tolia gave Mama a bottle of ninety-six percent pure spirit and showed her how to dilute it with water to make vodka. He stole the spirits from his workplace fearing jail if anyone discovered his theft. He took only small amounts, thus taking him a long time to accumulate a liter.

Mama sold the homemade vodka on the black market. With the exception of the first two bottles, she split her earnings with Tolia. She started dealing on the black market by buying and selling small items at a profit. Mama became a *speculiantka*, a dealer on the black market, which violated the law and could result in a jail sentence. The authorities looked the other way. Since black market dealing equaled survival, the Soviet government realized it could not jail its entire population.

Mama's business was primarily with Soviet soldiers returning home from the war and eager to sell their military shirts, coats, and pants. They bought silk scarves, ladies blouses, silk stockings and other finer luxury items non-existent in Russia.

Mama, a very small *speculiantka*, bought and sold no more

than a few items at a time. With the profit, she bought bread, butter, and fruit. Our diet improved tremendously. A frequent meal for me in the summer was fresh bread and butter with sweet large cherries.

Soon after our arrival in Beltz, I obtained a job with a former colleague of Papa's as an accountant's apprentice. I entered large columns of numbers, adding or subtracting them, depending on the need to debit or credit. I performed the calculations using an abacus. Accuracy, speed, and neatness were very important on that job. I then realized that I liked working in an office as opposed to a shop. Although tedious, entry-level work, it was considered a white-collar job. I knew then that I wanted to be a professional, and not a tradesman or a blue-collar worker in a shop or factory. My father's insistence on clean hands, a suit and tie, and reading and studying to improve one's self had an impact on my goals for the future.

In Beltz, I also found my old friend, Benny, who had grown tall. Prior to the war, we'd called him Benny the *Karlik*, midget. We renewed our friendship. He'd become a lathe operator, which widened the gulf between us if we weren't reminiscing about the past. Before the war, we had been inseparable, even though we attended different schools. Papa had insisted that I attended school far from our neighborhood, whereas he'd attended the local school. Benny, like me, had survived the war by escaping to one of the Soviet Central Asian republics.

My cousin Bronia, Aunt Liza, and Uncle Shulim arrived in Beltz from their own personal hell in Uzbekistan shortly after us. After some time, Uncle Shulim found an abandoned house littered with feces. He cleaned it up, replaced the missing windows and doors, and they settled into it. The little house, in the Pominteni section, was located at the other end of town.

Bronia started school and I met one of her schoolmates, Anna. Her family settled in Beltz soon after the Soviets came into Bessarabia in June 1940. She was what we referred to as a true Soviet. They'd also survived the war at another location

in the Soviet Union, and then returned to Beltz after its liberation. We immediately became very good friends. In fact, she
was my first love.

While we lived in Beltz, an event of global proportions
for which we'd prayed during the previous four years finally
occurred. Too few of us lived to see that event. After everything
we'd endured, it was difficult to truly enjoy the collapse of the
Third Reich. With sorrow and pain in our hearts for our lost
relatives, we celebrated the anti-climactic German surrender
and the end of the war, *Den Pobedy,* (Victory Day), on May
9, 1945. The sun shone on that beautiful day in May, white
puffy clouds floated in the sky and a soft wind lightly touched
the faces of the multitude in the streets. Everyone watched the
military parade. I was no exception. A military band played
and soldiers marched while people celebrated and drank in the
streets.

For our family, however, it was a bittersweet event to
celebrate the downfall of the Nazis and our survival of four
years of horror and misery. Never in our lifetime would we
be subjected to that kind of tyranny again, at least not from
Germany. During the war, we doubted our nightmare would
ever end. The celebration came too late for the victims but
the survivors knew that we had triumphed over Hitler and the
Nazi murderers.

Many wept openly during the celebration, myself included
as I remembered my cousin Pesia, murdered at the age of
twelve. I wanted her to see the victory through my eyes. Even
though my sobbing stopped, the tears continued rolling involuntarily down my face. She, like Uncle Zioma and all the rest
of our family, had been perfectly innocent. We also listened
to stories about the atrocities committed against the Jewish
people in the concentration camps, although we didn't know
yet of the six million deaths. While time heals and pain dimin-
ishes, I will take to my grave the knowledge of this horrifying
period of man's inhumanity to man.

A monument erected in honor of the Red Army, which fought and liberated our city, was but a modest reminder of the war. Located in the center of Beltz, across the street from City Hall, many festivities took place near the monument. At the time, I thought, "Who needed to be reminded when one has lived through it?"

The poor living conditions in Beltz prompted Mama and me to make plans to leave our home at the earliest opportunity. We considered a move to Chernovitz because people who'd already moved there said it was easier to find a place to live. Once Papa was released from military service and joined us in Beltz, my parents decided that he would leave the next morning to explore Chernovitz. He wore his military uniform, having no other clothes to wear.

Chernovitz suffered relatively little damage during the war. It was a large modern city with more housing, better transportation, and a variety of business and school opportunities. We hoped that Papa, a soldier returning from the war, would have a better chance of demanding and receiving an apartment prior to having settled in with us. We believed that the government would be obligated to provide a higher preference to a discharged veteran than the resettlement of refugees. What's more, the one small room we lived in could not accommodate one more bed or person.

We wanted to leave the Soviet Union, intending to immigrate eventually to the United States. We equated the thought of going to America with utopia, the impossible dream. Yet we had a minute hope because we had known that Papa's cousins, Mosia, Matusia and Rose lived in the United States. We believed that they would send us an affidavit inviting us to America. Even that early in my life I equated America to a beacon of freedom and a place everyone dreamed of living. We knew from our cousins that America allowed immigration. Departing the Soviet Union for the United States of America translated into an act of treason for a Soviet citizen. Therefore, we would need to leave the USSR, and then apply for entry from another country. We also knew America had strict immigration quotas, which required a long waiting period of the applicants.

Before belonging to the Soviet Union, Chernovitz, in the region of Bucovina, was part of Romania. Before that, it had been part of the Austrian Empire. Beltz, on the other hand, was Russian until Romanian control. Our best course of action would be to escape from Bucovina, posing as Austrians or Romanians.

Even though Chernovitz was a part of the Soviet Union at the time, a large segment of the Chernovitz population considered itself either Austrian or Romanian, and felt occupied by Russia. It created an easier climate for planning an escape to the West from Chernovitz. The Soviet officials and the border guards on the Romanian border regarded people wanting to repatriate from Bucovina with less suspicion than those who wanted to cross the border from Bessarabia. Certain that our destiny was to escape from the Soviet Union we eagerly anticipated the next step in our odyssey – the move to Chernovitz. We had spent only six months in Beltz.

CHAPTER 14

CHERNOVITZ

PAPA arrived in Chernovitz in July 1945, wearing his military uniform. He showed the local authorities his discharge papers and explained that he was looking for an apartment for himself and his family. Within a week, he found an apartment with a glass-enclosed foyer, a kitchen, a fairly large room with an attractive ceramic fireplace in the far corner, and an indoor bathroom. He returned to Beltz to share his good news. We happily packed our few belongings and boarded the train for Chernovitz.

We were pleasantly surprised when we first saw the apartment. After all, we had not lived in decent quarters since the beginning of the war. Even though the apartment was much smaller than our pre-war home in Beltz, it was more modern, had taller ceilings, larger windows, and above all, a bathroom.

I don't know how or where my parents obtained used furniture, but they managed to acquire two beds, a table, chairs, and a wardrobe. The furniture occupied the one room, offering little privacy and not much space for my parents, but they didn't complain.

The apartment was on the ground level of a two-story building. The address was Khruschova 13, apartment #3.

Chernovitz was everything Beltz was not. A large, metropolitan, and clean city with hilly streets, wide boulevards, tall multi-story buildings designed in a classic architectural style, and most importantly, it had survived the war with little destruction. With transportation in the form of trolleys and buses, it also had retail stores, which periodically stocked goods for sale. I particularly remember a *konditerai* (bakery) that from time to time sold cookies and Viennese pastries. I treated myself to a pastry whenever possible.

The city uplifted our moods and we were relieved not to be exposed daily to the haunted ruins of once familiar places. Beltz had served as a constant reminder of our lost family members and friends. Chernovitz provided us with a fresh start and new hope for my future.

Shortly after our arrival, I applied and was accepted to a technical high school, which was equivalent to a combination seventh and eighth grade academic enrollment. I had not completed the seventh grade prior to leaving school in Stalinabad in 1943. At the technical school, I made new friends, three boys from Beltz. Fima, a head taller than me, and Mara became my best friends. We'd spent a lot of time together, often in our apartment doing homework and talking about girls.

Papa began buying and selling items on the black market. Our standard of living improved, and I finally had my own bed; I was fifteen. Mama bought a used military coat from a soldier, and a tailor converted it into an officer's style coat for me, along with a Cossack style, winter hat. The hat had a hard vertical, circular rim covered in a gray lambskin, and the top was made of black cloth. I felt that I cut quite a stylish figure as I went off to school. Uncle Tolia and Aunt Sonia also moved to Chernovitz, where they managed to secure a one-room apartment.

I missed Anna, having spent only two months with her before we'd moved to Chernovitz. After that, we stayed in touch by mail. During winter break, I took a train to Beltz to see her, staying at Bronia's home for the better part of a week. We had no place to be intimate, so we huddled together at the local theater, always afraid that people might recognize us and tell on us. Despite frigid temperatures, we walked for hours in the snow holding each other. We didn't feel the cold. When my family departed for Romania, I hadn't been able to even say goodbye to her, because we left secretly.

Three other apartments shared our courtyard. One neighbor, a recently discharged army colonel with a chest-full of decorations, happened to be Jewish. Two Gentile families occupied the other apartments, one a recently discharged wounded veteran with a missing leg. He used crutches, and he always seemed to be drunk.

One weekend, after a few drinks too many, the veteran attacked the colonel at the entry to our foyer. The disabled veteran began shouting insults, finally hitting the Jewish colonel with a crutch. In a loud drunken voice, he demanded, "Where did you buy your medals, on the Tashkent front? You f... *Jidy* did not serve in the army or fight the Germans. You hid in the far interior and bought these decorations."

The colonel defended himself by covering his head with his raised arm, unable to bring himself to strike a one legged man barely able to stand.

That type of behavior prevailed throughout the Soviet Union, and by no means an incident exclusive to one wounded drunk. The official Soviet Government policy stated the equality of all citizens. In reality, anti-Semitism ran rampant during the post-war years. The authorities always looked the other way. I have little doubt that they shared the sentiment.

These episodes made us cringe. How could we accept this behavior after all we had endured? We all questioned our long-term security in such an environment for any surviving Jew. Could we survive the undercurrent of hatred and bigotry? All the good feelings of my potentially successful future evaporated. Attending school and working hard for the future for a Jew felt like just another dream, an exercise in futility, similar to building a house on a foundation of shifting sand.

The writing on the wall became clearer with every passing

day. My parents and I felt the escalating tension, and we began to consider seeking freedom and safety in another country. Security was very important after all our suffering during the war. Even though we had found refuge from the Nazis in the USSR and our post-war lives had improved, we knew we had no future under the Soviet regime. We longed to immigrate to America, but we viewed that with distant hope and some skepticism. The decision to start running again, and illegally at that, was difficult to make. Meanwhile, time passed as we considered our options.

Papa's cousin, Lazar, arrived in Chernovitz after his discharge from the Red army. A short time later, he married his sweetheart Lena, the woman who had left Engels with Mama and me. Lazar experienced great difficulty in acquiring lodging in a very small room in someone else's apartment, because the city was overrun by returning refugees and discharged military.

Lazar and Lena's wedding consisted of a simple meal and a bottle of vodka in Uncle Tolia's one room apartment, with my parents and I in attendance. It was a bittersweet affair, most of our family absent, even though he had four brothers, including two in America. We hoped that they were alive, although we realized that men in Europe and United States had fought in the war as well. America had been fortunate not to have to defend or do battle on its own territory.

Lazar found employment in a sock factory. Lena also worked, but they earned little and struggled a lot. Like many veterans, his wardrobe didn't extend beyond his military uniform. He always wore his military coat with a big oil spot on the back, and tall army boots. Even though Lazar desperately wanted to join his brothers in America, his membership in the Communist Party made him fearful of being considered a traitor punishable by death. He suffered, although he finally made it to America some 45 years later, in the early 1990's. By then he was in his late seventies.

Uncle Tolia's wife, Sonia, had a brother in Bucharest, the

capital of Romania. There he managed to secure false documents indicating that Tolia had been born in Romania. The Soviet Government allowed them to repatriate to Romania so that Sonia could rejoin her family. After their arrival in Bucharest, Tolia passed on the information to my father, which served as the signal for us to begin a similar process in Chernovitz. Meanwhile, Lazar and Lena moved into Tolia's now vacant and larger apartment.

Tolia's successful escape to Romania inspired optimism and courage. My parents and I discussed the consequences of the risk we intended to undertake. We assessed the benefits of running to freedom versus the threat of lifelong imprisonment, deportation to Siberia, never to be seen again, or death as traitors to the state if caught with false papers. Our choice was either to run to the West or spend the rest of our lives under the Soviet regime, with its current lifestyle, and subjected to anti-Semitism.

We asked ourselves if we were willing to take the risk. We had no easy answer. Although a difficult decision, my parents concluded that, for my sake, we must take the risk. Nothing worthwhile comes easily or risk-free, does it?

Lazar advised us to leave, admitting that he wished he possessed the courage to do the same. As a member of the Communist party, he considered the benefit-to-risk ratio completely unacceptable.

Papa, along with friends in whom he could confide, started planning and plotting our escape. They met very quietly in our apartment at night with the window shades drawn. We had to make agonizing decisions. Could the providers of the false documents be trusted? Could someone be setting a trap to ensnare Jews who wished to flee the USSR? Were the documents good enough not to look false and withstand the scrutiny of the Soviet government authorities? We all worried a lot. After several months of excruciating concerns and investigation, Papa decided to proceed. He paid a man for a false document, which stated he'd been born in Romania. Upon obtaining the documents, he applied for permission to repatriate back to Romania. We nightly expected a knock on the door from the KGB. Time passed, and the permission arrived.

Papa sold our possessions and converted them into a few tsarist gold coins, not an easy task without being detected. In order to hide the coins, Mama made small incisions into the roots of a few onions and inserted the coins after a great deal of practice. Adding potatoes, beans, bread, and cheese to a bag, she further disguised the location of the coins. We packed few of our remaining belongings. We left the apartment in a condition that implied our ongoing occupancy. No one knew of our departure.

"You must not talk to or volunteer information to the Russian border guards," Papa instructed us. "Let me do all the talking and good luck to all of us."

We each carried a small bundle. If anyone asked our destination, the answer would be that we were going to Beltz to visit Uncle Shulim's family. Mama had made up the beds prior to our crack-of-dawn departure. We felt like thieves fleeing the scene of a crime, terrified of being caught. In fact, we were committing a crime. We were running illegally to freedom. Even if we managed to escape the Soviet Union, we had no idea if we would ever reach America. We were running again, just as we had run from Beltz at the beginning of the war.

PART THREE

THE ROAD TO AMERICA (1946 – 1950)

CHAPTER 15

ROMANIA

CHERNOVITZ had an impressive railroad station. As he purchased three tickets to the Romanian border, Papa feared the KGB would interrogate and stop us from leaving or, worst yet, arrest and send us to Siberia. Well aware that our permission papers to leave the Soviet Union were based on bogus documents, we were suspicious of every person on the station platform. We imagined being followed and spied upon. The half hour wait for our train strung our nerves as tight as piano wire. We spoke very little and avoided eye contact with the other passengers. We also worried about what would happen when we reached the frontier. To pass the time and calm myself I turned my attention to the time when the Russians entered Beltz. At the time, we regarded them as our saviors from the Romanian Fascists.

On June 28, 1940, I woke up to quite an unexpected spectacle, courtesy of the Red Army. They entered our town without firing a single shot. It was a hot sunny morning and the whole town watched with great interest and admiration the Soviet soldiers marching in.

I stood in front of our house and looked at the strange uniforms and odd-looking spears attached to the rifles. I was used to the Romanian soldiers with bayonets affixed to the rifle tips. These soldiers had thin, what looked like spears, about one and a half to two times longer than a bayonet. The cross section of these devices resembled a four-edged star. Instead of coats, they wore shirts over their riding pants and a belt around the waist over the shirts, a typical Russian custom. They also did not have epaulettes, their military ranks displayed on their collars. The Soviets considered epaulettes a mark of capitalists including the tsarist army. Yet years later, they switched to epaulettes.

Many soldiers waved to us and the population returned the greetings. They all came from the direction of the Turkish Bridge passing our house and moving toward City Hall and eventually to the military barracks. The procession lasted most of the day. There were tanks with open turrets, cavalry, trucks carrying soldiers, horses pulling artillery cannons, and plain infantry marching and singing Red Army songs. Some trucks pulled cannons while others pulled mobile kitchen stoves. The tanks created a lot of noise as they moved slowly over our cobblestone roads. The dark smoke exhausted by the tanks and trucks hung in the air well after they passed.

I watched with excitement because I understood that the USSR military were strong and brave, not like the Romanian army. That day I felt that we were a part of a large and powerful country, where all citizens were equal.

We were in a festive mood and at the same time, I felt apprehension. While people were talking of a change, I didn't comprehend what the change meant or what to expect and how to behave. Even children are afraid of a change. I started thinking, were these Soviet soldiers supposed to be our friends and liberators? How would my life be different tomorrow or a week later? What was their school like? I really couldn't imagine how my daily activities were going to be affected by simply being a Russian or Soviet citizen. Excited, it felt like a new adventure. I was going to be able to speak Russian, my mother tongue and not Romanian, and that made me happy. I felt we were truly Russians now.

The first administrative change renamed all the streets. Consequently, our address changed from Carol II No. 57, to

Lenina 57. Shortly thereafter, we realized that Bessarabia's annexation by the Soviets brought on many changes in our lives. A few were beneficial, the majority negative. The most positive change affecting the Jewish population made all citizens equal. We no longer felt threatened because the Fascist parties, namely the Romanian Iron Guard and the Cuzists, were outlawed under Russian regime. However, we didn't know that equality was mainly on paper. In practice, anti-Semitism was alive and well in the Soviet Union.

Another positive change for us personally occurred when Papa obtained the prestigious position of Director of Credit in the local Government Bank, his highest professional achievement. Some time after, he bought me a beautiful mandolin, which I never learned to play. The war took care of that.

The negative changes were numerous, and they affected the whole population, especially the Jewish religious way of life. The government discouraged and banned any religious activities including attending synagogues and even praying at home.

The immediate effect on me was to stop learning prayers at home with the rabbi. Instead, I started learning Yiddish writing and reading with a new rabbi, not forbidden, because it did not carry any religious implications. Soviet documents required each citizen to state a nationality. So as far as they were concerned, Jewish was a nationality like Uzbek, Tajik, Ukrainian, etc.

Of course, Simchas Torah celebrations in the streets, or Tashlikh were out of the question. Also all Zionist activities, such as collecting money for Palestine, now Israel, were forbidden. Practically every Jewish home had a blue metallic box with a white Star of David, the *Kehren Kayemet pishke*, for depositing coins for Palestine.

All students had to repeat the last school year, taught in Russian. Also all merchants and homeowners were heavily taxed, and referred to as capitalists. That included physicians

and others. Newly issued passports designated some as unde-
sirables, with the intent of exile to Siberia.

A serious impact was the disappearance of all goods,
clothing, and foodstuffs from the store shelves. Before our
so-called "liberation" by the Soviets, Bessarabia was a region
that had everything. The land was rich in agriculture; grain,
corn, fruit, poultry, lamb, sheep, and cattle were plentiful. The
finest wine, bread, dairy, cheeses, *Caracul* (Persian lambskins),
and wool were abundant. The region also had fine woolen
fabrics, and produced sugar, sunflower oil, and spirits.

As soon as the Soviets came to our region they started
buying everything they could lay their hands on, and sending
it home to Russia. Additionally, the producers and merchants
stopped or reduced producing and selling goods because of the
concern of high taxation or confiscation of their businesses.

Mama stopped stuffing me with butter, sour cream and
fish oil, and I lost some of my earlier fat. Mama also lost some
weight, but remained overweight. Mama's weight loss I considered a positive effect.

Prior to the Soviets' takeover, a few people in town had
short wave radios. Uncle Zioma had a *Telefunken*. We could
listen to news and music from all the neighboring countries.
Often we listened to classical music from Sofia, Budapest, and
Prague. After the Soviets' arrival, they confiscated all radios and
distributed to every household one single-station radio with
no tuning capability. The Soviet radio consisted of a hanging
paper speaker cone mounted on a magnet with a single knob
controlling only on/off and volume. The radios transmitted
only Soviet music, propaganda, and news.

The Soviets issued Uncle Zioma a passport designated as
paragraph 39 identifying him as an undesirable. He was among
the inhabitants who were well off, and consequently considered
capitalists by the Soviet regime. He was merely a practicing
physician, who had a beautiful house, and lived nicely. Most
physicians in town received those special types of passports,

identifying them as undesirable capitalists. Our family worried that the Soviets would deport him to Siberia.

Ironically, six years after we welcomed Russian troops into Beltz, in 1940, we were endangering our lives, illegally, to flee our liberators. Yet I found a profound sense of gratitude to the USSR. If not for our asylum deep inside Central Asia, we would have suffered the same fate as the eleven members of our family slaughtered by the Nazis and their sympathizers. I reminded myself that Papa had repaid our debt to the USSR by serving in the Red Army, and fighting and paying with his health, in the battles of Stalingrad.

Had it not been for widespread anti-Semitism in the USSR, Soviet oppression, no personal liberties or opportunities, and miserable living conditions, we might have remained in Chernovitz. Instead, we opted to embark on a risk-filled journey to freedom.

We reached the Romanian border on a beautiful sunny day. Along with many others, we stood in a line to await inspection by the Soviet border patrol. Our anxiety spiked as we finally approached the officers. One guard rummaged through our belongings. Another guard took our forged documents from Papa, scrutinized the papers, and asked questions. Papa could not control himself, stuttering terribly as he tried to answer the guard. Too frightened to think, I stood and gazed at Mama's hand. The first Soviet border officer opened our small burlap bag and stuck his hands into the collection of vegetables where we'd hidden our only money, Mama squeezed my hand involuntarily out of sheer terror. My heart briefly stopped, and I feared we were not going to survive the inspection. Those few minutes, dragged for an eternity of uncertainty.

"*Neblagodarnye Jydy* (Ungrateful Jews)," the border guard quietly grumbled as he returned the papers to Papa. "Running back to Romania." Then he released us from Russian control and we took a step closer to freedom. My hair turned prematurely gray that day.

From the border, we took a train to Bucharest where Uncle Tolia lived. Unlike the previous train ride, we actually relaxed and were able to decompress after our fearful border crossing. Uncle Tolia and Aunt Sonia greeted us happily as we entered their apartment. We briefly recounted our border crossing all thankful we'd been successful. While talking with Tolia and his wife's brother, they explained the lack of inexpensive living quarters and work in Bucharest, so we remained there only for a week. The city was large, with wide boulevards adorned with impressive statuary and architecturally stylish buildings. Although referred to as the Paris of the east, few apartments could be rented and there were few, if any, employment or business opportunities for Papa, who concluded that we would make our way to Galati, Romania.

During our brief stay in Bucharest, I became acquainted with a boy about two years my senior. We toured a little, and he showed me some very nice areas of the city. Our talk quickly turned to girls, and he told me, "Bucharest has some of the nicest bordellos. Have you ever been to one?"

"No," I replied timidly. "Don't you think I'm too young? I'm only fifteen."

"I've been there many times," he said, his voice filled with pride. "I was about fourteen when I first went. Let's go there now! It's not expensive, and you'll have the time of your life."

"Are you sure they won't throw me out?" I asked.

"Not a chance! Besides, the sooner you go, the sooner you become a man," he said as he laughed.

Eager to experience life, I was also terribly embarrassed and too ashamed to say no.

We entered a poorly lighted large room with all the windows covered with faded red drapes. Four scantily clad girls sat on chairs arranged around the periphery of the room. As we entered, a smiling, middle-aged madam approached us. I felt very awkward.

"Welcome boys," she said, recognizing my young age immediately. She asked us to pay in advance. "I have a special girl for each of you."

She escorted me into a small room with similarly faded drapes, a mirror, a bed, and a basin. The dark room smelled of cheap perfume and powder.

As soon as she left, in walked a plump woman of about thirty. She wore a red silk robe arranged to display her nude body. I was immediately disappointed. I'd expected a slim young girl. The woman removed her robe and lay down on the bed. She noticed my shyness and inexperience.

"Have you done this before?" she asked as she pulled me into the bed. Well, we had sex, and I "became a man." As first experiences go, it was disappointing. I'd often tried to imagine what my first experience would be like. This interlude definitely fell short of my wild and exaggerated expectations.

"Oh boy, my girl was great!" my newfound friend said when I walked out onto the dark street to join him a little while later.

"How was yours?"

"All right," I told him. He seemed to detect my disappointment and changed the subject.

After our goodbyes to the family, the next day Papa, Mama and I departed by train for Galati.

GALATI

Galati, in the southeastern section of Romania, was a fairly large city near the Soviet border and the southwest corner of Bessarabia, now the Republic of Moldova. All the trains going east stopped there before crossing into the Soviet Union, which made it a good place to do business with the Russian soldiers returning home from the war. This was Papa's primary reason for choosing Galati as our temporary residence.

We rented a one-room apartment in a third floor walk-up. Several other apartments on the same floor shared a bathroom. The entryway to the apartment as well as the bathroom could be reached from an exterior covered balcony area.

Papa met a man he'd known in Beltz, and they immediately went into business. They opened a shoe store in a small wooden kiosk near the railroad station. Each day, one partner stayed in the kiosk, while the other took bundles of shoes to the railroad platform. The intended buyers were primarily Russian soldiers. These soldiers understood the lack of most goods in Russia, so they bought anything and everything they could to take home.

Papa's business was successful from the very beginning. He purchased decent and fashionable shoes, and he sold them at a good profit. He and his partner spoke Russian, which gave them an advantage, although no hard selling was required. The soldiers simply grabbed the merchandise and paid the asking price.

Papa wrote to his cousin, Mosia, in New York, briefly described our situation, and asked if he would send us an affidavit to immigrate to America. Meantime we lived very sparingly, saved all we could, and dreamed that we might some day be fortunate enough to immigrate to America.

In Galati, I met a few Jewish boys, mostly older than myself, and members of a Zionist organization that recruited boys and girls to join a *kibbutz*, which is Hebrew for a collective farm. The organization didn't own a farm in Romania. The name *kibbutz* implied that they would eventually live on a communal farm in Israel. I was a perfect candidate for their organization, because I was a foreigner without any ties, had been through hell during the war and I had nothing to loose.

The senior recruiter and the group's leader was a man of about twenty-four named Itzhak. He seemed an exceptional individual. Built like a weightlifter, he sounded and acted like an intellectual. He spoke well, knew Jewish history and philosophy, and cared passionately about the establishment of a Jewish state in Palestine.

"There you will learn to live in a group of boys and girls with similar ideals and interests, and you will depend on each others' labor for sustenance. The organization's ultimate objective is to create a Jewish state in Palestine," he explained. "And the only way that can happen is if large numbers of young displaced Jews throughout Europe immigrate illegally, by necessity, to Palestine."

The concept sounded very idealistic for a Jew. It inspired me to build my own country and fight for it to make it happen. I wanted to be a part of the process. Even though going to America was the family's first priority, we had no guarantees that we would ever achieve such a goal.

After a discussion with my parents, I joined the organization and moved to a *kibbutz* in Bacau, another town in Romania.

BACAU – LIFE IN A KIBBUTZ

Bacau, located northwest of Galati was a medium sized, clean city. The house the *kibbutz* occupied was near the railroad station.

Life in the *kibbutz* challenged me, but I embraced the idealistic dreams and enjoyed myself. Above all, everyone treated me as an adult and an equal. We worked long hours, unloading railroad ties and other materials at the railroad station for minimal pay. We also solicited various businesses in town for employment or donations to our cause. We listened to frequent lectures, covering topics like socialism, how to live together, the process of sharing food and clothing, behaving in a mature manner, as well as the history of the Jewish people, current political affairs, Zionist ideology, and the Hebrew language.

With twenty young adults, boys and girls, living together in tight quarters, there was a high degree of social and sexual freedom, a new experience for me as the youngest member of the kibbutz. There was a lot of fooling around because for most of us it was our first experience living in common quarters with little supervision. From a social point of view, life was a blast in Bacau. A young girl of twenty-five managed the *kibbutz*. She shared everything with us although she had her own room.

There was also a very serious part of life in the *kibbutz*. We all had a common bond and ideology to reach Palestine. We were the future pioneers who would reclaim our ancestral, religious, and cultural homeland. We intended to make the desert green, to build a Jewish homeland, and to create the State of Israel. We were all children who survived the war under various circumstances, and were convinced that it was high time for the Jewish people to have a permanent home, just like other peoples of the world. That was the only way we could assure our survival. We wanted to gather the scattered survivors of the Holocaust into a permanent homeland, a place where we could live and defend ourselves if the need arose.

Shortly after I arrived in Bacau, the head of the *kibbutz* began to groom me for leadership. I attended a two-day seminar in Bucharest, along with the elite of the organization. There, I met with Itzhak, the young man who'd recruited me into the organization. After a warm handshake, he told me that he was impressed with my performance, and he believed I had a future in the organization. As a result, I rotated through several managerial jobs during my stay in the kibbutz as part of my training.

The separation was very hard on my mother, even though I'd left with her consent. After some time, Mama wrote that she wanted to visit me for a day. I encouraged her visit as I'd missed her too.

I met Mama at the railroad station. After a warm greeting, I escorted her to the *kibbutz*. She saw first hand my busy schedule and the responsibilities I had undertaken. She expressed her pride in me, and how much she'd missed me. At the time, I was responsible for securing and distributing all foodstuffs. She noticed the easy familiarity of my *kibbutz* family, and the way we shared everything, right down to somene taking the smoking cigarette from my lips, and even the food I nibbled. My friends felt that I had plenty of stuff because I was in charge of it, but it wasn't so. Prior to Mama's visit, I'd been in charge of obtaining and assigning people to outside jobs. I think Mama understood how much I truly enjoyed my life and the *kibbutz* environment. In truth, I thrived on my management responsibilities, and the trust they implied. Above all, I loved the social and the sexual freedom.

The *kibbutz* occupied a large, old, two-story house. Tables and chairs were situated in a combination dining and meeting hall. We also had a good size kitchen and several closets for our shared clothing. Sharing in the *kibbutz* extended to the point that no one objected when in the morning, a boy would pick the shirt he was going to wear independent of whose it was. Dorm-like sleeping quarters in several rooms allowed us to select a different bed practically each night with another girl, although such sleeping arrangements didn't always translate into sexual activity. I even slept one night with the leader of the *kibbutz*. There were a few committed couples, who intended to get married after immigrating to Palestine. They were *yachasim*, or betrothed, in the Hebrew language. I refused to commit to a single girl, saying, "I'm too young." As the youngest boy in the *kibbutz*, I felt some sort of privilege among the girls.

While working at the railroad station offloading railroad ties and clad in a pair of shorts, a chilly rain began to fall. By the time we got home, we were soaked and cold. My coughing and wheezing for the first time in my life signaled the start of my asthma.

The *kibbutz* received a donation from an American Jewish organization of several cardboard boxes filled with used clothing. I found the smallest leather jacket – the first leather jacket ever – and I enjoyed wearing it. Because it came from America, it implied style and adventure, and I thought it made me look more mature. I even managed to save a photo taken of me in that jacket.

When the organization selected the members who would travel to Palestine, the decision was made that I would remain in Bacau, help train new members, and allow others to make the first journey.

"You are the youngest and a future leader," the head of the *kibbutz* explained. "We have great plans for your future."

"Your plans conflict with mine," I protested angrily. "You know I joined the *kibbutz* to go Palestine at the earliest opportunity. I can get my leadership training there." I felt strongly that I should've been allowed to present my case before the final decision was made. I decided to resign from the *kibbutz* and wait, no matter how long it would take, to focus on immigrating to America, where I had relatives and could begin a new life in the most enviable country in the world. This was my parents' preference as well.

Shortly afterward, Mama and Papa informed me of a letter from Mosia, in which he explained that our chances of immigrating to the United States were much better from Italy. Obtaining a visa for America in Romania was practically impossible. At best it could take a very long time. Mosia encouraged us to leave Romania and make our way to Italy where we could wait for our quota to immigrate. I departed the *kibbutz* and returned to Galati.

CHAPTER 16

HUNGARY

"I have something extremely important to tell you," said Papa to us the evening I returned to Galati, "I have been in touch with a guide who will take us across the border to Hungary."

"A smuggler?" I interrupted.

"Yes, of course. He assures me that he has been doing this for some time."

"And you believe him?"

"We have no choice. If we want to reach America, we have to take the risk."

"It is a huge risk," worried Mama. "It could mean our lives."

"Believe me, I know that. We did not escape from the Soviets to live out our lives in Romania. We must take the next step while it is possible."

"I agree, but, Papa can you trust the man?"

"He came recommended by Jewish people, who told me they knew a family smuggled successfully out of Romania by this group of men. I made the decision to liquidate my little business, and we would have enough money to proceed."

"God has looked after us so far," Mama said, sighing with resignation. "Let's pray that He will not abandon us now."

I'm sure it was not an easy decision for Papa to make. I think we all doubted that anyone, even God, cared enough to protect us. We also knew that we would shoulder the burden of reaching Italy, where we would apply for visas to America. First, though, we needed to reach Hungary and then Austria. The only agonizing question remained, were the guides Papa wanted to trust honest men? Could we trust them with our lives? Our lives were hanging in the balance again. Since Papa knew no others, they would have to do.

As soon as Papa had liquidated his business, we left for Transylvania, in the northwestern region of Romania. Separated from the rest of the country by the Carpathian Mountains, the region bordered Hungary. We traveled by train to a town whose name I believe was Oradea, near the border. After checking into a hotel, we waited for the opportunity to cross the border.

Several days of uncertainty passed, which heightened our anxiety.

"I can't fall asleep," I complained in the middle of the night, as I heard my parents constantly tossing.

"Try to get some rest, Buma, it'll soon be over," said Papa without conviction.

I couldn't get the upcoming adventure off my mind.

A man contacted Papa and told him that our crossing would occur later that same night. The guides expected a dark, moonless night. We each carried a small bundle and followed the guide very closely, in the pitch-black of night. I feared being caught, first by the Romanian and then by the Hungarian border guards. I worried our guide might mislead us, rob us, or even kill us. How could Papa put our lives in the hands of a guide? What had made him trust a smuggler? While following the guides, I felt a wave of confidence return. *We'll make it.* I told myself repeatedly.

We walked endlessly, making several stops, hiding behind some bushes, and waiting for border guards to pass us by or change shifts. That night seemed interminable. Before dawn, exhausted and dirty, we arrived at a farmhouse, a location prearranged by our guide without our knowledge. The owners admitted us, showed us where to wash up and clean our mud-covered clothes. The farmer's wife fed us bread and fresh milk. After we rested, we received a set of false Hungarian passports with Hungarian names, photos that did not resemble us at all, and three railroad tickets to Budapest. We immediately started to memorize the names on the passports, as well as the birth dates and places of birth, while we prepared for the next stage of our journey.

Early the next morning, another guide arrived to transport us by a horse-drawn cart to a railroad station in the next town. He dropped us off a block from the station with only minutes to spare before the train's arrival to avoid suspicion. He also advised us to take any available seats in any third class car and, above all, not to converse with anyone on the train and pretend to sleep. He suggested that Papa hide his watch so no one would ask him for the time, since he couldn't understand or answer in Hungarian. Before dropping us off at the station, he told us that outside the Budapest railroad station, an individual who helped illegal refugees would meet and take care of us.

"I was assured that someone would escort us to Budapest and then hand us over to the next guide," Papa complained angrily.

"No one will accompany you!" the man replied, his voice harsh.

"How will we recognize him?"

"He will recognize you. Don't worry; you're not the first people we've smuggled this way!"

We possessed no bargaining power and no choice. We had come this far, and we couldn't turn back. As we walked to the station, we heard the train approaching. We moved briskly, arriving at the platform as the train pulled in. We took three seats together in a third class car. I believe the three of us occupied a bench that normally accommodated four passengers. There were no separate compartments. The seats consisted of wood-slatted benches placed perpendicular to the length of the car. They alternated between back to back and facing each other. The car was more than half-empty. Slowly the train started moving out of the station and gained speed. Initially, no one faced us. At later stops, the car filled up.

Frightened and exhausted we did not speak the language, and we carried false documents. A sixteen-year-old with light brown hair, I held the passport of a black haired, twenty-five-year old man. My parents' photos did not match their appearances either. To reduce the fear of my predicament I closed my eyes pretending to doze and hoped to fall asleep. I concentrated on the clacking of the wheels over the rails. In my mind, I transformed the rhythmic noise of the wheels hitting the track segments into a primitive metallic monotone symphony, and longed for the cabin's measured shaking to lull me to sleep. As time passed, the hypnotic effect started melting away my stress. In my state of self-induced trance, I sensed the slowing of the rhythm and the train came to a screeching halt.

Our biggest scare occurred when the conductor, accompanied by a Soviet soldier, stepped into our railroad car. The conductor said something in Hungarian and passengers started showing their papers and tickets. When they reached our seats, Papa handed the three passports and tickets, while Mama and I pretended to sleep. They opened the passports, looked at the photos, returned them to Papa, and walked to the next aisle. From the time the conductor and the Russian soldier approached our row of seats until they left, my heart pounded mercilessly and beads of sweat dotted my forehead. I was afraid that the pounding and my shaking while pretending to be asleep would give me away.

I had little time to recuperate from the first inspection when the train slowed and stopped again. Two Soviet soldiers entered our car. One sat down on an empty spot across from us, while the other soldier addressed me, *"Podnemaisia! ya hochoo seedet* (Get up! I want to sit down)."

I gestured that I didn't understand Russian. He grabbed me by the arm, pulled me off my seat, and sat down. He then shook his head side-to-side, *"Beztolkovyi malenkyi Yesusyk* (Stupid little Jesus)!" He called out to the other soldier. I pretended not to understand him. What else could I do? I would have loved to have replied in Russian that his behavior was inappropriate for a member of the Red Army in an occupied country, and that he was a discredit to the Soviet Union. Instead, I felt grateful that he didn't demand my documents. I stood on the train for a long time, desperately hoping that no one would speak to me. I tried, unsuccessfully I thought, to control my nervous tension. Despite my panic and fear, we somehow made it.

We finally arrived in Budapest at a vast railroad station with multitudes of passengers rushing onto the platforms. As we approached the exit, we noticed Hungarian police, who stood at the station exits and observed those exiting the area. We immediately became terrified. We feared discovery and didn't know what to do. We knew to avoid drawing attention to ourselves. Without speaking, we separated, waited for a large crowd, joined them, and proceeded to the gate. As I passed under the watchful eyes of the police officers, I tried to be inconspicuous as I looked toward the exit. I inhaled deeply and took a sigh of relief as soon as I was outside the gate.

We paused on the large concrete steps outside the station, looked around, and then made our way to a position behind a structure that concealed us from the police. We did not know the identity of our next guide, nor where or when or if he would meet us, so we simply waited on the busy thoroughfare. We tried to behave nonchalantly but on the inside, we were shaking with trepidation. We wanted to be invisible to the police, but detected by whoever was supposed to pick us up. I felt like a spy in a movie, waiting for an unknown contact while the authorities looked everywhere for me. I lacked the training or nerves of a spy. We also didn't know friend from foe or whom to trust. Would our promised contact come through for us now? We were desperately lost if nobody picked us up as promised. We had no Hungarian money.

After an endless half hour, a truck covered with a tarp slowly passed us and stopped several yards away. A young man jumped out of the truck's cabin and approached us. He studied us over before he said,

"*Do radst Yiddish* (Do you speak Yiddish)?"

"*Ya,*" Papa answered tentatively.

"Get into the back of the truck, quickly!"

We didn't question the man's instructions. We simply obeyed, immediately felt saved and grateful for his rescue. Our intense anxiety began to ease. He helped us climb into the empty back of the truck and then took us to Buda, across the Danube from Pest. The truck stopped next to a large bombed-out building that may have once been a castle. The driver came to the back of the truck, opened a corner of the tarp, and spoke quietly.

"Listen carefully. Do what I say and you'll be alright. Get out of the truck. Hide in the ruins. Lay low. Don't go anywhere or talk to anyone. Someone will pick you up at night and take you across Hungary into Austria."

We spent a warm, sunny day hiding in the ruins. We could see into Pest, because Buda is on higher ground than Pest. We periodically heard voices. At first, we feared not being found, then realized there were other people hiding in neighboring ruins. The day seemed to last forever. We ate what remained of the few apples and bread given to us in the farmhouse after we crossed the Hungarian border from Romania. At dusk, it began to rain, and we focused on staying dry.

Before dawn, a large military looking truck covered with a khaki tarp pulled up. A man dressed in a military uniform asked us to get into the truck. It was loaded with people who sat on wooden benches. As we squeezed in, the man told us to remain quiet. In the front cabin, three men wore British military uniforms. A man clad in an officer's uniform spoke to us in Yiddish. To each other, the men spoke Hebrew. These men were from a military organization in Palestine, the Jewish Brigade, which had fought alongside the British against Germany. Yet England refused to allow Jews to immigrate to Palestine because their sympathies were with the Arabs.

When we embarked on our illegal border crossing from Romania to Hungary we were not aware of the Jewish Brigade network in the British Army or of other Jewish people throughout Europe specifically dispatched to aid illegal refugees to reach their destinations. God bless them for their efforts. Without them, we wouldn't have survived.

It rained very hard that entire day. Under the tarp, the sounds of the raindrops magnified. I felt as though I'd taken up residence inside a drum. It was also hot and sticky, and several people became ill. We pushed the corner of the tarp open in order to get some fresh air and to look outside. Due to the weather, the streets of the various towns through which we passed were deserted. We helped ourselves to water, and bread and cheese in a bag on the floor of the truck. A few times, the truck stopped and we descended to quickly relieve ourselves. Ladies first, then men.

At nightfall, we arrived near the border. The truck stopped, and we heard Russian spoken. I assumed it was a checkpoint. The same young man in the British officer's uniform spoke some Russian. After some discussion and perhaps a payoff, the truck proceeded forward. We stopped several more times, and we heard German spoken. Someone opened a corner of the tarp and shined a flashlight into the truck, blinding us. Frightened and concerned, we worried what might happen next. After ten minutes of discussion, the truck continued its journey to Vienna, arriving there the next morning.

CHAPTER 17

AUSTRIA – VIENNA

I N April 1947, the truck arrived in the American zone, one of the four zones of occupation in Vienna, at a transit camp that housed countless refugees. I didn't realize the large number of people seeking refuge in Vienna. We were not alone. I felt some sort of security in numbers compared to our border crossing into Hungary, one family by ourselves.

During registration, we were asked a variety of questions, including where we'd been born, which country we desired to immigrate to, if we had relatives or affidavits from relatives in our desired country. Papa displayed the documents from our American relatives.

After the registration process, we settled into a large room filled with bunk beds made of rough unfinished wood. We received blankets, hot meals, and used clothing.

This was our introduction to the Displaced Persons (DP) camps of post-World War II Europe. We lived in DP camps for several years, which gave us the status of international refugees. I disliked the label, not exactly an honorable distinction or something to be proud of, but I didn't complain. We lived among many refugees from a variety of countries. Numerous organizations took responsibility for our well-being.

The HIAS (Hebrew Immigrant Aid Society) and UNRRA (United Nations Relief and Rehabilitation Administration) provided our housing, fed and clothed us, and endowed us with minimal internationally recognized legal rights. UNRRA managed the DP camps. They issued identification cards to each refugee, which the local authorities of the host country recognized. Both UNRRA and HIAS assisted us when we relocated to Italy and helped us apply for a visa to the American consulate. The HIAS bore a large portion of the financial burden and UNRRA provided us with international legitimacy. Our documents classified us as "stateless." Even with the international backing of UNRRA, I found it awkward to live in a foreign country as a non-invited guest on a temporary basis.

We met refugees from every Eastern European country, Poland, Russia, Romania, Ukraine, Yugoslavia, Bulgaria, Hungary, and Czechoslovakia. The overwhelming majority of refugees were Jewish. We had a common reason for our refugee status, but each person's circumstances were unique. We all possessed similar objectives: to reach safe havens and resettle, to escape persecution, to be free to develop our lives and professions based on our individual abilities, and to prosper in peace.

The interminable waiting and lack of privacy were the most difficult aspects of life in the DP camp. Since we were no longer hungry, passing the time became our primary daily endeavor. In Stalinabad, I had no privacy because I shared two very cramped rooms with four women. Here I had my own bunk, but I often lived in a large room with a hundred men, women, and children. We stood in lines for breakfast, lunch, dinner, the bathroom, and to conduct business with the camp administrative personnel. How long would we have to stay here? What could we do to reduce our wait? There were no answers to these questions. In a way, it felt like a prison term, crossing off each day on a calendar, except we'd committed no crimes. I knew the DP camps were necessary steps toward my ultimate destination, but I hated having my life put on hold forever. I also didn't know where I would end up and prayed that we would make our way to America. We also knew that

America maintained the most stringent immigration laws, for a good reason, since everyone wanted to live there.

"Anything new on the bulletin board?" I'd ask Papa.

"Not last time I looked."

"I'll go and look again," I would say, setting off to examine the list of those scheduled to depart the camp.

I experienced many firsts in Vienna. I saw an American Jeep driven by American military personnel. I also saw an African-American man for the first time. He wore an American military uniform, was very tall, and had large hands and feet. This giant of a man sat relaxed in a Jeep with a folded windshield, one foot stretched over the hood. He offered us some chewing gum, which was another first for me. We'd had homemade unsweetened chewing gum in the Soviet Union. In the Vienna DP camp, we received two kinds of canned food, which we never had before. One was corned beef hash and the other evaporated milk. They appeared to be army rations. I liked them both. We boiled the can of milk in water until it turned into a beige colored sweet dessert, almost like caramel.

I had mixed emotions about living in a German language country, including fear and curiosity. I felt a strange satisfaction however to realize that both Germany and its ally Austria, had been vanquished by the Allies.

We were free to roam around in the buildings and in the courtyard. I also recall various inspections for the purpose of obtaining a physical headcount and verifying the documents of the residents in the DP camp. I can only surmise that the people who ran the camp had a quota on the number of people permitted by the Austrian authorities or that a stipend was paid the authorities for each refugee. Several times, the camp administrators sent us to hide in the attic. I spent several nights sleeping on blankets until the inspections were over. The attic, full of refugees, had to be very quiet while the authorities visited the camp. Once they departed, we vacated the attic and returned to our assigned quarters.

One evening, an employee of HIAS took several of us to the opera. The Vienna Opera performed Offenbach's *"Orpheus in der Unterwelt."* The performance held in the *Stadt Opera Gebäude,* the State Opera Building. For that occasion, I received a new light blue denim shirt and matching pants, and a pair of used British army boots, too big for my small feet. We had box seats.

I felt uncomfortable and embarrassed in the inappropriate clothing for an opera performance. Papa's past insistence on an appropriate wardrobe at all times haunted me. People stared at us when we entered the ornate theater, whose impressive staircase and chandeliers I still remember. While I appreciated going to the theater, I could hardly watch the performance. I was envious of the nicely dressed local people. Then I remembered that these same Austrians had joined Hitler in their atrocities against our people. They'd lost the war, yet they lived very well. One would not think that they had suffered defeat, not according to their dress.

One day, a couple of young boys and I decided to leave the DP compound to see the *"Prater,"* the large Ferris wheel in Vienna. Nobody questioned or tried to stop us when we crossed into the Russian military occupation zone, which was off limits for us to enter. We saw several Russian soldiers walking around, but they ignored us for the most part. It was pretty stupid, going on a dare, taking a foolish risk out of pure boredom.

We spent three months in Vienna. When our departure turn arrived, it was to move to the Italian border. A truck took us to Linz and Salzburg, then to a small border village in the Austrian Alps by the name of Salfelden.

During the week we spent there, we received strict instructions not to stray from the housing they provided. We could go for a short walk in the village as long as we were quiet and didn't travel in large groups. We were told we would cross the Alps on foot. I could not believe that it was possible, but we received assurances that many people before us had already done it successfully.

"How could I possibly cross these huge mountains on foot?" asked a worried Mama, looking at the gigantic snow covered peaks. "I'm in no shape, I'll never make it."

"None of us are mountain climbers," Papa said as he tried to calm her. "They tell us that all kinds of people young and old have already done it."

"Don't worry, Mama," I chimed in, "you've survived worse things. In no time we'll be in Italy, and then America."

"I'll certainly give it my best," she smiled, "God willing."

CHAPTER 18

THE ALPS

EVERYONE must be rested and ready to depart shortly after dawn, we were told one evening.

At dawn, four youthful members of an Israeli military organization, probably the Jewish Brigade of the British Army, gathered nearly one hundred refugees for our journey across the Alps. They spoke Hebrew to each other and Yiddish to us. They knew their way through the Alps from many previous trips, and insisted on our adherence to strict discipline. We would follow their instructions to the letter, and we would observe total silence at all times. The threat of detection by the border guards sobered us all. We wore street clothes, and had no special climbing gear or attire.

Climbing began with relative ease at the beginning. We walked in groups of twos and threes, led by our guides up a path into the mountains, one in front of the line, one bringing up the rear, and two wherever needed. After some time we reached the top of the first mountain, only to be disappointed to see another, taller mountain looming before us, previously hidden from our view. Unfortunately, as this pattern unfolded we grew accustomed to discover mountains that we had yet to scale.

We rested a few minutes at unpredictable intervals, always on the alert for either the Austrian or Italian border patrol guards. Our guides were familiar with the border patrol schedules and continued to monitor the guards' movement. They also scouted the terrain, adjusting our pace, depending on the distance we had to cover to avoid the border patrol.

As the day wore on, the walking and climbing became more tiring and difficult for me. Exhaustion, a consequence of our constant climbing and the thinner air at high altitudes, took its toll, especially on Mama. After many hours of hard climbing, we finally arrived at the last mountaintop, on the Italian side of the border, and our guides allowed us to rest. A combination of exhaustion, fear, anxiety, and the high altitude hit Mama hard, and she fainted.

"Mama, Mama!" I cried, dropping to my knees beside her and holding her head in my hands. "Someone, help me! Get some water!"

Papa poured water on her face and other people helped. Utterly distraught, I felt helpless, crying and watching Mama lying lifeless on the ground, fearful that she might not survive the Alps crossing. For the first time in my life, I witnessed Mama faint. After long and painful efforts to revive her, she fainted a second time, then again, and again. I couldn't help thinking of all the things we'd survived since the start of the war, and it struck me as profoundly unfair that she might die in the middle of a wilderness. While I prayed, she slowly regained her strength. Although delayed by her collapse the group set off again in less than one hour, with Mama, Papa and I trailing behind.

Our food consisted of canned sardines and crackers, cans of evaporated milk, and water. Our diet constipated everyone, which may have also contributed to Mama's fainting. The trip downhill consisted of going fast, slipping and sliding, then hiding until given a signal to start moving again.

Whenever we took rest breaks, my gaze roamed over the snow-covered mountains, and the ever undulating, sprawling green valleys below. Sometimes I saw grazing cattle in those lush valleys. Streams rushed and foamed as they hit boulders in their paths. We frequently crossed meandering mountain brooks with crystal-clear cold water, pausing to fill our canteens with that good tasting pure water. We washed in the frigid water, which felt invigorating and gave us renewed strength and hope.

The experience of crossing the Alps made me promise myself that I would avoid mountains for the rest of my life – a rash promise, made at a time when the mountains represented danger, fatigue, fear, uncertainty, and despair, despite the magnificent scenery and their sheer colossal size. As we approached each new mountain range, I hated what it represented, yet I admired its splendor. Deep inside, I also thought that they represented steps closer to freedom.

We crossed several wooden bridges that spanned larger streams patrolled by border guards. The tumultuous mountain rapids pummeled over boulders spewing a shower of water and white foam as they sped onward with a roar reverberating in the valleys. It became obvious that we had to cross when the guards were absent. Crossing those bridges undetected, spoke to the skill of our guides as they led us safely to our destination.

Several hours after dark, we arrived at an encampment high in the Alps where we found and joined other refugees. It was nicknamed "Yoine's Castle," after the Jewish man from Palestine who ran the camp. He was short, wiry, and energetic. After handing us American army blankets, we spread them out on the ground. Completely exhausted, I slept like a baby.

The next morning, we awakened in a beautiful wooded area, and discovered that several log cabins in the vicinity were part of the same complex. The next few days we spent resting and recuperating. While at Yoine's, we received daily visits from the Italian border guards, the *carabinieri*. I was surprised by their awareness of us. A rumor circulated that the United Jewish Appeal paid the border guards for each refugee who passed through the area. However, the Italian border guards couldn't permit everyone to cross the border into Italy. An arrangement existed with Yoine, whereby a certain percentage of the refugees had to return to Austria. In order to protect the women, children and the elderly, Yoine selected a group of able-bodied young people to send back across the Austrian border. I was included in this group of unfortunate returnees.

The thought of trekking back across the Alps to Austria was daunting. In order not to jeopardize the others, I cooperated in spite of my parents' obvious distress and my own anxiety. The reality became apparent when the *carabinieri* with rifles in hand lined us up in two's to escort us back to the Austrian border. That brought into focus the miserable task ahead. I was scared and worried. I know that it was even more emotionally painful for Mama to see me led by armed Italian military. I didn't know if, how, or when we would return, although we were secretly assured that we would all be back by midnight. Among our numbers was a young Israeli to guide us back. The Italian guards became abusive, striking one man with a walking stick because he did not respond immediately when ordered, in Italian, to move. His arm swelled up like a balloon after absorbing a direct hit meant for his head.

The c*arabinieri* treated us like a column of prisoners for the most part of the day. As we neared the Austrian border, they pointed at it. "*Attraversa la frontiera e non retorna mai a Italia* (Cross the border and don't ever come back to Italy)!" they ordered in a menacing tone.

We continued in the direction of Austria until we lost sight of the carabinieri.

"Gather around and listen carefully," instructed our Israeli guide, his expression stern. No one doubted that he was in command. "Stay close to me so I don't lose anyone. I have no time to look after you. We will be moving very fast." He looked at his watch. "We have very little time if we're going to avoid another encounter with the Italian border guards. Do as I say and we'll be back at Yoine's by midnight." Then he raised his fist for emphasis. "We cannot be captured. Good luck to us all! Now follow me!"

He set off at a hard run and we followed.

The trip back consisted of running, sliding down steep terrain and trying to avoid slamming into huge boulders as the sky darkened. Out of breath, exhausted and scared, I stayed close to the leader at all times, determined not to get lost. Adrenalin flooded our bodies as we scrambled up slopes, scaled over rocks, crossed mountain streams, and crept across bridges throughout the long night. I used every bit of strength I possessed, sometimes too fatigued to do anything but slide and tumble as new bruises accumulated across my body. The physical and mental strain never diminished. At midnight, just as our leader predicted, we finally made it back to Yoine's Castle, relieved that this unfortunate, dangerous adventure was over.

I wore my total possession, two pairs of pants one atop the other. By the time I returned to Yoine's, the backside and the knees of both pair were ripped to shreds. I sported a collection of bumps, black and blue marks, and scratches. My parents were relieved to see me.

Mama hugged and kissed me, "Thank God that I see you again! Are you alright?"

"I'm fine," I answered, "but I need sleep. I'm exhausted."

During my absence, a group of people departed Yoine's Castle for Milan, which freed up floor space on the wooden balcony of one of the mountain cabins. My parents had secured a spot for us. Overtired, I tossed and turned for a couple of hours before falling asleep. I tried to imagine what Italy would be like as I lay on a blanket. So far, I had only experienced the mountains, and I saw little difference in the terrain between Austria and Italy. I knew that Rome was a historic city and the home of the Vatican, while Venice was a city on water, and that Italian operas were world famous.

Romanian history had taught me that in ancient times

the Romans had invaded and occupied a country called *Daci*, pronounced Dutch. They had intermarried, and the resulting country had become known as Romania. In my Romanian school, I had also learned the story of the twins, Romulus and Remus, who'd been nursed by a she-wolf. This is part of the history of ancient Rome.

In the morning, Yoine's helpers told me to rest because Papa, Mama, and I would depart the next day.

Again, we set off on foot. It took us half a day to reach a main road. Two new looking streamlined buses awaited us. We boarded the bus, which would take us to Milan. The thought of being in Italy filled me with excitement and anticipation.

The future suddenly seemed to possess possibilities that, until now, we had only dreamed about.

CHAPTER 19

ITALY

MILAN

THE sun shone brightly, the sky was blue with puffy white clouds, and the countryside looked painted in every shade of green as we traveled on the serpentine mountain roads of the Alps. Several breathtaking lakes, their rippled surfaces reflecting the sunlight, formed golden dancing lights, emphasizing the beauty of our surroundings. On clean roads, we crossed numerous bridges and tunnels, encountering few vehicles. Every time I spotted a convertible sports car driven by good-looking, nicely dressed young Italian men and women, I thought, "This is the definition of the good life." Of course, at the time I did not yet know the expression *la dolce vita*. I also did not realize that we were traveling through one of the wealthy areas of Italy, the playground of the Italian rich and famous. I vacillated between gratitude for having made it this far, and the envious desire for a better life. Difficult for me to accept the fact that some people were living in luxury, I wondered if I'd ever experience a life of luxury.

The buses brought us to a notable building in the center of Milan. We passed through neighborhoods and shopping areas that surprised and impressed me. At *Via dei Unioni* No 5, a large wooden gate led into a cobblestone courtyard, surrounded on three sides by the building. A multitude of refugees roamed around the building and small front yard.

The first several nights, we slept on US Army blankets spread on the cobblestones in the courtyard because the facility lacked sufficient accommodations for us. Then we moved into a large room filled wall-to-wall with wooden bunk beds similar to those in Vienna. The refugees used the same US Army blankets to enclose their beds for as much privacy as possible.

The room housed everyone from the elderly to small children. We often said, *"Prekrasnaya komnata... plokho chto noojno delit yeyo s sotney lyudmy* (Nice room... too bad I have to share it with a hundred other people)." UNRRA and HIAS also operated this transit refugee camp. Sometime later, a new organization called IRO (International Refugee Organization) replaced UNNRA. We loved living at *Via Unioni* because of its location in the center of town, but for the same reason we thought the Italian government might consider it inappropriate for housing refugees. We were too visible and might have upset the neighborhood. Only a few blocks from *Via Unioni* on the grand *Piazza del Duomo,* in white marble shimmering splendor in the sun, stood the famous colossal *Catedrala Duomo.* The streets housed beautiful and exclusive stores. *Corso Vittorio Emanuele* and *Corso Venezia* contained cafes and fashionable shops. On one corner close to *Piazza Duomo* stood a famous bakery of sweets, cakes, and cookies called *Panettone Motta.* In front of it was a trolley stop.

From the first day that I arrived in Italy, I loved the Italian people. I never felt any discrimination at all from them, either for being Jewish or as a poor foreign refugee.

A few days after our arrival in Milan, my parents sent me to expedite a registered letter to Mosia in New York. I walked out of the DP Camp at *Via Unioni,* still wearing torn pants from my crossings of the Alps. I reached the trolley stop in front of the *Panettone Motta.* Because of my attire and lack of Italian language skill, I felt too embarrassed to ask for assistance from strangers on the street.

I finally set aside my pride and approached an impeccably dressed gentleman in his fifties.

"Posta, America," I said as I showed him the letter.

"Ho capito." He nodded and took me by my hand. We boarded the trolley, and he paid my fare. After a couple of stops, we got off. He escorted me to the post office and helped me to send the letter, then returned with me aboard the trolley to the stop in front of the *Panettone Motta.* He refused to accept the payment I offered.

"Grazie, grazie," I thanked him profusely as I bowed.

I have not encountered other Italians quite like him. However, he is a good example of the reason I love the Italian people.

Shortly after our arrival, I was given a pair of trousers and a shirt, to replace my torn clothing. While we were housed on *Via Unioni* I had plenty of free time and we were not restricted to the camp's premises. Since we were centrally located, I was able to roam, take in the sights, and familiarize myself with Milan. I went to the *Duomo,* which is the most magnificent cathedral in Milan. Adjacent to the huge *Piazza Duomo* stood a large indoor mall called the *Galleria,* its entrance lined with an impressive row of columns. It was probably the first, if not the only, large enclosed mall in Italy. It contained high-end retail stores, a restaurant, cafes, and a *gelato* parlor. A black market money exchange thrived outside the *Galleria,* Italians offering a favorable exchange of dollars for Italian liras.

My parents and I spent less than two months at *Via Unioni.* We then transferred to *Scoala Cadorna,* a decommissioned school used to house refugees, our home for less than three months. Located in a suburb of Milan, I no longer had the convenience of exploring the inner city. There was nothing of interest in the vicinity, and not much for us to do there. On Sundays, the local boys played soccer at the school's soccer field. We did not feel comfortable watching the games, because we thought we might be intruding. We were also afraid they would make fun of us. Most refugees feared offending the citizens of our host country as well as being misunderstood or ridiculed.

Again, we settled into large barracks-style rooms and gyms filled with multiple rows of wooden bunk beds. The school, larger than *Via Unioni,* had the beds spread further apart. We enjoyed the expanded space because it afforded us additional privacy.

We received three meals daily, but nothing more than basic staples and canned food. People tried to earn money by selling whatever they could, and they supplemented their diets by buying fresh fruit, vegetables, and other items otherwise unavailable.

We decided to make and sell cigarettes. With very little money, we purchased cigarette paper and tobacco. Out of a piece of wood the size of a pencil, I chiseled a cylinder the thickness of a cigarette with a longer handle at one end to form the cigarette. Mama or I rolled the paper around the wooden cylinder, glued the edge with egg white, and let it dry. Then I rolled tobacco in a hard paper, which was narrower in diameter than the glued cigarette paper. I stuffed the pointy end of the rolled cardboard with tobacco into one end of the cigarette paper shell, and pushed the tobacco from the hard paper into the cigarette paper shell with a piece of wood resembling a chopstick. I cut off the excess tobacco from each end, the result a viable cigarette. I had learned that process in Stalinabad when Mama and I made cigarettes for sale on the black market.

We kept the cigarettes in a small, open cardboard box on the bed. The large room housed many people who milled around, and some bought one or two cigarettes from the box. Our meager earnings enabled us to buy fresh fruit and other items, as well as to replenish our supply of cigarette paper and tobacco.

In the DP Camp at *Scoala Cadorna,* my parents and I met the same cross section of refugees from various parts of the world that we had encountered on *Via Unioni.* We made several new friends.

Our major objective of course remained to register with the American Embassy and make sure that we were eligible to immigrate to the United States. Papa corresponded with Mosia, who persuaded their cousin, Rose's husband, Phil Schechtman, to send us an affidavit, which invited us to live in the US under their sponsorship. Since Rose and Phil married in the USA, my father hadn't met Phil. They lived in White Plains, New York. I didn't understand why Mosia, who had grown up with my father, didn't send us the affidavit himself. I can only assume he did not want to be responsible for us if we didn't find work and became a financial burden.

We registered the affidavit under the Russian quota. Then, we waited for our turn to come. At about the same time, the US Congress, with President Truman's approval, enacted a law creating another quota for displaced stateless war refugees. We also registered for that quota system. We would use whichever came through first. However, we felt extremely grateful to Phil for sending us the affidavit. To reach America no longer seemed like the impossible dream. In spite of all the uncertainties, new hope took root deep inside me. We may make it to America yet, I began to think.

One day a camp administrator asked the boys and younger men to help clean up and wash the floors of several rooms after they were painted. A couple of weeks earlier, I had made friends with a Yugoslavian boy several years older than me. We washed the floors together. Suddenly, I noticed my new friend standing with his back against the wall. He was stiff and trembling, saliva foamed from his mouth. Then I noticed an electrical wire hanged on the wall where he stood, the stripped end was touching the back of his neck. Impulsively, I swatted the wire away from him, and in the excitement, I touched the stripped end, and received a jolt. In that instant, I thought that in trying to save him, I would also end up electrocuted. However, due to the electric jolt I slipped and fell on the wet floor onto my back. Since the electric wire wasn't long enough to reach the floor, it slid free of my hand, which saved my life. I became an unwitting hero, and my friend was taken to the infirmary with a small hole burned into the back of his neck. He couldn't thank me enough for having saved his life.

CREMONA

Only months after we moved to *Scoala Cadorna,* it also became a transient refugee camp. I assume the authorities dealing with refugees found it easier or cheaper to keep the DP camps in smaller towns, which kept us from intruding upon metropolitan life in large cities like Milan or Rome. On the outskirts of Rome, in *Cinecita,* was another DP Camp. *Cinecita* translates to the "movie city," Italy's version of Hollywood. Here too, its proximity to Rome caused it to become a transit camp. In our case, we were sent from *Scoala Cadorna* to Cremona, a town of sixty thousand, and 75 kilometers southeast of Milan.

The refugee camp in Cremona consisted of several buildings surrounding a larger courtyard, and accessed through wooden gates. The kitchen was in one building, offices in another, and living quarters spread among several other buildings. A separate dormitory for boys, *Kinderzimmer,* where I stayed, and a room for girls, kitty-corner from the boys, occupied a corner of the only building that possessed any notable architectural character. A two-story structure, it distinguished itself from the others by brick circular arches at one corner of the second floor, which enclosed a balcony. Our quarters occupied that corner of the building. The rest of the buildings in the complex looked ordinary and old. A few had a second floor. The large courtyard covered partly in cobblestone or concrete connected the buildings. The camp housed hundreds of refugees, the living quarters filled with the same double-deck unfinished wood bunks as in the previous DP camps. Again, for privacy, we nailed US military blankets to the bunks to form partitions. A few small rough wooden tables sparsely placed between the bunks were in great demand. Sometimes a family managed to get a table for their private use, but we usually shared them with those lodged near us.

The boys and girls quarters were nicer. Instead of bunks, we slept in single cots. In contrast to the large rooms housing the adult refugees, we were less crowded and enjoyed more light and fresh air because our long and narrow room had several windows. One building in the camp housed the ORT school.

During the winter months in most of Italy, with the exception of the mountainous north, the weather was mild with rain showers that lasted for days or even weeks at a time. A sweater and raincoat was all one needed, however, I never had any rain-wear all the time I lived in Italy. In addition to rain, Milan and its surrounding environs received a lot of fog. The summers were warm, the heat increasing further south. We didn't feel uncomfortable due to lack of air conditioning in the Cremona DP camp. We were free to roam, and that made up for the inconvenience of everyday life.

ORT, a Jewish supported institution whose full name was the Organization for Rehabilitation and Training survived on philanthropic donations. It had existed for many years. The ORT school objective in the refugee camps was to train refugees to become self-sufficient, able to earn a living wherever they might immigrate. They offered courses in mechanics, cabinet making, radio repair, and electricity. I enrolled in the electrician course, based on aptitude and the skills I had acquired in Stalinabad and Engels. ORT had an additional effect of reducing idle time, which plagued all the refugees in the DP camps.

The classes at the ORT consisted of both theory and hands-on practice in installing electricity, using circuits with multiple switches, relays, etc. Our first project was to build a primitive electromechanical doorbell. I cut out a circular piece of copper and hammered it into a semi-sphere to make the bell. I wound a coil of wire and made an electromagnet. I made the little hammer with its appropriate contacts to strike the bell, and finally assembled it on a rectangular piece of wood.

The schoolwork was familiar and easy for me, so I ended up with lots of free time on my hands. I started volunteering in the ORT office. I was able to do some drafting, as well as to study algebra and physics on my own. I also studied more advanced electricity and electromagnetism than was taught in the classrooms. I actually enjoyed my work and developed a good relationship with the senior personnel in the office.

After the formal course ended, I continued to study on my own. Then, ORT announced of a decision to open a school called *Central ORT Institute,* near Geneva, Switzerland. It would be an international showplace as the World ORT head-quarters was located in Geneva. Its objective was to train instructors for the various ORT schools.

The ORT school administrator at Cremona urged me to apply to the Institute because he felt I was a good candidate. Four hundred people applied throughout Italy. The ORT gave us a set of informal exams, emphasizing intelligence more than technical knowledge. I remember one specific question. "As a student of electricity, how would you explain what electricity is to two different people? Assume the first person was technically educated. The second person is an extremely intelligent black African, who has never seen or heard the word electricity." In the first case, I defined electricity as a stream of electrons. In the second, I tried to explain in terms of a force created by a flowing river.

Several months after the exams, they informed me that out of the 400 people, my friend Max and I were accepted. I felt a great sense of accomplishment. I was elated. Years earlier in Chernovitz I had attended school and thought that I was on the right track until I encountered terrible anti-Semitism. Now, I felt I would have a future as an instructor in a technical school. Perhaps one day in the future, I'd advance from that position. I believed the Institute was my sole chance for an education. I knew that even in America, I had no chance for a college education without the means to pay for it. Unfortunately, the Institute opening date kept slipping.

Upon completing the electrician course, no other courses were offered in the electrical field. Time passed. ORT hired an Italian instructor to teach a course in electrical motor winding. By that time, I spoke Italian fluently. The previous course had been taught in Yiddish and Polish. I signed up because I wanted to stay with the ORT school until the Institute in Switzerland opened. After the motor winding course started, ORT decided to move the course to Iesi, a small town near Ancona on the Adriatic coast. I left my parents in Cremona and moved to Iesi.

The ORT school was the only source of education available to the youth of the DP camps. While ORT taught us a trade, it didn't provide a formal education, yet we couldn't attend regular Italian schools. Upon arrival in Italy, we didn't speak the language, weren't citizens and were there on a temporary basis. We all knew it wasn't the responsibility of the Italian government to provide us with a free education. In addition to losing years while waiting to immigrate, it's a pity that I had to waste valuable time without an education, school regimentation, and social life, which is part of growing up and fitting into a normal society. There was nothing normal about our existence.

Life grew boring and time hung in suspension for the refugees in our DP camp in Cremona. Adults and children alike merely existed one day to the next. A few younger people became engaged, their intention to marry after reaching Palestine. I had an easier time than most. Busy with ORT school, I made friends easily. We stepped out of the camp in the evenings, hung out in the center of town, and took in a movie, whereas my parents did not. My family remained uninvolved in the affairs of our host country, and we didn't socialize with the local Italian population. With whatever money we had, we'd infrequently purchased fruit or delicious tomatoes to supplement our diet. While we were grateful for three meals a day and a roof over our heads, the waiting uncertainties regarding immigration to America made us keenly aware of the strict U.S. immigration quotas.

We periodically received packages during our stay in Cremona from various American Jewish organizations. They contained canned foods and used clothing. In time for *Passover*, a cardboard package marked *Matzos* arrived. We opened the outer box, which contained several one-pound factory enclosed boxes of matzos. However, each box felt lighter than a pound. Upon opening the first box, we were shocked and pleasantly surprised to find the box filled with packs of Pall Mall cigarettes. In fact, all the boxes contained Pall Malls, a tremendous gift, because American cigarettes were very expensive and in high demand throughout Europe. We sold the cigarettes for a sizable sum of Italian liras, which helped us for many months. We weren't in a position to thank our benefactors, because we didn't know their identity. We were, however, extremely grateful, blessing them every time we used the money. We thought of the cigarettes and resulting funds as our *manna* from heaven.

In Cremona I made many friends. About fifteen boys from various parts of the world, each with a unique background lived in the *Kinderzimmer*. Many were survivors of German concentration camps. I was the only one with living parents. One Polish survivor, whose name was Josek, had one living relative, an aunt in South Africa. She sent him five dollars every month. He bought a used red bicycle, and managed to live rather well by our standards. Some time later, he received passage on a ship associated with the *Betar* and *Irgun* Zionist organizations sailing to Palestine. The *Hagannah*, the Jewish fledgling army, intercepted the ship in Tel Aviv harbor, fearing *Irgun* would take over the country. He jumped ship and escaped wearing just swimming trunks, he later wrote to us.

I particularly recall one boy from Hungary. An American army captain liberated him from a concentration camp. The boy spent several months in a hospital, recuperating and gaining weight. The captain visited him often, developed a great liking for the boy, and felt personally responsible for his well-being. After his discharge from the army, the Captain returned to his wife and child in Chicago, where he ran an exclusive school. He continued corresponding with the boy and promised to adopt him and bring him to America.

A Christian, the Captain sent an affidavit promising to bring up the boy in the Jewish faith. Monthly, he sent the boy money to hire a teacher to study liberal arts and science because he wanted to teach the boy correct English in his school in Chicago. Eventually he brought the boy to Chicago, and adopted him as his son. This boy symbolized success to all of us. He corresponded with one of the boys in the *Kinderzimmer* after going to America. His newly adopted family insisted that he learn Hebrew and Jewish prayers and practice his faith. They also gave him a new car, which he drove into a tree. Heart broken, he contemplated running away from home. His new family assured him that the insurance would replace the destroyed car with a new one.

In Cremona I also met Itzhak Sladovnick, who lived with his father. His mother had not survived the Holocaust. We played basketball together. Rather wild, I ended up being hurt or bleeding during practically every game.

Interested in dentistry, Itzhak worked with a dentist in

our DP camp. He exhibited a fascination with other people's mouths. When he realized that I had one small yellowish baby tooth in my lower front jaw that had not been replaced by a new permanent tooth, Itzhak insisted, and I finally agreed, to have him make a stainless steel crown for the tooth.

Another boy in the *Kinderzimmer* named Itzik had survived Auschwitz. Short in stature, stocky, and strong like an ox, he had the personality of a pit bull. I believe Auschwitz created his personality, outlook and behavior. His entire family, including his parents and siblings, perished there. He was one mean dude. Two brothers, who lost their parents and were inseparable, also lived in the boys' room. We shared our living quarters, lived amiably and all minded our own business.

The girls' room, located in the same building, also on the second floor, perpendicular to the boys' room housed about fifteen girls. The majority were from Poland.

Popular pastimes in Cremona were the movies and the houses of prostitution, the latter called *casino(s)* in Italian. The refugees referred to them as *shpigelech*, which means mirrors in Yiddish, because in the center of Milan, not far from *Piazza Duomo* and *Via Unioni*, was an elegant *casino* full of mirrors. The refugees who went there were impressed. They asked one another, "Have you visited the mirrors yet?" The word caught on, and among the refugees, the word *shpigelech* meant *casinos*. It started as a secret code word, but before long, men and women alike knew its real meaning.

The Italian government officially recognized and licensed the *casinos* as legitimate businesses. To prevent prostitution on the streets, crime, corruption, and venereal diseases, the Italian government legalized and controlled the *casinos*. The girls were inspected twice each month. They also rotated from town to town, from casino to casino, and were not allowed to work in the streets. Consequently, the streets remained free of prostitutes.

Each casino had an "off limits" for the Allied forces stamped on its wall next to the entrance to discourage the soldiers from frequenting those houses. The sign consisted of a circle with a line drawn diagonally at forty-five degrees across it, which became the advertising sign for the brothels instead of a red light. Often these stamps were in a neighborhood where small children played. Mothers and grandmothers sat outside watching people go by while keeping an eye on their children, further proof of their acceptance as a legitimate business by the local population.

While the casinos took care of the crime and health issue, it certainly did not address Judeo-Christian moral values.

Our pastime in Italy was to attend the cinema whenever possible, since it was rather affordable. When we first looked at ads in front of the movie houses, we saw posters with pictures of the actors or action depicted in the advertised film. They all were stamped *oggi* diagonally across them. A joke traveled around our DP camp that somebody thought that all movie houses were playing the movie "*oggi*." It implied the refugees did not know *oggi* meant 'today' in Italian. I went to the movies frequently, and I learned my Italian language skills while being entertained. I learned the language rather quickly without ever going to school. My knowledge of Romanian helped, because the languages are quite similar.

In our DP camp, loudspeakers played popular Italian songs and issued news announcements. Everyone in camp, including me, followed with great interest the news about Palestine, conflicts between the Jews and Arabs, and the unfair bias against the Jews by the British occupation forces. I also followed the news about the *Hagannah*, as well as the activities of the *Irgun* and *Stern* groups. Reading and listening to the UN debates about the partitioning of Palestine into Jewish and Arab states was "a must" for everyone, independent of where one wanted to immigrate.

On May 16, 1948, we heard about the long awaited event: the establishment of the State of Israel. I find it hard to describe in words the exhilaration and happiness I felt. The DP camp exploded with joy. We danced, kissed, hugged each other, and wept with happiness. We congratulated each other with the words *"l'hitraot b'Yerushalaim"* (see you in Jerusalem), and *"mazel tov."* I started to think of what it meant to have a Jewish country, a place where I would not experience discrimination, with a Jewish army to defend me, and the absence of anti-Semitism. A Jewish country established after two thousand years of living in Diaspora. For two millennia, Jews had wandered the globe, unwelcome, forced to convert, or driven out of countries all over Europe. The majority of people in the world have their own countries even though they may voluntarily choose to live elsewhere. I was ecstatic. In Romania, I had joined a *kibbutz* in order to go to Palestine to help build our own country. Even though it had not happened, I celebrated fully.

The historic event of May 16, 1948 was of importance to every Jew across the globe. It was especially significant to the homeless and stateless survivors of the Holocaust. The war had decimated the European Jewry, many of whom lived in DP camps awaiting immigration to a place suitable to rebuild their broken lives. Many refugees, perhaps the overwhelming majority in the DP camps, wanted to go to Palestine, but had not been permitted to do so. The British stopped any ships carrying immigrants to Palestine, intercepting the ships, and interning the refugees on Cypress. That would no longer happen.

The DP camp organized a peaceful march through the streets of Cremona, a day to celebrate and to remember. We managed to save two photos, one of my father and the other of me marching in solidarity with the declaration of the State of Israel.

I've always been sentimental and a dreamer. That night I could not fall asleep. I questioned if I was doing the right thing by selecting to immigrate to the United States instead of to Israel. I thought that even though I would probably have a more financially awarding future in America, my place should be in Israel with my people due to my understanding of the struggle to survive as a young Jew during the war. The next morning I had a lengthy discussion with my parents about going to Israel instead of America. First, they said they would not go to America without me and they wanted to live in America for my sake more than their own. In the end, they convinced me that America was our future. We had no relatives in Israel, but both of my parents had cousins in the USA.

"We know that America is a highly developed democratic country. A real democracy protects its minority population," said Papa. "Therefore, we would not encounter discrimination or anti-Semitism there."

I really didn't need a lot of convincing. I'd seen many American movies showing tall skyscrapers of New York and beautiful people which made me dream and hope that one day I would live there too. America was the new center of the world and the place to be.

I was ecstatic when I learned that President Truman had immediately recognized the State of Israel. However, my happiness was short lived when I heard the Arabs did not recognize the partition and that all the neighboring Arab countries had attacked the newborn state. For the next several days, the major topic of conversation in the camp was the fighting. Everyone prayed for the Israelis. Many in our camp wanted to volunteer and join the fight but very few could implement their wishes. Itzhak, my would-be dentist friend tried, but his father prevented him.

Every six months we traveled to the American Consulate in Naples or Rome to check our status regarding our quota to immigrate to America. Papa, Mama, and I took those trips by train. We traveled third class with all kinds of Italians, farmers, peasants, and workers. The Italians were extremely nice sharing their food and drinks with us. They passed around bread, cheese, eggs, meats, and wine. Their generosity seemed to convey their acceptance of *profuggi* (refugees) in their country. The few I met were friendly and engaging, which meant the world to me after the devastation, hatred, and anti-Semitic behavior I'd experienced. It also seemed like every Italian could sing and they did not require special occasions to do so. They sang melodious and sentimental songs aboard trains, in the open market place tending their wares, or wherever the urge struck them.

Whenever we went to Rome or Naples, I toured and saw the various sites in these interesting cities. When I first saw the Vatican in Rome, I couldn't believe the architectural beauty and splendid art that existed in a single building. I also admired *Il Fuoro Romano* (the Roman Forum), the Coliseum, the statuary, and various fountains in Rome. I also heard for the first time the music of Raspiggi entitled, "The Fountains of Rome." Even though I did learn in school about the *Volcano Vesuvio* in Naples, I could not believe my eyes when I first saw it. I had also learned in school about the disaster in Pompei. Mama even reminded me of the internationally known Italian song about Sorrento in vicinity of Naples, which she used to sing in Russian before the war.

Cremona, as well as every small town throughout Italy enjoyed performances by touring opera companies. They were not first class quality but whenever they arrived, I went and delighted in the performances. Tickets were relatively inexpensive not much more than movies. I saw elderly men sitting in the cheapest seats, their eyes closed, and with their arms mimicking the *maestro*. They just loved their operas.

The lines to purchase tickets for the same evening's performance were lengthy and the people disorderly. When I sat down in my seat in the theater, after having been squeezed by the crowd while in line to buy tickets for *Rigoletto*, I realized my wallet was missing. Pickpockets lifted it while shoving in line. I had my identity papers in it. It resulted in several visits to the local police department with witnesses from the DP camp to vouch for me before they issued me new documents.

My stay in Italy aided me in my quest to learn as much about the world and culture as possible. Exposed to architecture, music, history, geography, political philosophies, foreign peoples and their customs, and the Italian language, I appreciated everything that I learned. A graduate of the school of hard knocks, I became perceptive and matured beyond my young age.

Classical music in general and opera in particular, became favorites of mine. I was taken by the melodious arias in Verdi's and Puccini's operas and the whimsical, allegro, staccato, comic melodies of Rossini. On the way home from the performances the melodies stayed in my mind as I hummed or whistled them. The most popular tenors at the time were Tito Gobbi and Bennymino Gigli. In addition to the roaming opera companies performing operas on local stages, the Italians filmed the most popular operas. Verdi's *"La Traviata,""Rigoletto,"* *"Il Trovatore"* and *"La Forza Del Destino,"* Puccini's *"Tosca,"* *"La Boheme"* and *"Madame Butterfly,"* Rossinni's *"The Barber of Seville,"* Leoncavallo's *"I Pagliacci,"* together with Mascagni's *"Cavalleria Rusticana"* played frequently in Cremona's movie houses. It seems like they were always in high demand and I've seen them many times. Love of music and bel canto stayed with me for the rest of my life. I was young and impressionable absorbing everything like a sponge. When I lived in Brooklyn with my parents, our radio stayed always tuned to WQXR, the classical music station. Even though I enjoyed music, many years passed before I learned that Cremona was the home of Stradivarius and his world famous violins.

I was extremely happy and puzzled not to be subject to discrimination or anti-Semitism in a formerly Fascist country dominated by the Vatican. I discovered that mostly women frequented the churches. Men seldom attended, the Communist Party strong and popular with all male workers.

Yet, many Italians openly praised Mussolini for having built beautiful roads throughout the country.

In Cremona at times a local person would ask me my identity, I replied that I was *Ebreo,* which is "Jewish" in Italian. They didn't seem to know the meaning of the word. Instead, the locals referred to us as *Polacchi* since the early refugees were Polish.

Soccer and bicycle racing were very popular in Italy. Many young people rode multi-speed racing bikes, wearing colorful cyclist jerseys with pockets on the lower back and sides. The country was also fashion minded. Their shoes, especially loafers were made of fine leather, light in weight, flexible and impeccably designed. Men's suits in fine lightweight woolens were beautifully finished, as were dress shirts and silk neckties.

Even the ordinary worker owned at least one single nice suit, dress shirt and tie. On weekends, he'd spiff up in the only suit he had, come out to the center of town for a walk, people watching, enjoying a café, or attending a movie. There weren't many cars, and the Alfa Romeo was king. Almost everyone rode a motor scooter, the Vespa and Lombretta most popular. Italian women wore suits made of the finest leather, and were resplendent in their attire. The young women were beautiful.

Several years later, when I arrived in America I was able to compare the U.S. and Italian cultures. Practically everyone owned a car in America. There were no scooters to speak of, and the bicycles were heavy and made by Schwinn. I rarely ever saw lightweight ten-speed bikes. Neither biking nor soccer were popular sports. The shoes were heavy and the penny loafer was popular.

Years later, due to free trade, advances in communication and television, the U.S. and most European countries became more similar and universal. America imported beautiful shoes from Italy and the whole world now wears jeans. Literally thousands of young people can be seen on racing bikes on the streets, and even soccer caught on with school-children. In

Italy, I would have been happy to own a bike. In America, I wanted and needed a car.

Iesi

After living in Cremona for over a year, I moved to Iesi to attend a course in electric motor winding at the ORT school. In September 1948, I was eighteen years old and lived on my own. Mama and Papa remained in Cremona. Our ORT instructor came from northern Italy. He didn't like southern Italians, didn't understand their dialect and called them Arabs.

"Loro non sono i miei fratelli, ma sono Arabi (They're not my brothers, they're Arabs)."

Iesi, was a small town near Ancona, a larger city and a major port on the Adriatic Sea. The refugee camp in Iesi was very small, housed in a former nunnery outside of town, and situated on a hill that provided beautiful vistas.

I spent most of my time attending classes at the ORT school. The head of the camp was an American Army Captain who lived in a private three-story building with a water tank on its roof, which supplied water for the Captain. Outside the basement, a manual pump would bring the water up to the roof tank.

I obtained a job to make sure the tank always had water. It entailed my turning 5000 revolutions of the crank handle daily, a boring job I hated, but I liked receiving the few liras it paid monthly. The first thing each morning and sometimes in the evening I stood at the pump and turned the handle. I planned to install an electric motor to do the job, but I never managed the task. Besides, I would have lost my only income. For a month or two, I also had a second job as a guard at the DP camp. A few nights each week, I stood watch for several hours. I also walked around the periphery of the camp with a flashlight in one hand and a stick in the other, making sure there were no intruders or unusual activity.

On those nights that I did not work as a guard, I went into town in late afternoons and evenings to sightsee or go to a movie. The walk into town took half an hour. The DP Camp was quiet with no activities going on. I endured the boredom because I still hoped to become a student someday at the Central ORT Institute in Switzerland.

After as little as four months, the DP camp in Iesi closed and we relocated south to Barletta. Earlier, the Cremona DP camp closed and all refugees moved to Barletta as well. When I arrived in Barletta my parents were already there.

BARLETTA

Barletta, a small town of about fifty thousand inhabitants was on the Adriatic coast in southern Italy, about 40 kilometers north of the large city of Bari. Just south of Barletta was a smaller town called Trani, which also had a DP camp. I went once by bike to visit friends residing there. Soon after, the Trani DP camp also closed and the inhabitants consolidated in Barletta. I finally received word while in Barletta that the Central ORT Institute was at last opening and that I'd be going there soon.

I was extremely glad. My dreams seemed about to materialize. I had waited a very long time for that happy day to arrive, but I remained concerned that something might go wrong at the last minute. My parents however, had mixed emotions about my impending departure. They wanted me to receive a good education but weren't eager for us to be separated again.

"You just returned to us from Iesi," Mama sadly noted, "and now you are going to leave for another country."

"Let him go, Sonia," Papa intervened. "He deserves the opportunity to be educated."

"It's the best thing that's happened to me," I reminded her. "I'll get a free education, something I would never otherwise be given."

"We won't stand in your way, Buma, but you must promise that if we receive our visas to America, you will return and join us." Mama continued. "For us, America will happen fairly late in life. You are our reason for going. You have your whole future ahead of you, and we want to see you enjoy a successful and happy life."

"I promise, Mama, I promise."

"Then go, and may God bless you!" she said with obvious reluctance and pain in her heart.

Within less than a week, I received notice that I should get ready to travel, as my documents were being prepared. It was the happiest time of my life when I realized that within a few days I would leave the refugee camp and travel to Switzerland to study. In my mind, I began to see the light at the end of the proverbial tunnel. Never again would I live in a DP camp. With an education, I would live a normal life. I was on cloud nine. I kept on repeating to myself, "I made it, I made it!"

February 2, 1949, the International Refugee Organization, IRO, issued me an Emergency Identity Certificate in lieu of a passport. I was classified as a citizen of no country, "stateless." A few days later, I was given a train ticket to Geneva with a stop in Milan. I took a night train on February 9, arriving in Milan on the 10th. An ORT representative met me and took me to the Swiss Consulate in Milan, where I obtained a travel visa to Geneva. I departed immediately. The trip by train was very exciting. I traveled through many tunnels and saw countless mountains covered with snow. I was very impatient, and I couldn't wait to experience Geneva and the Central ORT Institute.

CHAPTER 20

SWITZERLAND

THE CENTRAL ORT INSTITUTE

I arrived in Geneva on February 11, 1949. I'm able to quote the exact dates because I still have the documents with the stamped entry date to Switzerland. An ORT representative met me at the Geneva railroad station and took me by car to the Institute. The school, in a beautiful picturesque village near Lake Geneva, was located a couple of hundred yards from the French border. The village called Anières près Genève meant Anieres near Geneva.

The school occupied a new building, surrounded by trees and rolling lawns and a small forest in the schoolyard. The building once used as a sanatorium for the mentally impaired was beautifully renovated into a technical school with two stories and a basement, containing classrooms, dormitories, and laboratories. Wide steps in front of the main entry enlarged the tall façade. The ORT insignia, made of a mosaic of tile and inscribed in the terrazzo floor of the lobby, reminded us of its existence. The Institute, also referred to as the Dr. Aron Syngalowski Center, honored the head of the World ORT Organization. Shortly after our arrival, he came to personally meet with and welcome all the students. He explained that the Institute had been his life's dream.

A sparkling new and spacious room with two beds and a very attractive loft that included two additional beds became my new home. The floors and staircase to the loft, as well as the rail across the loft overlooking the room below, were made of light color polished wood. My friend Max, one of the 400 applicants from Italy, decided to occupy the loft with me. A large window brought the sunlight into the room.

Within a week, Vittorio Pavoncelli, a native of Rome arrived. Since Vittorio spoke only Italian, he became our roommate to facilitate his need for translators. Most of the boys in the Institute spoke two or more languages but not Italian. Vittorio occupied a bed downstairs. Our room represented the Italian contingent.

At first sight, Max and I could not believe that Vittorio was Jewish. After sharing our room for about a week, he told us that although his family was thoroughly assimilated, his grandfather took him every year during the High Holidays to a synagogue. "Mussolini also considered us Jewish," he said. "He made us move out of Rome during the war. I was forbidden to go to school during that time."

I still considered Vittorio a Jew in name only. He knew very little about being Jewish and he and his parents hadn't practiced their religion. I also knew that as far as the Nazis were concerned it didn't matter if you practiced Judaism. If the Nazis believed you were Jewish, you would be mistreated. Having the Pavoncelli family barred from their home in Rome was wrong, discriminating, abusive, insulting, and degrading. One cannot condone the behavior of the Italian government. However, to the Italian government's credit, it was not on par with the suffering Jews had endured in other countries under Nazi control.

Some time later Max and I found out that Vittorio's older sister worked at the ORT in Rome. Because of her connections, he had been accepted to the Institute. At the age of seventeen, he was the youngest student in the school. I was eighteen at the time.

Within a couple of months after Vittorio's arrival at the Institute a national tragedy befell Italy. One of their major soccer teams perished in an airplane accident. All of Italy went into mourning. The accident effected Vittorio badly. He wept for a week, stopped eating, and didn't attend classes. At first, we tried to console him but we soon realized that our words were of no use. He needed time to mourn.

It was ironic to me that one could define the word "tragedy" using different yardsticks. For a country to lose an entire soccer team is tragic and I felt sorrow and sympathized with Vittorio's mourning. However, I was amazed at the entire country's strong reaction to that unfortunate event. Perhaps I'd been hardened by the Jewish tragedy of the Holocaust. I recalled that the world had shown very little sympathy for a tragedy of completely different and previously unheard of proportions.

The inaugural class consisted of sixty-three boys from various countries and with different life experiences. We thought of ourselves as a mini-United Nations. Among us were four boys born in Poland who had ended up in the Buchenwald concentration camp. The Swiss Jewry had rescued them and brought them to Switzerland where they'd lived for several years before the Institute opened. Consequently, they spoke French, wore nice clothes, and held temporary jobs in Switzerland. They even owned robes and slippers, which I considered luxury items at the time. There were three boys from Belgium who spoke French and Flemish, two from Casablanca, Morocco, who spoke French and Arabic, one from Holland, one from Denmark, one from Rio de Janeiro, Brazil, who spoke only Portuguese, six from Bulgaria, one from Hungary, and several from Poland.

All of our classes were taught in French, even though the teachers spoke other languages. In the classroom, they refused to translate anything. They pretended to know only French.

Outside the classroom, they spoke to us in a variety of other languages.

"Professor, I'm sure you know it is hard enough for us to comprehend a technically difficult subject even when it is taught in a language we understand," I said during a break to one of the instructors who taught us electricity. "Don't you think it is unfair and makes it so much tougher when you teach exclusively in French?"

"I know and even agree with you," he said as he smiled. "However, it is imperative that you learn the French language as soon as possible, and so we teach only in French."

"Professor, th-th-th that's easy for you to say," jokingly I stuttered, "but I'm at the receiving end." We both laughed.

"Those are the rules, and they're for your own good."

It was extremely hard to compete with boys whose native tongue was French. When we started school we knew nothing or very little French but within less than six months everyone became fluent. In my case, I'd had one year of French in Liceu Comercial in Beltz and I spoke Romanian and Italian, both romance languages. The transition to French was easier for me and I mastered it relatively quickly. When it came to math and physics, I was able to rely on the equations and symbols which are universal. The Institute gave us dictionaries to help us with translations of material into our own languages. However, they had no French – Russian dictionary. I received a French – German dictionary, which was of limited use. For a short time, I shared a physics book written in Portuguese with the boy from Rio de Janeiro even though I did not know the language.

When we arrived at the Institute, the building had just been completed. The laboratories in the basement were finished with the exception of the installation of the machinery. The students in the mechanics class helped to install lathes and other equipment in the machine shop. We helped with the electrical wiring under the direction of the instructors.

Many of our instructors taught at the Institute on a part time basis. The rest of the time, they taught in Swiss colleges and universities in Geneva. We had a very dedicated old professor teaching us the French language. He resembled a caricature of a typical old professor. Tall, slim, with hair like Albert Einstein, he wore his glasses on the tip of his rather pronounced nose. He made our classroom instruction unique, because he acted out much of what he said to his students.

"On ne peut pas ouvrir la porte quand elle est fermé à clef." In order to explain (you cannot open the door when it is locked), he hit the door so hard with his shoulder, the door's central panel cracked. To demonstrate *"le couleur de mes chaussettes est rouge,"* (his socks are red), he displayed his red socks by putting his foot on the podium. To explain how one summons a taxi in Paris, he put two fingers in his mouth, whistled loudly, signaled with his hand, and shouted *"ici!"* (here!)

We attended classes five days a week from early morning after breakfast until five in the afternoon with a break for lunch and a snack around three o'clock. With the exception of French language instruction, all other classes were on technical subjects. All of us worked hard, and a terrific esprit de corps evolved among the students. "You are the crème de la crème, the backbone, and the future of ORT," complimented our teachers, uplifting and inspiring us to do our very best. We loved being there.

At the entry to the grounds of the Institute was a building where the gatekeepers, a married couple, lived. He also maintained the grounds. His wife had a young beautiful blond sister from France and she lived with them. She worked as a housekeeper in the dormitory. Max and I flirted with her. I called her Angelina. That was not her name, but she liked being called little angel.

One morning I faked illness to avoid going to my classes. When she came into the room, I was the only one there, and in bed. We had a great time, although I was afraid that someone might come into the room and find us. About a month later, she did not look too well and I was naive enough to think that she might have been pregnant. I worried for a while until she looked fine again.

We were provided with all our meals, books, instructors, clean sheets, housekeepers and a monthly stipend of five Swiss francs, which wouldn't even cover the cost of cigarettes. Unfortunately, I smoked at the time. After a couple of months, they stopped the stipend and in protest, the majority of students stopped shaving and grew beards.

Life at the Institute was wonderful, an idyllic place of security on the heels of war, where many of us had experienced near starvation, deprivation, and DP camps. The contrast was unbelievable. For the first time I had self-respect. I felt confident when I looked in the mirror, liking the young man I saw. There is nothing more invigorating to the soul and the human spirit than hope and the prospect of a good future.

As international students, we lived in a highly civilized and technically advanced society. On weekends, many of us toured Geneva. Once I bought a daily pass on the trolley, using it to travel to Geneva and back. The trip by trolley took about an hour each way. After a student used his daily trolley pass he'd give it to another student, but mostly we hitchhiked.

We walked less than a couple of hundred yards to reach the border, where the guards knew us. From the Swiss border guard booth, the road continued into France in a straight line as far as the eye could see. The two-lane road lined with tall poplar trees resembled sentinels whose silvery leaves shimmered in the breeze.

"*Bonjour, monsieur,*" I'd address the guard at the border booth, "it would be nice if I could get a ride into Geneva."

"*Bien sûr* (Of course, they would reply)." Those who knew us well would smile.

"You're here for a ride to Geneva. It must be the weekend."

Cars arriving from France stopped at the border.

"Do you mind giving this student a ride to Geneva?" the guard would ask.

Most people agreed to transport us. We thanked the guard and then the driver for agreeing to give us a ride.

In 1949, a new international airport opened outside Geneva. A huge celebration of the inauguration of the airport ensued. On that weekend numerous people arrived from France thus passing through the border patrol near our Institute, a good opportunity for several Institute students to get a lift from the border to the airport. The ride was fun despite shivering from the cold while riding in a rumble seat. The inauguration ceremony included a military band that played the Swiss national anthem. Several dignitaries gave speeches.

I felt mixed emotions when I recognized the deposed King Michael of Romania in the crowd. I easily recognized him even though he was now a grown man, broad-shouldered, handsome and wearing a grey suit instead of a uniform. He had the same wide nose and light complexion as when he was the young King. The fact that he spoke Romanian to his companions further convinced me that he was *Mihai*. I'd also read he lived in Switzerland at the time.

"Look, the man in the grey suit standing there is Michael, the former king of Romania. He was a fascist," I told my friend, "and I hate his guts."

"He does not look like a king to me," my surprised friend said.

"You should have seen his official photos in regal uniform. He looked rather impressive."

A few days later, my friend showed me a local newspaper article, which reported Michael's presence at the airport inauguration.

The countryside between Anieres and Geneva was positively magnificent. On the way to Geneva, the terrain sloped from left to right with small hills and on one side and the shining lake on the other. Both sides displayed magnificent homes. Dense foliage partly obstructed houses on the right side and afforded them privacy. Where the trees were sparser, I could see spreads of large estates, some with tennis courts and boats on the private beaches of the lake.

Chauffeur driven cars drove many of the locals home for lunch and then back to their businesses in the late afternoon. While walking to the trolley one day a chauffeur driven car stopped to offer me a lift into Geneva. I sat next to the owner in the back seat.

"And what do you do here young man?" he asked.

"I'm a student from Italy."

"What a coincidence," he replied, "my son is currently studying architecture in Italy. I hope someone would give him a lift as well, when he needs it."

"Yes, I'm sure they will," I said. "People are nice all over, especially in Italy."

We had a little more conversation about my studies.

"My son believes that Italy is the place to study architecture while living among the works of the old masters."

"I agree."

The Institute introduced the students to what I thought as an unusual Swiss snack. In addition to the three meals a day, we received at 3 o'clock in the afternoon a slice of bread and a chocolate bar. I eventually adjusted to that Swiss standard but I developed a preference for the chocolate.

Despite the beauty and relative peace of the village, I didn't expect and couldn't get used to anti-Semitism. As we walked in Anieres, nicely dressed mostly in suits, little local boys of the age of about six or seven ran by and yelled at us, *"sale Juif* (dirty Jew)!" in French. Obviously, at their tender ages, they didn't express their own opinions, but the opinions of their parents.

We met a few local girls who seemed to like us. We flirted

with them and enjoyed their company. However, they refused
to be seen with us in the village.

"How come you are hiding when we're together?" I asked
the girl.

"The priest in church warned us not to associate with the
students in the Institute, because they are Jews. He called
the Jews subhuman degenerates, and survivors of concentration camps. But I can't believe it," she confided after some
hesitation.

I was shocked to hear such remarks from someone who lived
in a civilized country, which relied on its neutrality, commerce,
and diplomacy to coexist in peace and prosperity for nearly
seven hundred years. It put on the brakes to my hopes for the
future, clipped my wings, and crashed the highflying optimism
I felt earlier. It brought me back to earth. Reality in the form
of discrimination and anti-Semitic sentiments by many people
thrived in a so-called "neutral" country.

On the other hand, most villagers were polite and didn't
mistreat us. Their manners were perfect, covering up their true
feelings. In Switzerland, cigarettes were sold without matches
and we had to buy them separately. When I bought two books
of matches for one Swiss cent, the local storeowner told me
many times, *"Merci bien,"* or *"Merci beaucoup, monsieur."* Not
entirely a sincere thank you because of the great profit earned
with the one-cent sale. I believe in this case that the Swiss
merchant's gracious "thank you" is innate in their culture and
without sincerity.

I discovered that Swiss laws were exclusively for the Swiss.
If a foreigner living in Switzerland obtained with great difficulty a work permit, it was a qualified permit; it allowed a Swiss
citizen to claim the job and displace the foreigner. One cannot
become a Swiss citizen by merely being born on Swiss soil.
Neither does one obtain citizenship by marriage. One must
have Swiss parents. Some people justify these laws because
Switzerland is a very small country with limited raw materials

and resources. Their laws, therefore, must protect their citizens. Others would prefer to call their laws selfish or self-centered, socially backward and non-progressive.

Switzerland is a beautiful, small country made up of mountains, lakes, and borders. If one travels, it does not take long to encounter one, two, or all three.

The city of Geneva is quite attractive. Lake Geneva or *Lac Leman* as it's called in French, plays a prominent role. The League of Nations and the International Red Cross on the shores of the lake stand near a fountain in the shape of a needle, which shoots water 465 feet high into the sky. *Jet d'Eau*, the manmade geyser is four times higher than Old Faithful. Many times, I stood on *Pont de Mont Blanc*, the main bridge, admiring the white snow-covered mountain peak whose name it bears. The little island, called *"Ile de Jean-Jacque Rousseau,"* displays the famous sculpture of "The Thinker" by Rodin. Nearby, swans glide gracefully over the water. I spent hours fascinated with everything around me. What a difference from Beltz, where I spent the first ten years of my life. This place overflowed with splendor and culture, I thought. Seeing the wonderful surroundings and high standard of living of the Swiss motivated me to be and to do my best. They weren't any different from me, except they'd had opportunities not available to me. Surviving the dreadful war years had made me a stronger, more focused and ambitious person, more cognizant of what I was missing and what others had. As long as I was spared and stayed alive, why shouldn't I be able to live the same high standards? Am I less capable or deserving? I decided to work as hard as humanly possible, to compete, to strive and to succeed, or to die trying.

It always impressed me that a small country such as Switzerland functioned successfully with four languages, German, French, Italian, and Romansh (a dialect – a mixture of the latter two). When I strolled the streets of Geneva, I heard Russian spoken by richly dressed older people. Later, I learned that a large contingent of the Russian aristocracy had escaped to Geneva during the Soviet revolution in 1918. Several were in the Swiss watch business.

When I needed my first haircut, I went to Geneva to a barber who charged two Swiss francs and with an additional fifty cents tip I spent half of my monthly stipend. Later, my friends at the Institute and I started crossing the border into France. In the nearest French village, we found a barber who charged one hundred French francs, equivalent to one Swiss franc. Adding a twenty-five cent tip, it amounted to half of what I had to pay in Geneva. After that, we went to France for our haircuts.

One evening our students from Bulgaria sang Communist songs while on the French side of the border. The French police arrived, informing them firmly, "All students are forbidden to cross the border into France. You are not welcome here. If we ever catch any of you on French soil, we will put you in jail!"

After that episode, we were afraid to go into France, but to save some money we had to go there for our haircuts. We crossed the border where there were no guards present. By then we knew the locations of the border guards.

The difference between Switzerland and France amazed me. Perhaps a kilometer from Anieres, the first village in France displayed a tremendous difference in the standard of living. The people on both sides of the border were basically the same, spoke the same language, and practiced the same religion. Some French villagers commuted daily on their bicycles to work in Switzerland at menial jobs. Even blindfolded, I could tell when I left Switzerland and entered France. The Swiss side was quiet and cool. France seemed noisy, hot, and dusty. There were fewer trees. Chickens and ducks wandered on the streets, dogs barked. I attributed that to the economic differences between the two countries. France, the poorer country, had fewer paved streets, more dust, and people lived more primitively.

During my stay in Switzerland I frequently communicated with my parents by mail. One day, I received a letter that the American Consul had notified them that our long awaited visas were ready. I could not believe that only six months after my departure for Switzerland, America beckoned. At first, I didn't want to leave the Institute. I wrote to my parents, pleading that the ORT Institute might be my only chance to receive an education. I feared a life of poverty as an immigrant in America, sentenced to menial work and no opportunity for an education. The response from my parents was short and simple.

"Buma, if you won't go to America, neither will we."

In the end, I promised to accompany my parents to America.

While in Switzerland, I had corresponded with my father's cousin, Liova. He lived in Lyon, France. Although he invited me to visit him, I never made the trip because my family received the visa to America.

As a student of the ORT Institute, I will forever be grateful to them. The six months I spent, there were the nicest, most exciting since the war began. They gave me my start in life. I worked hard, learned, enjoyed my studies, made friends, and spoke passable French. I loved the life I experienced there, which was light-years from life in DP camps. The only downside was the anti-Semitism, and I learned that perfection, even for the much-lauded, beautiful Switzerland, is an illusion.

CHAPTER 21

BARLETTA –
THE SECOND TIME

O N July 17, 1949, I left the Central ORT Institute for Barletta. Upon my arrival my parents and I embraced, however Mama failed to demonstrate her overjoy of seeing me.

"Is something wrong?" I asked, puzzled.

"We've just received a letter from the American Consulate." Papa sighed. "There are only two visas waiting for us."

"How is that possible?" I asked, my shock evident. "What's wrong?"

"You weren't in Italy when the visas were issued," Papa explained. "The authorities knew you were attending school in Switzerland."

"Don't worry, Buma," Mama tried to assure me. "We won't leave without you." She put her arm around me.

"You must leave without me," I insisted. "Otherwise, you'll lose your visas and who knows how much longer you'll have to wait for new visas to be issued, even if they give you others after you refused the first."

"We aren't leaving without you," declared Mama, tears in her eyes. "You are our reason for going to America. For us, it is already too late."

I tried to behave with a calm I didn't feel. I felt it was imperative that my parents departed for America, even if I had to wait for several months or years to join them. I had to convince Mama I'd be alright. At the same time, I was extremely unhappy, angry and silently cursed the American Consul and the entire US immigration process. Why do they make it so difficult? Haven't I waited long enough? When am I going to be among the fortunate and go to America? Now that I've abandoned my studies, I discover that my departure for America is delayed, postponed, or in question altogether.

"Please let's be reasonable," I spoke quietly to my parents. "We all know how difficult it was to obtain these visas. We repeatedly risked our lives, we used false documents, we escaped from Russia, we illegally crossed borders, and we've endured years of waiting in Italy. You can't possibly refuse to go. Most people would do anything to reach America. In a short time, I'll receive my visa and join you in America. Please go and make a new home for all of us, Mama." I hugged her, wiping the tears off her cheeks.

"Sonia, Buma is right," said Papa. "He's young, strong, and capable. He'll be fine. He was alone in Switzerland, and nothing bad happened to him. Be reasonable, we cannot refuse our visas."

After a couple of hours of reasoning and pleading, Mama finally capitulated. Immigrating to America had been our *raison d'être* since our decision to flee the anti-Semitism of the Soviet Union. We had gone through hell, believing that our goal of immigrating to a safer, more tolerant environment had been a worthy endeavor.

Four months later, my parents received their visas and booking on a ship. They departed for America on December 14, 1949, arriving there on December 22, 1949, per the Declaration of Intention documents they filled out in Mount Vernon, Westchester, NY on March 18, 1950. In those formal documents, they registered their intention to become citizens of the United States.

I accompanied them by train to Bagnoli, their port of

embarkation near Naples. We slept there overnight. The next morning, they embarked on an old military transport ship called SS (or USAT) General A.W. Greeley.

The day of their departure the sky was gray, the wind gusted, and the rain-wet pier was slippery. The weather resembled my mood. Words are inadequate to describe my feelings while standing at the pier, with tears in my eyes as I watched their ship slip away from the dock. I stood measuring the separation between my parents and me until the sight of the ship faded. I wept, filled with sadness and uncertainty. I did not know how long it would take me to join them. The thought of returning alone to the DP camp in Barletta was unbearable. My feet refused to carry me. I felt like I was returning to jail. It depressed me, especially after I'd been exposed to the idyllic life at the Central ORT Institute. It was one of the saddest days in my life.

I returned to Barletta, waiting impatiently for my visa. I remained dispirited. I felt imprisoned without a known release date. For the sake of my sanity, and to earn money, I secured a position working for the DP camp as a clerk. I was responsible for the daily rationing of all the food for the camp's residents. I calculated and issued a daily food order, which was released from the warehouse to the kitchen in order to feed all of the refugees in camp. The calculations, prescribing various foodstuffs and amounts of food were based on the necessary caloric intake and other dietary requirements for each person, as well as the type of food available in the warehouse, including meat, milk, flour, cereals, rice, pasta, vegetables, sugar, oil, butter or margarine, and desserts. Two cigarettes per person per day were also allotted.

I reported to the Comptroller of the DP camp, Signor De Napoli, who was accountable to the camp director. Antonio De Napoli, a civilian employee of the DP camp, lived in Barletta with his wife and children. Short, slim, and fit, with his shiny black hair combed back and olive skin was always impeccably dressed in a suit and tie. He rode a Vespa to work. Intelligent and well-spoken, he had an upbeat disposition.

I enjoyed my job, which involved a lot of responsibility. I quickly discovered the prevalence of corruption, and had to be above any tempting offers. A clerk from Czechoslovakia, one of the few non-Jewish refugees in the camp, was assigned to me. He was responsible for the physical handling and distribution of the food based on my daily order. He repeatedly attempted to engage me as a resource for his black market activities, but I declined for two reasons. My parents had instilled in me a high moral code, and I refused to jeopardize my immigration to America. I did not report him or the others I suspected involved in the scheme.

"You're very young," he told me," if you were older, you'd understand the world better, and see it our way."

I felt isolated and lonely after my parents left for the United States. With no friends and no mentor for counsel or advice, I lived a solitary, lonely existence. After work, I wandered around town to a movie or just for a walk. I wanted to go to the *casino,* but felt uncomfortable going there without a friend.

Time passed very slowly. Each day, I waited for mail from the American Consulate. Each week felt like a month, and a month resembled an eternity. My prevailing thoughts centered on my visa. When would I receive it? Why am I not getting any notice? Is something wrong regarding my visa? I slept poorly at night, and preferred to work in order to stay busy and not dwell on worrisome thoughts about the future.

About four months after my parents' departure and nine months after my return from Switzerland, I received notice that my visa had been issued. The next problem was locating a ship for the Atlantic crossing. Finally, the happy day arrived. I received correspondence requesting my presence in Naples to pick up my visa. I was also informed that an Italian ship by the name of "Maria C" would depart from Genoa on May 4, 1950, and I had passage on it. HIAS paid for my passage. Oh, what joy! I don't even have anybody here to share it with. I immediately wrote a letter to my parents. I promised myself that I'd eventually repay HIAS, although they didn't request or expect remuneration. Several years later, I sent a check to HIAS. I felt proud to do so.

After a total stay of ten months, I left Barletta for Naples to pick up my visa. My entire outlook on life changed on the day that I received my visa at the American Consulate. I became the happiest person on the face of the earth. It sounds ridiculous now, but my only concern at the time was to arrive in America nicely dressed. I vaguely remembered reading that early immigrants had come off the boat shabbily dressed and carrying a teapot. I was not going to be one of those. In Naples, I shopped with the money I had accumulated while working and saving. I bought a new gabardine suit, a dress shirt, a tie, a pair of fine leather loafers, pajamas, and a pair of slippers. I remember that I'd been impressed when I'd seen the boys from Buchenwald wearing slippers, pajamas, and a robe prior to shaving and showering in our shared bathroom at the Central ORT Institute. These purchases were a first for me with my own money. It was bad enough that I was coming to the United States as a poor immigrant. At least I wanted to look good.

Walking from the American Consulate in Naples, a young man holding a Parker ink pen approached me.

"I come from a nearby town with my sick wife. She is in the hospital, and I have no money at all." He begged, "Please buy my pen. It is the only thing I have. Please buy it, I beg you."

After refusing several times, he followed me for a block, begging me to buy it. I finally gave in, bought the pen, and put it in my shirt pocket. By the time I reached the hotel, I realized the pen was leaking and had spotted my shirt. The pen was a fake. I should have known better than to do business with a con artist on the streets of Naples.

CHAPTER 22

VOYAGE TO AMERICA

EFORE departing for Genoa, I came down with a cold and ran a low fever. I worried I might not pass the medical examination prior to embarkation, which would force me to wait again for another ship. An American immigration department physician or nurse checked primarily for trachoma in the eyes. I was concerned as my eyes were always red from allergies. I knew a cold would make them appear even worse.

I didn't succeed in staying calm, even though I tried extra hard. The question of whether I'd be going to America depended on that medical exam. It wasn't fair, I thought, to be refused admission after all the delays. The most important issue in my life was to board that ship.

"Come si senti (How do you feel)?" Asked a woman in a white coat.

"Sto bene (I'm fine)!" My teeth chattered as I spoke.

"Vostri occhi sono un po' rossi. Allergia (Your eyes are a bit red. Allergy)?" She studied my eyes.

"Si."

"Può salire a bordo (You can go on board)."

I was so relieved I could hardly contain my emotions.

Once I boarded the ship, I realized that I was on a small mercantile vessel, which had only twelve passengers. I was assigned a private cabin with two sets of bunk beds and a small circular window. The other passengers included a couple of opera singers returning to America and a young former marine, who'd served as a guard at the American Embassy, and his beautiful Italian bride. They were traveling to his family home in Texas. Since she called him "Honey," I assumed that was his name. When I called him by that name, he explained the endearment. I flushed and we all shared a laugh.

There was a young Italian female doctor who was returning to the US to get married, and an older wealthy American woman, who traveled extensively on merchant ships. A family of four immigrants and one other refugee from Barletta completed the list. We ate our meals with the Captain, and the food was excellent.

The ship left Genoa on schedule on May 4, 1950. The weather was perfect, warm, sunny, and a brilliant blue sky overhead. I felt ecstatic as we set sail that day. I noticed sometimes the weather and mood go hand in hand. When my parents sailed to the US and I had to remain in Italy, the cold wind and grey sky were in perfect harmony with my mood. I recalled the anxiety of the war years. I reminded myself the worst is over. Hitler, the Nazis, and all of their supporters are dead and consigned to history. I'm on my way to America and new beginnings. I didn't want to think about the unknown difficulties that awaited me in America. I knew that I would begin my life there as a penniless new immigrant.

I told myself that I would overcome the difficulties I would face in America. I had overcome the war. Learning one more language, English, should not be that difficult since I had learned new languages beginning at the age of five at which time I spoke only Russian. I'd already learned Yiddish, Romanian, a little German and Ukrainian, Italian and French. Finding a job should not be insurmountable. I was alive and I was going to the greatest country in the world. I would be an American in the country of opportunities. I was grateful to America and its immigration policies.

Our ship stopped at *Livorno* (Leghorn) to load barrels of

olive oil, and then onto *Napoli*. From Naples we journeyed to Malaga, Spain. I stood on the deck by the railing, watching the cranes load large bundles of sheets of cork. The process took the better part of a day. Next, we passed the Straits of Gibraltar and into the Atlantic Ocean. It was already May 8. In the Atlantic, the weather changed. The sky turned dark; wind and rain followed.

The small ship had no stabilizers. The waves grew high, and the ship took quite a beating. After a couple of days in the Atlantic, the storm became ferocious and the pounding so bad, the captain informed us that he had changed course to improve our situation. For several days, the ship turned about, steaming southeastward in order to reduce the time spent in the storm. All that time I ran a fever and suffered bouts of seasickness. The waves were very high and the ship rolled and pitched constantly, adding to our collective misery. Every minute the ship went up and then dropped like in free fall. Plates slid off the tables and liquid spilled. All of the passengers were prohibited from going on deck for fear they would fall overboard. I saw sailors dressed in rain gear and secured with rope harnesses move on the deck. I had difficulty walking inside the ship, and was nauseated all the time.

The only doctor on board was the young Italian female whom I befriended. She took care of me. She even slept in my cabin for several nights. No medications were available. An oil tanker passed fairly close to our ship, steaming in the opposite direction.

"Our ship's communication officer contacted the tanker and inquired if they had medication on board that would help you," the Italian doctor told me. "Unfortunately the answer was negative."

"You mean to say our ship went to the trouble of asking another ship for help?"

"Yes, I asked for it. I'm surprised that the Maria C does

not carry adequate medication on board," she said, her anger palpable.

"I appreciate your effort and am grateful for all you're doing for me."

"I do what I can. I'm a physician." Then, with a big grin on her face, she added, "Besides, I like you."

I smiled back at her and thought that she was quite a remarkable woman.

When the storm subsided, the ship was redirected to dock in Baltimore instead of New York, as originally intended. Twenty-three days passed before we reached Baltimore; an unheard of length of time for an Atlantic crossing.

When people ask me why it took so long, I jokingly replied the Maria C was related to the three famous ships, the Niña, the Pinto and especially the Santa Maria.

When I wasn't ill, I enjoyed my time aboard the Maria C. The Italian female doctor was a highpoint of the weeks at sea. Most of the passengers kept to themselves, other than the marine and his bride. I read the book *Ethan Frome,* by Edith Wharton, in English, although I labored over the language. I thought it was important to improve my English skills. I bought a bottle of *Chianti* prior to boarding, which I never opened due to my illness. I gave it to the sailors on board; they toasted to my health. *"La vostra salute!"*

We arrived in Baltimore early in the morning on May 27, 1950, a date forever etched in my memory. It was a glorious sunny day. How do I begin to describe my feelings of joy and disbelief that I'd finally arrived in America? I was overwhelmed with emotion. At first, I wanted to jump up and down and shout, "I am in America! I made it!" However, I felt too embarrassed to indulge such a reaction and somewhat uncertain. I did not know what to expect after building up in my mind a "promised land" image. I watched the workers around the port, who did not look any different from workers in other parts of the world. I also watched the stevedores as they off-loaded the cargo from our ship.

I observed those strong men with tattoos on their arms, whistling, yelling, and signaling to one another in the process of handling the cranes. For a while, I felt as though I was in the Soviet Union, where I'd seen similar muscled men with tattoos, mannerisms and gestures. For some reason, I'd expected more refined looking men in America.

I returned to my cabin and changed into my new clothes. I didn't intend to step onto American soil looking like a poor immigrant. I also wanted to impress my parents, and was impatient to see them. After packing my valise, I was ready to disembark, even though I did not know how I would make the trip to Brooklyn from Baltimore. I spoke to one of the American immigration officials while still onboard the ship in Baltimore harbor.

"Since the ship was supposed to dock in New York instead of Baltimore," I said, "could you please tell me how to get to New York?"

"You can take the railroad," he answered. "Do you have money for a ticket?"

"Yes, I have twenty dollars, but how do I get to the railroad station?"

"You can take a taxi."

He noticed I wasn't exactly elated with his answer. "If you wait until I'm finished with my business, I'll give you a lift in my car to the railroad station."

"Thank you very much. I'll wait."

The twenty-dollar bill was all the money I possessed. At the railroad station, I bought a ticket to New York Grand Central Station for seven dollars and change.

My father Gregory and my mother Sonia. Photos taken
for US visa applications – Italy 1948

My mother's parents.
Grandpa Zeilig and Grandma Hannah. Beltz, circa 1940

My great grandfather Benzion Eisenstein, father of my grandmother Sura, my father's mother. Photo taken in Mogilev Podolsk, Ukraine.

My father Gregory in his school uniform

1

Uncle Tolia
and
Aunt Sonia.
Beltz, 1940

Uncle Shulim,
Bronia,
Aunt Liza,
and
Alexander
Fleishman.
Circa 1948

Uncle Zioma in Beltz 1939. His brother Shulim by Zioma's grave in
Beltz. Zioma was exhumed from a mass grave in Bershad in 1944

Monument to the Jewish victims
of genocide by the Fascists
during WWII. The monument
was erected in Beltz and the
inscription is in Romanian

Uncle Tolia's grave in Israel.
He died in 1979

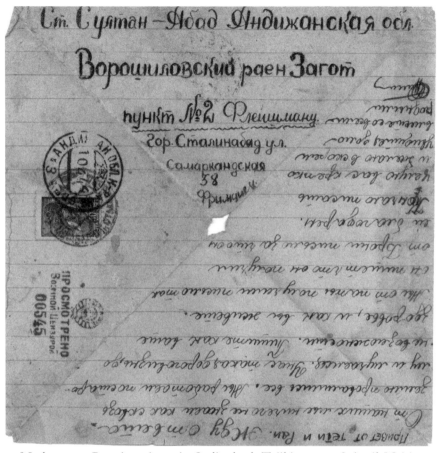

My letter to Bronia written in Stalinabad, Tajikistan on 3 April 1944
and sent to a kolhoz in Uzbekistan. The stamp "prosmotreno" 00545
on the lower left corner verifies that the letter was reviewed and
approved by the Soviet Union's military censorship

Aunt Sheiva with whom we lived in
Stalinabad, Tajikistan until August 1944.
Photo taken in May 1952 in Stalinabad

With members of the kibbutz in Bacau, Romania in 1946, I am on the left holding a hoe. Girl in the center was the head of the kibbutz.

My first girlfriend Anna (left) with my cousin Bronia in Beltz 1947. Bronia brought photo on her visit to Los Angeles in 1994

I'm wearing my first leather jacket donated by American Jewry. Pin is a kibbutz insignia.
Bacau, Romania, 1946

Cremona, 16 May 1948.
Most people in the DP camp in Cremona, Italy, marched in support
of the establishment of the State of Israel. My father is in the photo
above. I am in the photo below. The sign in back of me reads: Long
live Italy, always hospitable and generous to the Jews

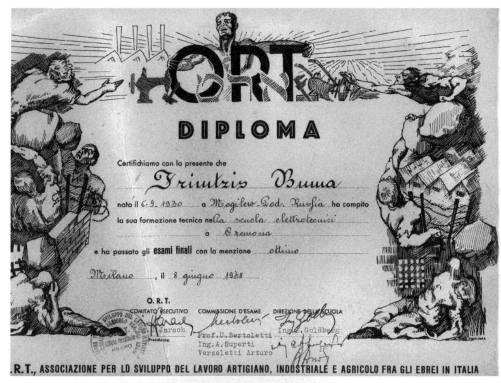

ORT
DIPLOMA

Certifichiamo con la presente che

Friutzis Buma

nato il 6-9. 1930 a Mogilew Pod. Russia ha compito
la sua formazione tecnica nella scuola elettrotecnici
a Cremona

e ha passato gli **esami finali** con la menzione ottimo

Milano, il 8 giugno 1948

O. R. T.

COMITATO ESECUTIVO   COMMISSIONE D'ESAME   DIREZIONE DELLA SCUOLA

Jarach
(Presidente)
Prof.U.Bertoletti   Ing.G.Goldberg
Ing.A.Superti
Verzeletti Arturo

R.T., ASSOCIAZIONE PER LO SVILUPPO DEL LAVORO ARTIGIANO, INDUSTRIALE E AGRICOLO FRA GLI EBREI IN ITALIA

UNION MONDIALE
DES SOCIÉTÉS POUR LE DÉVELOPPEMENT
DU TRAVAIL ARTISANAL, INDUSTRIEL
ET AGRICOLE PARMI LES JUIFS

ORT

WORLD UNION
OF SOCIETIES FOR THE PROMOTION OF
HANDICRAFTS AND OF INDUSTRIAL AND
AGRICULTURAL WORK AMONG THE JEWS

EXÉCUTIF CENTRAL
COMITÉ ADMINISTRATIF

Ref. AI./Bn

No *11077*

CENTRAL EXECUTIVE
ADMINISTRATIVE COMMITTEE

GENÈVE, le 16 juillet 1949.
6, RUE EYNARD - Tél. 5 72 34-35

ATTESTATION

Nous certifions, par la présente, que
Monsieur **Bumi FRIMTZIS**
est un élève de l'Institut Central ORT (section
électro-technique II) à Anières près Genève.

INSPECTION CENTRALE

L. Alcimih

UNION ORT

Above: My first diploma after the start of WWII. ORT Cremona, Italy, 1948

Below: Affidavit certifying my status as a student at the Central ORT Institute. Geneva, Switzerland 1949

Photo for immigration to
the US, 1949

DP camp Iesi, Italy, 1948

Photo taken as a student at the
ORTCentral Institute in Anieres,
Switzerland, 1949

DP camp Cremona, Italy, 1948

Graduation photo. CCNY June 1956

Top: Mama and Tolia, Palos Verdes, California 1975

Left: Mother's 89th birthday with Bronia, Rancho Santa Fe, California, 1994

Bottom: My father's cousin Lazar, his wife Lena, mother and I in 1995. I had not seen Lazar for 50 years

Our wedding photo.
Brooklyn, New York
February 2, 1957

The Frimtzis family at our wedding anniversary – February 2, 2007.
Rancho Santa Fe , California

PART FOUR

LIFE IN AMERICA
(1950 -)

CHAPTER 23

BROOKLYN

W HEN I finally set foot on American soil, I was both thrilled and curious, but I was also anxious about everything, I didn't know what to expect, except that my life would change. After all, this was America. I anticipated the reunion with my parents, and seeing the sights of New York. During the train ride, I took in the American countryside. The scenery reminded me of Europe, but I was not disappointed. I reasoned, grass is the same all over, so are grazing cows, trees and little streams.

When I entered New York Grand Central Station, the sprawling building, and the cavernous space it occupied, with thousands of people hurrying in all directions impressed me. After taking it all in, I followed the signs to the streets and hailed a taxi.

"Can you take me to Brooklyn to … Sackman Street?" I asked the cab driver, giving him my parents' address.

"Sure thing," the cabby said. "Hop in!"

On the way to Brooklyn, I marveled at the skyscrapers and all the traffic. It looked familiar somehow, maybe from all the American movies I'd enjoyed in Italy. Nevertheless, I looked at everything as if through magic glasses. I couldn't believe I was really in America. I felt like I was dreaming. Then, we crossed a bridge, and the driver said, "We're now in Brooklyn."

I felt impatient to see my parents.

At last, the taxi pulled up in front of the tenement building where my parents lived. I paid the cabby five dollars, including a tip, which left me seven dollars and some change. I wanted to remember the amount of money I started with my new life in America. I would one day marvel at what I had accomplished with it. Nervously, I climbed the several steps and rang the doorbell.

"Oh, my God, you're here! Oh, thank God that I finally see you! Grisha, he's here! It's Buma!"

Mama was so excited, I thought she might faint or have a heart attack. She embraced me, simultaneously crying and kissing me.

"Thank God I see you! Thank God, you're here!" she said, still holding on to me and crying. Papa also embraced, and kissed me.

"Don't be so hysterical. He's here for good!" he told Mama.

I hugged both of them tightly, glad to be with my family again.

"Why did your crossing take so long?" Mama asked. "We expected you weeks ago. I was going out of my mind, worrying about you. Our crossing took only a week. Are you alright?"

"I'm fine. I was on a small mercantile ship, and it made many stops. We were also rerouted due to bad weather."

"Let's not question his trip," Papa interjected. "He's here, that's the main thing."

"Please pinch me, Mama. I want to make sure that I am awake." She smiled and embraced me again as I grinned at her. "Are we really all in America?"

"Yes, my son. Our trip through hell took us an awful long time, but we're finally here. God bless Phil for the affidavit, and America who allowed us in."

"It feels really good to hear you say that, Mama. You know how long we've dreamed of this day." We held each other for a long time, both of us weeping tears of joy.

"Too bad our joy is saddened," she said, sighing as we let

go of one another, "by the fact that Zioma, my mother, Pesia and her family did not live to see it."

These minutes I hold dear. I will remember this reunion for as long as I live.

I looked around my parent's apartment, which consisted of a living room, bedroom, kitchen, and bathroom. The floors of all rooms covered in linoleum in a floral design, I'm sure represented a fashion statement. Mama insisted that I eat something. I was actually rather hungry. I believe she gave me a chicken salad sandwich on a Kaiser roll. I remember it because I questioned why she'd put lettuce in the sandwich. At home, before the war, we hadn't used lettuce in our sandwiches.

While I ate, Papa called Mosia to tell him I had arrived. I sat down with Mama on the couch in the living room. Papa sat on the matching chair.

We talked for a long time. I told them how I'd spent the five months in Barletta after their departure for America, but I was more interested in what had happened with them since their arrival. I wanted to know if Papa had secured a job, and what reception they'd received from our relatives.

"Phil Schechtman, who did not even know us, was more helpful than Mosia and Matusia, who grew up with Papa," Mama told me.

I glanced at Papa. His eyes dropped to the floor. He did not want to meet my gaze.

"Mosia gave me a job on his construction project," he said quietly. "I guess I should be grateful."

"You don't sound grateful or happy. What kind of work do you do for him?"

"All my life I used a pen and pencil, now I'm using a broom and shovel. I clean the houses between the various phases of construction. I guess I'm of no other use to him."

I didn't want to continue the conversation because I realized that Papa was hurt and bitter.

"Why don't you take off your coat, tie, and shoes? Make yourself comfortable," suggested Mama.

"I want Mosia to see me looking good." I responded. "I want to impress him with the things I bought with my hard earned money"

After a couple of hours Mosia arrived by car. He was glad to see me, but he seemed somewhat surprised and disappointed that I wore a suit and tie. From his comment, I deduced he expected me to wear some hand me down dilapidated clothes.

"That's a pretty fancy suit you're wearing."

"I bought it with the money I earned in the DP camp, Mosia. I wanted to impress you, and arrive in America wearing nice clothes."

"He really surprised me," Mama told Mosia. "I answered the doorbell ring, and there stood Buma. I was so excited, I was afraid I would faint."

"How did you get to the apartment?" Mosia asked me.

"I took a taxi from Grand Central Station," I replied.

"Didn't you see the subway station at Grand Central? Surely, you could have taken the subway instead of spending money on a taxi. I use the subway."

"I was afraid to try it for the first time with luggage. I thought I might get lost," I answered, somewhat guilty.

He obviously did not think that someone arriving for the first time in New York City with a valise in his hands and speaking little English should have trouble navigating the New York subway system. It looked like I started on the wrong foot with him. He must have thought I did not know the value of money; that I had spent the years in Europe in luxury, while my parents wrote letters to him saying how bad off we were. Perhaps I was much better at spending than at earning. After all, he really did not know me. I wondered if I had made a mistake by arriving in Brooklyn nicely dressed.

Sackman Street in Brooklyn was in a neighborhood where

earlier Jewish immigrants as well as newcomers had lived. Close by was Belmont Avenue, known for the Belmont market. In addition to thrift stores, pushcarts lined the street. One could buy articles of clothing as well as food. Prices were reasonable there. Many people spoke Yiddish in addition to accented English. My parents felt comfortable in the area, because they could communicate in Yiddish. They could not speak much English.

My parents told me that prior to moving to Brooklyn, they had an apartment in Mount Vernon, close to White Plains, where the Schechtmans lived. The area was less Jewish and they couldn't communicate. As a result, they felt out of place.

A few days after my arrival, I was taken to Philip and Rose Schechtman. I met their son Jerry and his fiancée Margie. They received us nicely even though we had never met them before. I told him how much I appreciated his sending us an affidavit. We also met Matusia (Mathew) and Helen, who lived in Wycoff, New Jersey.

Shortly after my arrival, I also met Mama's relatives, Harry (Herschel) and Julie Fleishman, and their children Dolly and Roy. Roy was about twelve and a half years old because I believe that year he was a Bar Mitzvah. I also met Paul and Sarah Margolies and their children, Donald and Allan. Sarah and Harry were siblings, and Mama's cousins. Harry was a plumber, and Julia a bookkeeper. Paul, I believe, was in the clothing business. They also lived in Brooklyn.

A few days later, Mosia invited us for dinner. After we finished eating, he explained to me that he was building houses. In reality, he was developing large areas on Long Island.

"Go to an army surplus store," he instructed me, "and buy a pair of heavy army boots and some work clothes. Then come to me, and I will give you a job on my construction projects. I'll start you at the bottom and pay you $25 per week. We'll see how you're doing and then we'll go from there."

"I really appreciate your offer and thank you very much,

but I would like to pursue a job in the electrical field, in which I have some experience."

He'd made the identical offer to me as he made to Papa. I was hurt and offended. He obviously did not think much of me, or my abilities. Nor did he ask for my job experience and my plans. With the exception of a dinner now and then at his house, Mosia offered no assistance to me or my parents. Both he and Matusia were very friendly but that was all.

I immediately began to look for a job. My vocabulary was rather limited, I knew less than two thousand words in English, and I had no connections. I took the subway to the Williamsburg area of Brooklyn, where there were several electrician shops. I went door to door and inquired if they would employ me.

"I am looking for a job," I would tell the owners. "I have some experience as an electrician in Europe. Could you use me?"

After a couple of days, one owner responded kindly.

"I have a little work," he said as he looked me over, "but I cannot hire you. My employees must be members of the Electrician's Union."

"Can I join the union?" I asked.

"It is hard to join the union without a sponsor, but I promise to get you into the union after you work for me for a short time. I know the union well. Meantime, I will give you a little pocket money for the work you'll do for me, but you will not be my employee, and I don't need your social security number."

"Will you hire me after you help me join the union?"

"Yes! Is that okay?"

"Okay!" I answered.

"Can you start tomorrow morning at 8:00?"

"Yes."

I returned home, informing Mama and Papa that I would be able to earn a little money and gain experience as an electrician's helper. I also told them about the man's promise to sponsor me into the Electricians' Union. I privately questioned his motives. I knew that if I became a union member, he'd have to officially hire me and pay me union wages.

My first day at work fell on a Wednesday. He asked me to clean up and rearrange the interior of the store, the various parts, brackets, pipes, elbows, insulators, switches, and other supplies. I worked hard because I wanted to impress him. The next two days he sent me out on a job with another electrician to repair the air-conditioner in a restaurant. The job involved working in the attic. The fans were heavy and greasy. We removed and replaced the air-conditioning fans and cleaned the grease from the unit and the compressor. The attic was little more than a crawl space. It was extremely hot. Soaked in sweat, I had difficulty breathing.

On Friday at the end of the working day, we returned to the store. Both the electrician and I were filthy with grease all over our clothes, our bodies, faces, and hands. The owner took me aside, gave me $15 cash, and said, "Here is some spending money."

I worked for that storeowner for three weeks. At the end of the second week, he gave me $25. He called it pocket money, paying me the same at the end of the third week. That amounted to 63 cents an hour, whereas the minimum wage was 75 cents an hour, or $30 per week.

"He'll never help you into the union. As a union member, he'd have to pay you union wages," advised other employees, who'd worked for him for some time. "You're the third person to whom he's made the same promise. The two others had worked for him several months before they'd wised up."

I knew that my boss never considered me an employee. He had merely found a way to have people work for him for menial pay. I resigned immediately.

Next, I found employment at Airking, a company that built television sets. I had to wire and solder two or three resistors, capacitors and a few wires into each TV chassis as it moved to my position on the assembly line. I obtained that job only after being timed as I performed the task. I had to be quick. Otherwise, I would hold up the line. I couldn't even take a bathroom break without having the supervisor replace me.

I earned 75 cents hour, $30 per week. I worked there until before Christmas, when the company laid off people so it wouldn't have to pay for Christmas and New Year's holiday time off.

"You would be hired in January," we were informed.

In January 1951, I applied for a job at Freed Transformer Company. Again, I was paid the minimum wage, 75 cents an hour. My work consisted of testing transformers against a given set of test specifications. If they met the specs, I passed them. If not, I rejected them. Then another employee determined which ones could be fixed, and which ones would need to be disassembled to save the usable parts. The work was somewhat more interesting, and no longer chained me to an assembly line.

Papa's cousin Rose, her husband Phil, and their son Jerry Schechtman, lived in a nice house in White Plains. Shortly before my arrival to the US, they purchased an old country home in Bedford Village, near Mount Kisco in Westchester County, New York. The house was located in an exclusive area, where affluent people with old money lived. There were no houses on either side of them, or across the road.

Rose and Phil were told that George Washington had slept in their aging country house. The property included a small lake and beautiful wooded grounds. There was an apartment above the detached garages, where their groundskeeper Rudy lived. On several Saturdays, either Jerry or Phil took me along to spend the weekend. At times, I helped Rudy pull weeds or did some other chores on the grounds. I felt that this was the only way I could repay in a very small way their hospitality towards my family.

On one clear lazy Sunday afternoon, the sun reflected in the lake and there was hardly a breeze in the air. Margie decided that we should all go for a swim. We spread out towels by the lakeside and she applied a clear liquid on my back.

"Baby oil?" I asked surprised as I read the label on the bottle. "I'm not a baby."

"We use baby oil to prevent burning and get a tan," Margie laughed. "You don't have to be a baby."

I meant to imply I was too tough and grown up for that stuff. They're still reminding me about the baby oil and tease me that I pronounced it "bebe oil."

At that time, Jerry was engaged to Margie. I always felt awkward about my poor command of the English language despite their friendliness, and ashamed of my social and economic standing. Because of my status in life, I felt that Jerry and I had very little in common, other than being related. Jerry was a college graduate with a degree in accounting from New York University, lived in a beautiful house, belonged to a financially well-established family, had a wonderful future ahead of him, and many friends.

By contrast, my situation was not enviable and my future was very much in question, although my past had provided me with a great deal of experience. I'd seen much of the world, and I understood life from a more mature prospective than my age would imply. However, I didn't feel that mattered in America as long as my English was as poor as my financial status.

One weekend when I was at the Schechtman house in Bedford Village, Jerry started to fool around playfully with Margie. Teasingly, she told him to stop.

"Say, Buma," Jerry asked, jokingly, "don't you think an engaged couple is allowed to fool around?"

"Definitely, according to European standards," I replied, laughingly.

Unbeknown to me, Margie told Jerry's mother Rose, what I said.

"You're a bad influence on Jerry and I want you to know that European standards do not apply in America!" Rose scolded me later that evening.

Surprised by Margie's misunderstanding of my joke and reporting it to Rose, I was less surprised that Rose had reprimanded me. I felt insulted, but didn't say anything in my defense. I felt further belittled, and lowered in status and my self-esteem. My ego hurt for a long time. After that episode, I didn't joke in Margie's presence for fear she would misinterpret what I said.

In September 1950, Jerry and Margie were married. They invited me to be an usher in the wedding party. The wedding, held at the Ritz-Carlton in New York City, was the most beautiful event that I'd ever seen, other than in the movies. I wore a white dinner jacket, and I met several of Margie and Jerry's friends.

On one occasion, Jerry and Margie invited me to my first college football game. Jerry explained the rules of the game. At first sight, it seemed a rather disorganized activity where everybody ran and piled up on each other. The next plays seemed similar, except for a kicked, tossed, or carried ball. That was my impression of the most exciting and popular American sport. It began to rain and I watched the teams playing in the mud. After a while, with all players covered in mud, I could hardly tell the teams apart. After the game, we went to the house of one of Margie and Jerry's friends, Barbara. I guess they were trying to fix me up with her. Again, I felt out of place because I had no car or money and spoke English poorly. I couldn't ask her out on a date, and I never called her, even though she had a sweet disposition and a pretty face. That, to me, served as further proof that I belonged to a lower social class, and it reinforced my unhappiness.

At summer's end, my parents and I moved out of our apartment on Sackman Street. It was scheduled to be demolished and replaced by a housing project. We moved to 573 Saratoga

Avenue, between Pitkin and Sutter Avenues. The apartment, on the first floor in a large tenement building, consisted of a kitchen, a living room, a bedroom, a bathroom, and a very small room off the kitchen. The small room, which was my room, had a window facing the interior opening (an atrium) providing scant daylight. No doors led to this small atrium with a concrete floor and drainage grate into the rat-infested sewer system. Linoleum covered the floors in all the rooms of our apartment. In my room, a very small wooden desk faced the atrium, a single bed leaned against the wall, and a wooden chair squeezed between the bed and the desk. The apartment was only half a block from Pitkin Avenue, a main commercial street with the Loews Pitkin movie theater and many fashionable men's stores. People came from as far away as Long Island to shop on Pitkin Avenue.

Shortly after Mama's arrival in the United States, she began to look for work. She spoke very little English and had no real work skills. She inquired, and eventually found a social club called the Beltzer Society, where earlier immigrants from Beltz socialized. She met people there from Beltz who'd known her as a young girl as well as her entire family.

One such individual was Moishe Yosel. He'd immigrated to the United States some twenty years earlier and now owned a shop sewing ladies' dresses. After talking about the old days, Mama broached the subject of employment.

"Moishe Yosel, you know I am no seamstress, but is it possible that you could employ me in your shop?"

"Every woman knows how to sew on a button or shorten a hem on a dress," he told her, "which would make you a 'finisher' in my shop. I have many such finishers who sew by hand. I can use one more."

She thanked him profusely and followed his suggestion.

He paid the finishers several cents per dress, considered piecework pay. To make a living, Mama learned to sew fast. Delighted that Moishe Yosel offered her a job, she worked for him during all the years she lived in Brooklyn. Papa, on the other hand, experienced greater difficulty in his adjustment to the United States as he sought employment.

Prior to World War II, he'd worked in an office in either an accounting, bookkeeping or other managerial capacity. In Beltz he held a prestigious position. Of course, in Beltz, he spoke the language. In the United States, his command of English was poor. In addition, young girls with a minimum of high school education or a few years of college occupied these clerical or low-end managerial positions.

He worked at various menial manual labor jobs when he first arrived in the United States.

At one time, Papa opened a luncheonette selling sodas, coffee, candy and some sandwiches. He started the store with Mama, but it only lasted a few months until they realized they could not earn a living. Later he started a store of fresh eggs with some money given by Phil. After a short time, the business also folded. Papa took a course and became a wallpaper hanger. Again, he could not get enough work and he must have been slow at it.

After seven years in the United States, he decided to become a real estate broker. He worked hard and obtained a broker's license. Papa was very good at math. He could calculate and analyze various schemes of buying and selling real estate. He failed, however, to be an effective salesman. His limited English and Eastern European manner served as a detriment to convince potential clients and customers.

In New York, he made several successful deals and saved some money. After his move to California, he couldn't make a living in the real estate business. Papa tried hard, but he failed to succeed in any professional endeavor. In his later years, he was practically destitute, but too proud to ask for help or admit failure.

He had a terrible life in the United States and I carry some guilt because I wasn't able to help him more. I was in no position to help much because I was also struggling at the time. Later, I had to take care of my own family. I also was unable to communicate with my father on a business level. If I did not agree with him about a certain business scheme he was proposing, he became insulted. After all, he was my father and of course, he knew best. What made me think I knew things better than he? Since when did I become such an expert to dispute his professional opinion?

At one time, based on his proposal and against my better judgment, I joined him in the purchase of a building in Watts, a suburb of Los Angeles. When he urged me to trade it for land in Palm Springs Panorama, I did. Later, I had to purchase his lot adjacent to mine because he could not keep up the payments. The developers later abandoned the land and I couldn't sell the two lots at any price. Thirty years later, I sold them at a substantial profit.

Like my grandfather Rubin, who'd been unable to earn a living in America and had returned to Ataki, my own father experienced the same failure in America. Sadly, it was a case of "like father, like son" for my father and grandfather. I was determined not to allow history to repeat itself, and I dedicated myself to hard work and success.

CHAPTER 24

THOMAS JEFFERSON
HIGH SCHOOL

S HORTLY after my arrival, I decided to go to school to learn English. The only high school open that summer was Erasmus Hall High School in the Flatbush section of Brooklyn. I approached the young girl at the registration desk and explained that I wanted to register for an English class. Realizing how poor my English was, she directed me across the street.

When I got there, I became aware she sent me to grade school. Stunned, my ego wounded, I decided that even if I never learned English, I would not go to elementary school. I'd known minimal French when I began my classes at the Central ORT Institute, and yet, in less than six months I spoke French fluently. That gave me self-confidence. I knew that I could accomplish the same with English. Thus, I lost the summer of 1950 without attending school and without learning English, which greatly troubled me.

"I'm wasting valuable time," I complained to Mama. "Next to working, learning English is the most important thing I should be doing."

"Stop worrying. You are doing the best you can. A couple of months delay until September won't make a big difference." Mama continued with a smile, *"Meshiakh vil kimmen a por monat speiter,"* in Yiddish, "Messiah will arrive a few months later."

Before the summer was over, I went to the City College of New York (CCNY) to inquire what it would take to register in college. The registrar, a woman in her sixties, was either sympathetic to my problem or actually felt sorry for me. After I showed her my papers, written in French, for one semester at the Central ORT Institute in Switzerland, she explained that while she believed I had an education, the documents were not adequate to serve as a basis for admission to CCNY.

"What would you recommend?" I asked.

"I could admit you as a non-matriculated student," she replied.

For a split second, I was embarrassed. I didn't know what she meant.

"What does a non-matriculated student mean? Please explain."

"You would have to take fifteen credits and receive a B grade or better to become fully matriculated. You would also have to pay $9 per credit," she explained.

"That would be $135," I quickly calculated. "I cannot afford that."

"I could consider you as a 'special' student, which means that you would have to pay only $5 per credit."

"I cannot afford to pay that, either," I answered dejectedly.

"In that case, you will have to finish high school."

"To finish high school will take four years, just because of English and American history," I said somewhat confused. Surely, she didn't mean that, I thought.

"You come and see me if you'll be missing only English and American history." She encouraged me further by saying, "I really believe you can do it. Come back and see me, and good luck!"

I thanked her.

In September 1950, some four months after my arrival in America and after having lost the summer without enrolling to learn English, I went to Thomas Jefferson High School, located on Pennsylvania Avenue in Brooklyn and a considerable distance from our apartment. I intended to register for night school. Again, I brought my papers from the Central ORT Institute, which everyone ignored.

"I want to register in the last course of each sequence, so that after finishing the course, I can take the State Regents Exams for the entire course sequence," I told the man at the registration desk.

"You can't do that," he answered, obviously annoyed. "I don't know what you are talking about."

"Let me be more specific," I said, determined despite his resistance. "I want to register in Algebra II, Geometry II, and Physics II, without taking Algebra I, Geometry I and Physics I."

"No way!"

"May I speak to the person in charge of the registration, the registrar?" I finally asked after some arguing.

He pointed out the registrar in a little windowed partition. I knocked on the open door and entered. I showed the registrar my documents from Switzerland and explained my situation to him. "I took the equivalent of Algebra I, Geometry I, and Physics I at the Central ORT Institute in Switzerland therefore I want to register in Algebra II, Geometry II, and Physics II."

"We cannot recognize your documents from Switzerland. They are not official in the USA," he said.

"Look, I want to assure you that I won't give you any trouble. If my grades are bad, I'll withdraw from classes. I won't wait to be kicked out. I won't waste my time and yours." I somehow finally prevailed. The registrar sensed my commitment, or perhaps he felt sorry for me. I didn't care which. He registered me, and I thanked him.

The same month that I registered in high school, I also filled out a document titled, "United States of America – Declaration of Intention," the formal paper an immigrant with permanent residency status is required to complete and sign in front of a US District Court clerk, which indicates an immigrant's intention to become a US citizen. In the document, I had written my name as Robert Frimtzis. Under the name used at the port of entry, I wrote Buma. The clerk watched me sign my name as Buma Frimtzis. He said to me, "Now is the time to change your name, if you so desire."

I crossed out the name Buma and signed Robert. I still have that document, dated 29 September 1950. I believe the clerk meant that I could change both my first and last names, but I did not understand him.

That first semester I finished with grades in the 90s in Algebra and Geometry, and in the 60s in English and History. It is hard to describe the difficulties I endured in my English 5 class. Perhaps a better way to express it is that it would be comical if it hadn't been so painful. We studied Shakespeare. I possessed a vocabulary of maybe a few thousand words in English. I remember appealing to my teacher's sense of fairness.

"Mr. Meyers, I believe it would be fair if you grade my papers on the basis of content, not my vocabulary and spelling. You said that you'd be evaluating our critique and understanding of the play."

"What you say is true, however I can't ignore your poor English and spelling. This is a course in English," answered the teacher.

"Please, Mr. Meyers," I said in a frustrated and pleading tone. "This is a course in Shakespeare, not spelling. You're penalizing me for my spelling."

In the end, I think he gave me a minimal passing grade out of compassion, because I had worked so hard.

Although I worked full time during the day and attended

school at night, I studied as much as I could every night after coming home from school and on the weekends. At the end of the semester, I took the Regents Exams for Algebra I and II, and Geometry I and II, receiving higher grades than in the high school. During an exam in Algebra, we were asked to solve five out of six given problems. I did not understand the instructions, so I solved all six.

Encouraged by the results of my first semester, I continued the process for the second semester. I took Intermediate Algebra, Physics II, English 6, and History. Again, I successfully completed the second semester with similar grades as in the first semester. Then I took the Regents Exams for Intermediate Algebra and Physics I and II, and received grades in the 90s. Thus, I made up the major and toughest high school courses in two semesters at night while working full time during the day. I never finished English and American history, and of course, I never obtained a high school diploma.

In high school, I met other immigrant students who were taking night classes. Most of them had arrived in the United States before me. Consequently, they spoke better English. I developed life-long friendships with some of these young men.

Each one had survived the war under somewhat different circumstances. Nevertheless, we were all recent immigrants with similar objectives, aspirations, and problems to overcome. We saw each other socially at night and on weekends. Since they had immigrated earlier, they earned more money. One of the young men even managed to buy a used Ford. That car meant a lot to all of us. It became our pleasure car, a status symbol, and it made meeting girls a lot easier. My parents' house became our meeting place on weekends. After a short time, my friends and I became inseparable.

On weekends, we walked around Eastern Parkway, trying to pick up girls. We saw movies in the local theaters, or strolled along Pitkin Avenue. During the summer, we went to Brighton

Beach. Most new immigrants gathered at Bay 5, the *"greener"* beach. The veteran or more seasoned immigrants called the new immigrants, *"greene,"* the same derogatory name they'd been called when they'd first arrived in America. It implied that they were green, not ripe and didn't know the ropes.

The Korean War broke out shortly after my arrival in the United States. We were all worried about being drafted into the Army. We believed that we had an obligation to serve and protect our new country, but we didn't feel mentally or emotionally capable of becoming combatants so soon after what we'd endured during and after the Holocaust of World War II. We also had not yet truly partaken of the good life in America. I arrived in the United States on May 27, and the war had started less then a month later, on June 25.

The first of my friends to receive "greetings" from Uncle Sam was Sheldon. He reported to the Selective Service asking to be excused because he was in the United States on a student visa. The U.S. Immigration and Naturalization Service revoked his visa, forcing him to put up a bond and eventually leave the country. The United States could not deport him to Poland, so they agreed to allow him to go to Canada where he had an old uncle.

The last night before his departure Sheldon, another friend and I spent the entire night together. We repeatedly assured him that he would be alright. I remember that he cried like a child.

"Why me?" he kept on asking. "After all I went through. I lost my family and I'm finally trying to start a new life, and now I have to leave for the unknown."

Moritz and I took turns to encourage him,

"Don't worry, Sheldon, you're a hardworking, capable guy. You'll do well in Canada. You'll be alright."

"But I know nothing about Canada," he cried. "You guys realize how tough it will be to start all over again?"

"You knew less when you arrived in the US and you

didn't speak any English. At least you speak English now," we reminded him.

As it happened, Sheldon became rather successful in Canada. Now he does not regret his deportation. One other friend was drafted into the army and served his term. The rest of us were, somehow spared after interviews with the Selective Service. We surmised the Selective Service concluded we were not ready psychologically to go to war. I could not cope with the idea of being in the army. In fact, I know that I will never forget the ordeal of World War II, and it will affect me for the rest of my life.

CHAPTER 25

THE COLLEGE YEARS

RMED with the documents, which proved I'd had completed two semesters of high school and passed the Regents Exams, I returned to the City College of New York, CCNY, where I spoke to the same admissions director whom I'd spoken to a year earlier.

"Hello," I said, "My name is Robert Frimtzis. I hope you remember I was in your office last summer. At that time, you told me that if I finish high school, with the exception of English and American History, I should come and see you. Well, here I am."

"Oh yes, I remember you," she answered, "and I am also pleased that you followed my advice. Excellent, you made it in only one year."

I showed her my grades for the two semesters and the Regents Exams.

"Your Regents Exams grades are excellent, but the English and history grades are not so good."

"Well, what do I do now? Can I be admitted to college?" I asked, frowning.

"Not so fast, young man," she smiled, "I'll tell you what I'm going to do. I'll allow you to take the college entrance exams. If you pass, you will be admitted as a fully matriculated student."

"Is there another choice?"

"I'm afraid not. Don't worry, you'll do just fine."

The entrance exams were given in a large gym room that housed the basketball court and lasted a full day. The exams ordinarily established a baseline prior to entering college and determined each student's aptitude. In my case, however, it was a matter of being admitted to college. While everybody was guessing multiple-choice math and physics questions, I sat with paper and pencil and tried to calculate the answers instead of taking a guess.

A certain amount of time was allotted for each section of the exam. When the time expired, the particular section was collected and the new one distributed. The time limits were set so that it was impossible to complete a section. It was a race against the clock to correctly answer as many questions as possible.

After the exams were graded, I received a letter for an appointment with the director of admissions. What now? I worried. Maybe I hadn't passed the entrance exam. Surely, they could have just sent me a rejection notice. But then again, they could have also sent me a letter saying that I passed. I didn't know what to make of the letter. For the next couple of days, I agonized over the appointment.

I entered her office, fuelled by adrenaline, my heart racing. The woman smiled at me. I tried to relax but I couldn't.

"Please take a seat." After I sat down, she continued, "In all my experience, I have never seen such distorted exam results. You scored very high in math and physical sciences, but your English, social sciences and history were the worst I have ever seen." Then she stopped for an instant and looked me in the eyes, "After averaging your scores, the totals resulted in a passing grade. Congratulations! You will be admitted to CCNY as a fully matriculated student."

I heard the director announce the greatest news ever, but I was shocked and momentarily robbed of the ability to reason or speak. Then, I managed to say, "Thank you very much."

I believe she grasped my anxiety. She continued to smile.

"I am rarely mistaken about people. When I talked to you the first time, I saw a young man who was very serious, ambitious, and humble. I had a good feeling about you. I know you will do well. Good luck!"

By then I relaxed. I stood up and shook her hand. "You'll never know how much getting into CCNY means to me," I said, "and how grateful I am for your advice. I want to thank you again."

I left her office on cloud nine. I closed the door, took a couple of steps, looked around, and made sure I was alone. I jumped up and screamed.

"Yes! Yes, I made it!" I just could not hold in my joy any longer, not for a single moment. Words cannot describe the extent of my happiness.

Registration fee per semester was five dollars.

Being accepted to college is still one of the greatest highlights of my life. My emotions ran extremely high. Education meant everything to me. I never wanted to spend my life working in a shop as an electrician or as a blue-collar worker. Now I knew that I wouldn't have to.

When I left the Central ORT Institute in Switzerland, I had resigned myself to the idea of never being able to afford college in America, yet I had actually made it on my own. I was so proud of myself.

I needed seventy-five dollars, which I did not have. I did not want to ask anyone for a loan. At the time, I was angry about having lost a year going to night school. I now believe that the high school year was not a loss. It allowed me to reinforce my math and sciences, which I'd never formally studied. Above all, I had learned more English. Without that year, my college studies would have been much more difficult than they were, if such a thing were possible.

In September 1951, I registered at Brooklyn College as a fully matriculated student. I chose Brooklyn College because it was closer to my home than CCNY. It saved me about one and a half hours per day traveling time. Brooklyn College was part of the City of New York colleges with the same status as CCNY. Brooklyn College did not have an engineering school. However, it had a two-year pre-engineering curriculum, which after successful completion allowed one to continue at CCNY as a junior. At the time, I did not know that the English classes at Brooklyn College were more difficult than at CCNY, because we took the same classes as the liberal arts and English majors.

At CCNY, the English classes for engineering students were easier. In addition, I was required to take, without college credit, a speech clinic class. I started going to school at night while working at Freed Transformer full-time. I found school to be no picnic after a full day's work.

In no time at all, I developed a complex. I was embarrassed to take part in any class discussions due to my poor accented English. Any time I opened my mouth to respond to a question, I noticed that other students turned their heads and watched me, thinking, "Who is this foreigner who talks so funny?"

I was very self-conscious about my accent. Instead of it being a mark of distinction in a positive sense, I felt embarrassed. It was my Scarlet Letter. I felt like I wore a big sign that read, "Another unfortunate refugee, an immigrant! So go ahead, look down on him!"

I knew America was a country built by immigrants – that's what made it great, a democracy and a real melting pot. That implied that an immigrant should not feel ashamed for being different. He was, or would be, the contributor and builder of the country. Unfortunately, I felt like a second-class citizen. I felt that the statement about America built by immigrants, implying that there was nothing wrong being an immigrant, was appropriate to be made only by those who were not immigrants. They did not have to walk in an immigrant's shoes, work hard to achieve seemingly little, struggle with the language, feel embarrassed for not knowing the local mores, live with an accent that identified a foreigner, or with the stigma of poverty and lower social status. As a new immigrant, I couldn't see when I would be able to improve my life and how I could possibly contribute to the greatness of America.

Meantime I progressed at work and promoted to supervisor of the testing department with a twenty-cent hourly raise. Since I didn't pay for room and food from the time I started college, I was able to save a good percentage of my earnings. I accumulated as much as I could for over a year, from the time I started working at Freed Transformer Company in January 1951, until my completion of the first semester at Brooklyn College in February 1952.

"Mama, I figured out that if I continue college at night, it would take me approximately ten years or even longer to complete the courses."

"That long?" she asked, completely surprised. "That is a very long time."

"Mama, I doubt that I would have the patience, courage, and willpower to stick it out for that long."

"What can you do?" Mama looked worried.

"I would like to try going full time during the day."

"What about money? What about your job?"

"I have accumulated five hundred dollars. I would like to try day school for one semester and see how far the money lasts. I think I'll be able to work at Freed Transformer part-time. If I run out of money I'll switch back to night school."

"You do what you think is best. I'll support you as long as I can." She gave me a hug and a kiss.

"Thank you, Mama. I knew you'd agree with my decision."

I transferred to day school and registered for classes beginning February 1952. Then I went to speak to the engineer in charge of production at Freed Transformer Company. He knew that I was attending Brooklyn College at night with the intent of becoming an electrical engineer.

"Mr. Katzman, I just transferred to day school, and I would appreciate it if I could work here part-time."

"Why do you want to do that?" he asked me, "You have a good future here. Whenever you get your degree will be fine."

"My decision to go to school full-time is irreversible," I told him. "I just want to know if I can work here part-time."

"Certainly, Bob, you will always have a job with us. You understand that you won't be able to supervise the testing department on a part-time basis," he replied.

"I agree, but could I continue testing transformers?"

"I have a better idea," said Mr. Katzman. "You would be of greater value to the company if, in addition to testing, you would try to repair rejected transformers. Even if you only fix a few each day, you'll earn your pay. You have enough knowledge to be able to do that. Are you willing to give it a try?"

"Of course I will," I agreed enthusiastically.

"Then it's a deal!"

He shook my hand, and I left his office. I was grateful to have a job, and I appreciated his confidence in me. I did not realize until after my first paycheck that my salary had been cut by twenty cents per hour. I did not think that was fair, but I had no recourse. I was glad to have the job.

I signed up for a full slate of classes, but I picked them in such a way as to have Tuesdays and Thursdays free. These were days that the school fraternities and sororities had their social activities, so classes were sparse anyway. This allowed me to work on Tuesdays, Thursdays, and Saturdays, and still maintain my grades.

During summer school breaks, I worked full-time. My boss reinstated my title of supervisor, and I managed the testing department. I also received an increased hourly wage of twenty-five, and then thirty cents per hour. When I returned to school,

I reverted to part-time status again, at a reduced salary. Later, I also started working closely with the engineers and gained design experience. I managed to continue college on a full-time basis until I graduated from CCNY in June 1956.

Toward the end, I worked only on Saturdays or Sundays. Often on Sundays, I was the only person at work. Periodically one of the owners, Irving Freed, also worked. He filled the transformers with potting compound. That black potting material was heated to liquefy, then in a hot smelly liquid state, poured into the canned transformers. A physically hard and dirty job, Irv was usually the man who did it. Most of the time, nobody supervised my work or checked on me. I would find a stack of transformers that did not meet specifications and a note that said, "Bob, see what you can do." During the several hours I worked, I managed to fix many transformers, which saved the company an appreciable amount of money.

During my years at Freed, I befriended many people. One of them was John Hutter, an engineer and a Holocaust survivor, specifically from the Matthausen Concentration Camp. He frequently helped me with technical problems and encouraged me to continue my studies. I also met Paul Erman, a refugee from Germany. A Christian family in Holland had hidden and saved Paul and three of his brothers. Before the war, they'd lived in Germany in a beautiful house, and his father had owned and operated a chemical factory that produced shoe polish. His house is still there. We've remained friends to this day.

After I finished my pre-engineering coursework at Brooklyn College, I transferred to CCNY. Travel by subway to CCNY from our apartment in Brooklyn took an hour and a quarter each way. While commuting by subway to CCNY, I completed all of my reading assignments. Most of the time I managed to get a seat on the subway for the duration of the trip. When I could not get a seat, I stood with my leather briefcase on the floor wedged between my feet so nobody would snatch it. One hand stretched high holding on to the overhead strap, while the other held an open book. Wouldn't you know it, this usually happened when I was studying for a quiz or a test to be given the same day.

At home, I sat at the little desk in my small room in front of the window until late at night doing my homework. With the exception of weekend nights, studying well past midnight was pretty much the norm. The neighbors used to see me through their windows and ask my mother, "How can he study so much? Doesn't he sleep? Whenever we go to bed, we see him studying."

People normally refer to their college days as "the good old days." They remember socializing, partying, friendships, and the fun of campus life. I could never make such a statement. My college years were very difficult. In addition to working, difficulties with English, my accent, my home environment, lack of money, and social status made up my other hardships. I had no time to join a fraternity or to participate in any other social activities in college.

The severe psychological complex I developed followed me for a long time. I felt that I deserved more than I got for working so hard. I also thought I was more mature, smarter, more perceptive, and more capable than the average American student in my classes. I was convinced that the English language and my accent, which I hated, held me back. I resented having to work harder than the others. Although I must admit, everybody had to work hard to keep up with the tough engineering curriculum and the CCNY environment.

Since CCNY was a tuition free college, the professors and staff reminded the students every step of the way, "For every student currently in school, there are ten others trying to enroll. What's more, they are more deserving than you." Such comments further discouraged the students, making life at CCNY more difficult than it needed to be. It may not make sense, but even as a senior with good grades, I worried constantly about graduating. I was not the only one to feel this uncertainty, since this general atmosphere prevailed at CCNY engineering school. The school attitude beat us down emotionally. My major goal during those years was to graduate and to obtain a respectable job, which would lead to financial security and a normal life.

Before the war, I attended school because my parents sent me. At the age of nine or ten, I was not very interested in school. I would have much rather played. My only motivation for good grades was embarrassment in front of the other students and the fear that Papa would punish me. During our escape, when we were running for our lives, some nights I would lie and think. "How I wish I could be in school now. I promise, if I survive, I will go to school and love it." Because of the events of World War II, I was strongly motivated to study and graduate. I promised myself that nothing would thwart my goal. As any young man, I was interested in entertainment and girls, but I avoided commitments of any kind until I got my degree. I kept that promise.

When I first saw how Papa's cousins Mosia, Matusia and Phil lived, I felt as though we came from a different planet. I feared that I would never achieve that standard of living. I thought they lived ordinary lives in nice environments, pursuing their daily activities. Then I realized that Papa's cousins were very successful. They lived well above the American standard at that time. They all had beautiful homes in exclusive neighborhoods and financial security.

I thought if one does not work hard for some objective, the achievement does not taste as sweet. This mental outlook justified my perseverance. If things were provided by one's parents and came easily, there is little appreciation. Although, I thought, I wouldn't mind being in that position.

All obstacles I'd overcome to survive and the conditions I'd been exposed throughout Europe matured me to see and recognize the stark contrast between my life and that of others. I even thought that I was in a better position than

Papa's cousins, and especially their children, to appreciate the lives they enjoyed. I believed they became accustomed to their good lives and consequently didn't give it much thought. I also wished I hadn't seen their living standards. If someone is exposed to only one lifestyle, he may not be aware that another, better or worse exists.

In "Pygmalion," George Bernard Shaw beautifully illustrates the fact that after having been shown a new and better life it was difficult and even tragic to have to revert to the old. Eliza Dolittle was perfectly happy selling flowers on the streets of London. Being poor and uneducated did not bother her. After she had seen the life of a high society, she could not return to her old lifestyle of selling flowers. Similarly, Henry Higgins could not understand how Eliza was originally satisfied with her life.

I'm aware that I was extremely fortunate to come to America. I will forever be grateful to this country for allowing me to immigrate, and for the opportunities it made available to me. I never thought that I would be able to obtain a free education in the United States. The propaganda in Europe at that time implied that America had fine universities, but that they were exclusively for the rich. Yet, I knew no path to success other than through education.

I became very impatient. I could not see any significant improvement in my lifestyle. The impatience led to doubts, which brought about a terrible psychological complex. While I was glad to bc in America, I felt envy, impatience, insecurity, frustration, ambition, and pride, all at the same time. I was happy to be in America, but not happy about *who* I was in America. I feared failure, doomed to forever struggle, just to survive. That fear haunted me for a very long time.

Speaking poor English made me feel inadequate. I did not plan to become a linguist. Oddly, out of necessity, I spoke several languages, but being multi-lingual gave me no distinction, advantage, or benefit in America. I would have gladly traded all the languages in my repertoire for English. That was a time before Spanish was a second language in America and before immigrants, legal or illegal, did not care to Americanize.I felt an urgent need to make up for lost time and opportunities. I wanted a nicer home than the little two by nothing room in my parents' apartment in the tenement building. I longed for a car, nice clothes, and more opportunity with the young women. After the horrors of World War II and the postwar experience, I should have been happy living in America. After all, there were no bombs falling and no hunger or persecution. I was grateful, but I was both unhappy and unfulfilled.

I find it hard to explain all of these simultaneously conflicting emotions. I would probably make a great patient for a psychologist. One plausible explanation could be derived from the fact that, during the war years, we just wanted to survive. Following our escape from the Soviet Union and waiting in displaced persons camps, our lives were in a state of limbo. We were impatient, but we could accept anything, because we felt everything was temporary. We were frozen in suspension. We had hope that the day would come when we would arrive in America and our real lives would begin.

Once in America, all of my patience evaporated. The clock started ticking on the attainment of the good life. What's more, I felt I had a lot of catching up to do. I was so low in my socioeconomic standing, compared to where I wanted to be, the gap seemed insurmountable. I wanted it all immediately. I knew I was using an unrealistic timescale, but I couldn't seem to help myself.

Frequently when I saw a young person driving a beautiful new car, especially a convertible or a sports car, I asked myself, "Will I ever be able to afford that?" When a successful looking, smartly dressed young man carrying a briefcase passed by, I thought with envy, "Now that's what I'd like to look like, but when?" When I passed an upscale neighborhood, I thought, "Will I ever live in a place like that?" My aspirations made me resolve to work harder. I became ambitious. When success did not happen quickly or easily, doubts, dissatisfaction, and unhappiness crept into my mind. I questioned my abilities. I was conscientious and worked hard, yet progress seemed painfully slow.

I compared myself to other Americans, those who did not go through the school of hard knocks, those fed with a silver spoon. I felt that my past provided me two diametrically opposed psychological outlooks on life, one positive and one negative. On one hand, superiority derived from maturity, worldliness, and appreciation of life. On the other hand, inferiority, shame, and fear that someone might discover the real me, the youth who'd lived a subhuman existence, run for his life, hidden from flying bullets, lived in the fields, slept on a grave in a cemetery, picked rotten food off railroad tracks, and was hungry and dirty. My shame included having to sleep in a single bed with my mother until the age of fourteen, where my lice killed the baby goat, Borka, tied to my bed.

I felt that I carried a deep, dark, ugly secret, and I feared it might somehow slip out, embarrass and belittle me, and display my true inferiority. I felt insecure, having had no exposure to the niceties of the American lifestyle. Uncertain of my social graces, and behavior in the company of people my age who'd had the privilege of being born in the United States. I feared people discover that I wasn't with it. I might have been mature and worldly in Europe, but in America, I was not hip.

I knew nothing about the American pastimes of baseball or football, which would have served me better than knowledge of foreign languages or operas. Being sensitive, I was not sure how to behave. Should I crawl into my shell for protection so my ignorance or uncertainty wouldn't show? However, then I'd lose my presence. I'd become invisible and cease to exist in American society. Under those conditions, I knew I would never learn the things I needed to know or was unsure of.

These mental conflicts, combined with my father's past

insistence that I strive to be the very best, made me extremely ambitious. I had a desperate need to succeed, to prove to myself and to the rest of the world that I was not inferior to the people of my newly adopted country. These psychological conflicts stayed with me to various degrees for many years. They gradually diminished when I started my professional career.

In plain street vernacular, my behavior could be called "crazy." In psychological terms "neurotic," or more politely, "confused." I was unhappy. However, that behavior, no matter what you call it, strengthened my resolve and drive. It also sharpened my concentration on study, competitiveness, and hard work as a method of achieving success. Envy and impatience served as catalysts.

I never revealed most of these thoughts. I agonized about them but couldn't tell anyone. From time to time, I might have touched lightly on the subject with some of my new immigrant friends. For the most part, I kept my feelings to myself, deep in my soul. I wish now that I'd opened up to someone. Someone trustworthy and knowledgeable, who wouldn't have ridiculed and might have lightened my burden.

Five years and a few months after my arrival in America a happy milestone occurred in my life. On November 17, 1955, I became a U.S. citizen. After having filled out an application, I was summoned to Federal Court on Whitehall Street in lower Manhattan. Many people stood in front of a judge. Some were asked simple questions about U.S. government, like who is the president of the United States of America? How many states are there in the USA? What is the Bill of Rights? Since the judge knew I was a college student at the time, he did not ask me any questions.

He instructed all of us: "Please rise, raise your right hand, and repeat after me the Pledge of Allegiance!" After that, he said, "I pronounce you new United States Citizens! Congratulations and good luck!"

That important event in my life occurred when I was twenty-five years old.

THE CCNY EXPERIENCE

My college experience at CCNY was interesting and challenging. On campus was a building called Army Hall used to train military personnel during World War II. It was in a state of disrepair. The entry to some classrooms was through a rusty metal staircase, which resembled a fire escape. A few windows had broken glass panes. I remember having a civil engineering class with Professor Lorell in such a classroom. It was in the winter, and the room was frigid.

Civil engineering courses were not considered highly theoretical, very difficult, or of interest to electrical engineering students. A subject cannot be considered highly theoretical if, after performing some detailed calculations, the result has to be multiplied by anywhere from 10 to 1000 as a safety factor. That implied that the equations were based on empirical approximations and had uncertainties, thus requiring safety factors. Dr. Lorell, however, was extremely theoretical, and made the course very difficult.

The electrical engineering curriculum at CCNY required electrical engineering students to take several mechanical and civil engineering courses. That supposedly provided us with a rounded education in engineering. We all knew however, that we would never make use of the material taught in these non-electrical engineering courses. At times, a student or two would raise a hand and ask him, "Professor, how come you spend so much time at the blackboard deriving complex, lengthy equations. Yet, after you're finished, you use a large safety factor?"

"You must derive the equations in order to understand the

theory, but in a practical sense, you multiply by a safety factor. That is how civil engineering works," he replied.

One winter day, he distributed the results of an earlier quiz he'd given the students. Our class average grade of this quiz was 2 out of a maximum of 10. He then proceeded to make a speech to the class, which I will never forget.

"There always was, there currently is, and there always will be a need for engineers, but when I say engineers, I don't mean anyone in this classroom." He then pointed randomly at students sitting in front of him. "You, for instance, did you ever consider being a violinist? Or you! You could probably be an excellent doctor, maybe even a surgeon, since you have delicate fingers." Pointing to another student, he continued, "You, on the other hand, would make a famous artist. Why did you pick engineering? None of you will ever be engineers. There are so many young people more capable than you who can't even get into CCNY, and here you are, wasting time and the space of someone more deserving than you!"

While it was freezing cold in the classroom, all of us were perspiring as a result of his speech. We felt terrible. Professor Lorell, who was born in Belgium and had a slight accent, later became the head of the civil engineering department. I did not mean to single him out. In fact, he was a fine instructor. He just delivered the message of the CCNY attitude or culture. All the engineering students at CCNY felt the terrific pressure and competition of attending a free college.

Professor Egan Brenner had been born in Germany. Jewish, he escaped the Nazi regime before World War II. He had the reputation of being a very tough, demanding, and consequently a feared teacher in the electrical engineering department. Students tried to avoid registering for the classes he taught, as long as the same course offered by another instructor was available. Because there were too many students to accommodate into a single classroom, the same course was often taught by two or three teachers at different times, providing more scheduling flexibility. I was not lucky enough to escape Professor Brenner's courses; I ended up taking several.

One day at the end of his class, he asked me to follow him to his office. I became instantly concerned. As I entered his office, he closed the door and asked me to sit down. After he sat down behind his desk, he started in a somewhat apologetic tone, "Mister Frimtzis, I don't know if you are aware that the college has certain limited funds it can make available to needy students, and that you could get a loan of $300. Furthermore, there is nothing to be ashamed of, since it is a loan."

I turned red in the face. I was embarrassed, "Professor Brenner," awkwardly I managed to say, "I sincerely thank you very much for the offer, and I appreciate your thinking of me, but I can manage without a loan."

"I thought I could help," he replied. Before walking out of his office, I shook his hand and thanked him again. He must have surmised that I was in more dire financial straits than the other students, although none of the other students were overly rich. Not at CCNY.

After that episode, I had a completely different opinion of Dr. Brenner. Yet during registration at the start of my last senior semester, I had the audacity to ask him to register me in a closed class taught by another professor, while his class remained open for registration.

"Professor Brenner, I want to make sure I graduate this semester," I said, implying that if I took his class, I might not graduate this semester. He smiled and registered me in the already closed class.

Every semester registration was a nightmare, competition fierce to sign up for the classes one wanted and a struggle to obtain all the required courses based on the offered schedule. Often, two or more courses were offered at the same time or a huge time gap between classes occurred. This situation became further complicated when a student tried to avoid a class because a reputedly tough instructor offered it. Classes taught by professors with a so-called "good" reputation or those who were more lenient filled up and closed first, whereas those with the more demanding professors filled up last. Often, registration schedules were based on a student's seniority. Seniors registered first, followed by juniors, etcetera. One would assume that when I became a senior, I would have an easier time registering. That was not the case.

I have fond memories of Professors Del Toro and Herbert Taub in the electrical engineering department, who were not as strict as Dr. Brenner and were very fair. Professor Taub was finishing his famous textbook, *Pulse and Digital Circuits*, by Millman and Taub, later published by McGraw Hill, 1956. The book was considered the absolute authority on the subject even before its publication.

It may be of interest that Colin Powell, the former Head of the Joint Chiefs of Staff and National Security Adviser and later the Secretary of State under President George W. Bush attended CCNY during my tenure as a student. He graduated two years after me. He originally started as an engineering student, but he could not keep up with the severe demands of the engineering curriculum. He enrolled in ROTC, and switched to geology, an easier major. Even though he had a hard time at CCNY and barely graduated, the whole world now recognizes his name. He appears in an ROTC photo in my CCNY yearbook, the Microcosm. CCNY was a free school and takes pride in its share of famous alumni. To mention just two others: Bernard Baruch, financial and economic adviser to presidents, and Jonas Salk, inventor of the Salk polio vaccine. Andy Grove, the CEO of Intel Corporation, graduated from CCNY a few years after me. He is a bona fide immigrant success story.

The process to select and admit students to the various engineering honorary societies at CCNY also bothered me. These are the national honorary societies established to recognize outstanding students in the engineering field. At the time,

I considered the process unfair. While the primary criterion involved a student's grade point average, there was a secondary requirement that the student participate in college social activities. I considered the second requirement unjust. To become a candidate, students joined the staff of the engineering college newspaper, "Vector," various engineering organizations, and other fraternities.

I had the grades to be admitted to Eta Kappa Nu, the National Honorary Electrical Engineering Society, or Tau Beta Pi, the National Honorary Engineering Society. However, I had no time to participate in any of the college social activities because I was working while going to school.

I was hurt. It did not help my complex or the chip on my shoulder. It served as one more reason for my unhappiness. At the time, I resented being excluded from membership. I knew that I deserved the distinction of belonging to the engineering honorary society, but could not achieve it as a poor struggling immigrant concentrating on a job instead of pursuing extra-curricular activities.

It further hurt my ego when a good friend (my future wife), who had somewhat poorer grades than me, was admitted to Pi Tau Sigma, the Honorary Mechanical Engineering Society. While I was very happy for her, I was very unhappy for not being considered for a similar honor.

Honorary society membership bestowed a social status for the honoree in college, and additional opportunities for employment upon graduation. The powers to be however, thought that I obviously did not deserve to belong to an elite society. To me it was ample proof that the poor didn't have the same opportunities as those who could afford to go to school without having to work.

I've softened my attitude since then, because maturity has allowed me to understand that well rounded students generally become well balanced adults in the work environment. However, I still believe that the wrong criterion for defining a "rounded student" was used. I knew the students who were chosen and I'm less convinced than ever that belonging to a college newspaper or a fraternity made those students more rounded individuals. I also believe that a case can and should be made on behalf of the good and serious student who works and maintains a good scholastic average. Not to admit such a student serves to discourage him. I certainly felt discriminated against.

CHAPTER 26

ROMANCE

URING my upbringing, sex was not a subject of discussion with either my parents or other adults. I was brought up to believe that the subject was never appropriate to talk about or even less appropriate to write about. However, you will not be surprised to learn that it was ever present in my mind. Not surprising since I was a young man.

The world became more liberal regarding sexual behavior in post World War II Europe. After my arrival in Italy, I had no contact with Italian girls because of being isolated in displaced persons camps. Even though we were free to roam the streets, we originally did not know the language and had no opportunities to meet or to socialize. We were temporary wayfarers, and relationships seemed a low priority during those transitional young years I spent in Italy. I lived in Italy when I was sixteen through eighteen. We made friends with other people living in the camps. We went to the movies frequently because they were affordable, and the films served as a major method of learning the Italian language. Frequenting casinos was as commonly accepted and inexpensive as movies.

After arriving in America, even though I had major problems finding work, learning English, and the local customs, endeavoring to acquire an education, and in general, becoming integrated into American society, the opposite sex was never far from my mind. In fact, such thoughts often interfered with and were an obstacle to my studies.

Soon after my arrival in Brooklyn, I started meeting girls. My friends and I tried to strike up conversations with girls while promenading on Pitkin Avenue, on Eastern Parkway, or in and around the movie theaters. These were our normal hangouts in the neighborhood. While we met a few girls this way, overall we were not very successful. In the summertime, we went to the beach to meet girls. We met some girls on Bay 5 in Brighton Beach.

The first girl I was fixed up with was Fay. Her mother, Charna, knew my mother and her family from Beltz. Mama encountered her while attending a meeting at the Beltzer Society, a social club where immigrants reconnected or met with others from the same town or region. Charna, friendly and hospitable to my mother, invited my parents to her home in Brighton Beach.

Shortly after my arrival, Fay, her mother, father, and younger brother visited my parents' apartment. Fay was a nice looking girl, and she attended Brooklyn College at the time. We went out on several dates and enjoyed each other's company.

One Saturday night I took her to Radio City Music Hall in Manhattan, where we saw a variety show that included the famous Rockettes, followed by a movie. That evening, a pianist played George Gershwin's "Rhapsody in Blue." After we left the theater, we walked on Times Square, and Fay commented on the music.

"Bob, what kind of music do you like?"

"I like most music, but I love opera and classical music. I heard a lot of it in Italy."

"I just love Gershwin. I think that he's a great composer, the likes of the classic masters," she commented.

"I like him, too, but I wouldn't compare him to the masters of classical music. For one thing, his music is more modern and jazzy. I couldn't even compare him to a contemporary pianist and composer like Sergey Rachmaninoff."

"I also play Chopin and Mozart on my piano," in her defense, she answered, "but I love Gershwin."

I felt that perhaps I'd been too harsh in my opinion. I knew that I could not argue with her about things strictly American, because I still had a great deal to learn. However, when it came to music and a reference to European classics, I made a strong statement. I disagreed with her about Gershwin even though she had formal musical training and played the piano whereas I had neither. I only had become familiar with a lot of classical music, especially operas, in Italy. Consequently, I considered myself somewhat knowledgeable on the subject. To me she sounded like a typical, conceited American who knew very little about the rest of the world. That was the state of my mind at the time. Looking back, I made an unnecessary argument, but I had no other knowledge to impress her with or argue about. I believe that if it were not for my insecurity complex as a new immigrant in America that argument would have never happened.

At Brooklyn College, Fay was pursuing a degree in educa-tion. However, she told me she would eventually like to stay home and raise her children. That kind of talk scared me. While I had a long, uncertain road and struggle ahead of me, she had very normal thoughts based on her upbringing and environ-ment. I liked Fay, but I felt guilty because her mother had serious intentions regarding her and me. She told my mother that she liked me very much, and that she had "high hopes for us."

I, on the other hand, had no such intentions at the time with any girl. That resulted in too much pressure on me. I also felt uncomfortable because Fay knew me at my worst. I wasn't in college yet, my English was very poor, I knew very little about American favorite pastimes, and had an inferiority complex. I did not want to lead her on, so I started seeing her less often, and after a couple of more dates, I stopped seeing her. By that time, I was attending Brooklyn College at night.

After I saw Fay for the last time, I met Barbara. She lived in Brooklyn on Avenue H, but had girlfriends in our tenement building on 573 Saratoga Avenue. She was a slim, striking blond, one or two inches shorter than me, and I was immediately attracted to her. We started seeing each other and always had a great time. She was rather outgoing. Frequently, she came to our apartment and rang the doorbell.

"I'm here visiting my girlfriends and wanted to see what you're doing. Do you have some time?" Or if Mama answered the door she'd ask, "Is Bob home? I'm in the neighborhood, and I thought I'd say hello."

She lived with her parents in a nice apartment. Her father, a sharp dressing car salesman, wore a pinky ring and smoked cigars. I thought of him as a real sales type. Barbara worked in an office, was always smartly dressed, and wore a lot of makeup, which I didn't care for. While she was fun to be with, I thought less of her because she did not attend college. To me, that said a lot about her priorities and mental outlook on life.

"Have you ever considered going to college?" I asked her one time on the way home from a date.

"Yes, one of these days I'll apply," she said without much conviction.

"College would be relatively easy for you," I continued. "You wouldn't have to work while studying and you don't have problems with the English language. Think about it. If I can do it, you certainly could."

She looked into my eyes, took my hand in hers, and with a sweet smile, replied, "I find it hard to make the decision to go back to school. I like the independence and money I get from working, but I promise, I will."

"You know, your not going to college bothers me." I said, even though I thought that she really didn't care about education. "I hate to see you waste the opportunity. After I graduate I expect to do interesting, stimulating, and financially rewarding work."

"I'll look into it, I promise."

I didn't want to offend her, but I thought that she was shallow in her interests and that college would open up new horizons and an appreciation for cultural things. I became aware that she lacked any interest in bettering herself, or in becoming more worldly and refined. At times, she told me she was going to enroll in college, but I think that was mainly to appease me. We saw each other for the better part of a year before I ended our relationship. I'm sure she knew exactly why.

My friend Moritz and I met two girls who lived on the lower east side of Manhattan and were students at the CCNY downtown campus, which housed the liberal arts school. They lived in a very poor section of town. I dated the girl who was studying English literature, and Moritz dated the one pursuing a career in dance, primarily ballet. The girl I was interested in was a slim brunette, whereas the other had long beautiful red hair and freckles on her face. We double dated often. Moritz became seriously involved with his girl and fell in love with her. He was seeing her for longer than a year. I, on the other hand, remained true to my conviction of not becoming seriously involved with a girl while in college.

Soon after I transferred to CCNY engineering school in 1954, I met Annette. Walking on the college campus during a lunch break, I intended to get something to eat. Don, a civil engineering student, and another male student stood and talked to a young woman.

"Bob, are you going to the Greasy Spoon?" Don called out as I passed near them.

A student hangout across the street from the CCNY campus, the eatery was always crowded during lunch hours, and it was easier to get a table for four than for a larger or smaller group. Sitting four at a table squeezed a maximum number of students into their small place.

"Yes," I replied.

"Join us and we'll have a foursome!"

Don introduced me to Annette and the other student. We chatted briefly and then headed for the Greasy Spoon. During lunch, Annette talked mostly to me. I liked her from the very beginning. A brunette, five foot three, slim, with large brown eyes and a sweet disposition, she dressed smartly in an olive striped woolen top and a solid olive skirt to match. I remembered her attire because she was photographed in it soon after our first meeting. We did not have classes immediately after lunch, so Annette and I stayed and talked.

"I like your accent. It sounds continental. Where are you from?"

"Russia."

"You don't sound Russian."

"What do I sound like?" I asked.

"I thought your accent is western European," she said, still smiling.

"I spent the last several years before coming to the U.S. in Romania, Italy, and Switzerland, and I speak the languages of those countries. Perhaps those years modified my accent."

"That must be it. I wish I'd been to Europe. It sounds so interesting, worldly, and sophisticated. I've never stepped foot outside the United States. Some day, I hope to travel to Europe."

"If you'll be nice, I might be your guide," I joked.

Funny and upbeat, I thought she had character. I liked the fact that a girl was pursuing a college education in engineering, which was very difficult, and especially challenging for a female at the time. Both engineering students, we had a lot in common. Her obvious interest in me uplifted my spirits and excited me. She did not seem to mind that I was a recent immigrant, and she even envied my knowledge of several languages. I in turn wished I spoke better English. She told me that she liked the fact that I was older and more mature than most of the other students. All that gave me a boost and somewhat reduced my inferiority complex.

We often met for lunch at the Greasy Spoon. At times, she used to wait for me in front of my classes. Some of the students in my class teased me by announcing loudly, "Bob, your girlfriend is waiting for you!"

I discovered that she liked classical music, and that she played the piano. Our first formal date was at the Metropolitan Opera House. Since Annette knew I liked opera, she purchased two tickets to *Aida*. At the time, she did not know how to reach me by telephone or the spelling of my last name. She only knew it was somewhat unusual and started with the letter "F." During winter recess, she traveled an hour and a half each way from her home in Brooklyn to CCNY to inquire about me at the Electrical Engineering Department. She looked through the list of names of the electrical engineering class of '56, trying to determine my name and locate my phone number.

"I have two tickets to *Aida* at the Met for Saturday night at seven. I would like very much for you to accompany me," she said when she phoned me.

It was Friday about noontime when she called. Her invitation lifted my spirit and made me feel great. She sure knew how to get to me.

"I would be delighted, but I don't know where you live," I responded nonchalantly, while I was floating on air. No other girl had ever treated me so well.

"Meet me in front of the Met," she answered.

"I'll see you there at six-thirty, and thank you." I couldn't wait to go to the Met with her. I thought, this is a great girl. She has a lot of courage. She must like me a lot to go through all the trouble. She must be something special. I really like her, but I must be careful and not get too involved.

When I saw her in front of the Met, she wore a Persian lamb coat and a large brimmed hat with a long feather on it. I was somewhat embarrassed by her hat. It seemed inappropriate for a young college student. A more mature woman or a Hollywood personality should have worn it.

"I want to thank you for the tickets and the invitation. Where did you get the idea?"

"I thought you'd like it. You told me you loved opera, and I've never seen *Aida*."

"I do like it, and you're in for a wonderful time, because Aida is a great spectacle. It includes ballet and a live elephant on stage."

"I know, I read up on it," she told me.

"I didn't know you wore hats."

"This is to impress you," she said as she laughed.

"Perhaps you ought to take off your hat," I told Annette, once we sat down in our seats, "so it would not interfere with the people sitting behind you."

After that date, we spent most of our time together. However, I often reminded her that we were 'just friends.'

"I like you a lot," I told her at the very beginning, "but right now, I have only one objective. That is to graduate from college. Until I achieve that goal, I could not possibly get seriously involved with anyone."

In reality, she knew that we were more than friends. She said so many times because of her feelings toward me and because we saw each other exclusively. I in turn had strong feelings for Annette and demonstrated them on most occasions without saying, "I love you." I feared the words would imply a commitment, which I was trying to avoid.

At CCNY, most students dressed casually. A few wore ties and jackets. Most were younger than I. A few veterans of war were older and some relatively recent immigrants were my age. I became friendly with Percy Freedman, a World War II Air Force veteran. About forty years old, he wore a coat and tie to classes, and so did I. I wore a wine colored corduroy jacket, blue or gray slacks, often a light blue button down shirt, and a knit tie. I always carried a leather briefcase to class. I was about twenty-four years old. Annette told me at various times that she liked the fact that I wore a coat and tie, and that I looked professional and mature compared to the other nineteen or twenty-year-old students in my classes.

Percy lived several large city blocks away from our apartment. Before tests and final exams, he'd come to my apartment and we'd study together. After a couple of hours of deriving and memorizing equations and reviewing old problems, we'd take a break, and walk to an ice cream parlor on Pitkin Avenue and have an ice cream. We called this 'rewarding ourselves.'

"I can't wait to graduate and put an end to all this studying."

"Neither can I. Remember, I'm much older than you and no longer have much patience," he'd complain. "I dream of the day when I'll live in Santa Monica, California."

"Why there?" I asked.

He closed his eyes as if envisioning his future life.

"While I was in the service, I spent some time in Southern California. I loved it there. As soon as I graduate, I'm going to apply for a job with Douglass Aircraft Company in Santa Monica."

As soon as he graduated, he did exactly that. Years later, when Annette and I lived in Palos Verdes, we visited him. Married, he lived in Beverlywood, a suburb of Los Angeles.

When Annette told me that she was eighteen years old, I did not believe her. I thought that she was kidding. After all, she was in her third year of college, a junior. One evening when I was at her house, her mother showed me her birth certificate. That embarrassed me.

I took her aside and said, "I really didn't believe that you're eighteen, because you're a junior in college. On the other hand, I admire your accomplishment. But you've just embarrassed me by telling your mother that I didn't believe your age."

"I'm sorry. I didn't mean to do that."

I then realized that I was six years her senior and more mature than my age. I'd lived through things seldom experienced by a twenty-four year old. I thought that an eighteen-year-old girl was too young for me. Basically, a child. At that time, we started seeing each other exclusively. She made sure I saw her practically every day in school, even though we never attended the same classes. Later on, we did our homework together, but that did not work out. Our minds were elsewhere. We had a great time while the homework fell by the wayside.

During the summer of 1955, Annette accepted a part-time job counting rivets on the George Washington Bridge. She was actually counting rivets from the blueprint, but it sounded much funnier when she did not provide the explanation.

CHAPTER 27

FIRST ENGINEERING JOB

THE years of struggle at CCNY paid dividends when our class of '56 started job interviews as second semester seniors. We then realized we were very well prepared for the competition against students from other colleges. Many well-known companies recruited at CCNY as well as other college campuses. MIT (Massachusetts Institute of Technology) came to CCNY to recruit, but they did not recruit at Harvard, Cornell, Columbia, or NYU, just to mention a few.

During Easter recess, IBM in Poughkeepsie, NY invited me for an interview. I took Annette along for the ride. During our visit to IBM, Annette and I were invited to lunch in their executive dining room where we enjoyed a delicious ham dinner even though it was Passover. I thought they were inconsiderate for not offering a less obvious non-kosher meal, even though our home was not strictly kosher. However, the expression "political correctness" was yet unknown.

I received an attractive job offer from IBM, which I did not accept. I didn't want to live in a small town or be away from Annette.

I also interviewed with and toured the MIT Instrumentation Laboratory in Cambridge, Massachusetts. This lab was originally called the Draper Lab after its founder, Dr. Charles Stark Draper, who's credited with developing the gyroscope. In addition to the great prestige of working there, the employees had the opportunity to pursue their studies at MIT, which was highly desirable.

The CCNY class of 1956 graduated 176 electrical engineers; 73 graduated in February, and 103 in June. I graduated in the upper third of the June class. MIT made only seven job offers to students of my graduating class. I was the only one of the seven who did not accept the offer. While I was extremely proud to have received the offer, I wanted a higher salary. Even though a master's degree from Columbia University was not as prestigious as one from MIT, it allowed me to stay in New York earning more money.

During my trip to Boston for my MIT interview, I also accepted an invitation for an interview with Raytheon. They also made me a good offer, which I declined. If I had decided to live in the Boston area, I would have accepted MIT's offer.

Of all the employment offers, I accepted a job as a systems engineer at Curtis Wright Electronics Division in Carlstadt, New Jersey. I also enrolled at Columbia University in the electrical engineering master's degree program. Curtis Wright paid seventy-five percent of the tuition. My first salary after graduation in June 1956 was $115 a week. Of the total graduating class, only one other graduate received the same salary. The rest were paid about $100 a week. I believed that I deserved a higher salary since I had some work experience, and because I was older and more mature than most of my classmates.

I attended Columbia University at night. Columbia did not require a thesis for a master's degree. Instead, they required thirty-two credits to graduate. Each course was worth two credits. Therefore, it took four years going to school two nights per week.

After I got my first job, I realized that nobody was interested in my grades or honorary society membership. What mattered on the job was hard work, inventiveness, a willingness to learn, and an ability to get along with the other employees and management. At Curtis Wright, we were designing and building flight simulators used to train pilots to fly specific airplanes. Curtis Wright had contracts with American Airlines, Air France, Lufthansa, United and others. The company built flight simulators for the Lockheed Super-Constellation, Boeing 707, and Douglass DC-7 aircraft.

My work involved analyzing the flight equations, which represented the characteristics of specific airplanes, and then designing special-purpose analog computers to solve those equations. The design of analog computers was a subject I had learned as an electrical engineer, but I knew nothing about aircraft flight equations, taught only to aeronautical engineers.

I purchased a copy of *Airplane Performance Stability and Control,* by Perkins and Hage to study the characteristics of flight equations. I enjoyed my assignment, liked my supervisor, Aldo Benenatti, and the other engineers, and was happy to earn a good salary after so many years of hard work and sacrifice.

Curtis Wright occupied an old building. The engineering offices consisted of bullpen areas. Our section, flight analysis, occupied a glassed enclosure with about twenty desks. A Frieden calculator on top of each of our grey metal desks was used for arithmetic calculations, and a slide-rule was used for more complex operations.

Adjacent to our partition was an area with forty or fifty desks and drafting tables, which housed the other engineers and draftsmen. The project managers sat in individual glass enclosures, and the chief engineer, Dr. Dahmel, occupied the largest office with windows into the working areas. He held patents for flight simulators.

Curtis Wright built, assembled, and tested the simulators in a large hanger. Each simulator consisted of a cockpit with no nose or wings. Entry into the cockpit was up a primitive wooden staircase. The instruments inside the cockpit were identical to the specific aircraft being simulated. High on the walls hung a long paper sign with the statement, *"There is never enough time to do the job right the first time, but there is always enough time to redo it."* Early in my professional life, I've learned that fact and tried to avoid it.

Before graduating from CCNY, the students had been told by the college placement staff that it would be advantageous for us not to remain in our first or even second jobs longer than two years, unless we absolutely fell in love with that job. There were two reasons for this advice. First, we would have the opportunity to learn more than one set of skills and experience in more than one company's professional environment. Second, we would receive a meaningful raise in salary when hired by the next company. Since salary reviews and increases were done once a year, changing jobs provided the equivalent to one year jump in salary.

While employed on our first job, we could not evaluate other technical fields and other companies and decide where we should make a long-term commitment. Hence, the road for professional advancement might require several job changes after graduation. Even though I liked working at Curtis Wright, I followed that principle and changed employment after two years.

CHAPTER 28

ENGAGEMENT AND WEDDING

AS soon as I graduated, and became employed as an engineer with decent pay, my self-esteem and confidence improved. I still wanted more, because I had started with nothing, but I was also proud of my achievement. I worked as a professional, performing intellectually challenging work. I also no longer had an excuse regarding my relationship with Annette.

During a visit at Annette's house, her father sat me down on the step in front of the house, a common Brooklyn pastime, and embarked on an unexpected subject.

"Bob, I know you're aware Annette loves you, and we're fond of you too," he said in a serious but pleasant tone. "You have a fine future ahead of you, and I believe that it's time you make a commitment to Annette."

Caught by surprise, I quickly thought of a reply.

"I love Annette, but I still have very little materially. It will take time for me to accumulate some money."

"I had less than you when I married Annette's mother." He went on to say, "I also didn't have the kind of future you have. You are a fine young man with a college education, and I'm as sure as we're sitting here right now that you'll do very well. I'm not worried at all about you."

That very brief exchange put me on notice. It did not

provide me a lot of slack. I liked Annette's father. He always listened to and respected my opinions. I could talk to him more easily than to my own father. Often I used to kid him by reminding him of his pep talk and referring to it as, "Your talk with the shotgun in your hands." That invariably brought a laugh.

During my last semester, our romance blossomed. We were in love and inseparable. In February 1956, for Valentine's Day, we exchanged presents. Annette gave me an engraved cigarette lighter, and I gave her a gold bracelet with a charm in the form of a heart. Without my admitting it at the time, that was for me the start of a lifelong commitment. I thought I was ready for marriage, although I found the prospect daunting.

"Buma, it's time for you to marry," Mama said gleefully. "You know Annette loves you and you love her."

"Yes, Mama, I do, but it is a very serious step and I don't take it lightly. I want it to last a lifetime."

"Then marry her. She's a nice girl, and she'll make you a good wife. Besides, I can't wait for grandchildren."

When I decided to purchased an engagement ring, I spoke to my friend Martin, who'd become engaged a few months earlier.

"You know Annette admires the ring you gave Jane. Where did you buy it?"

"In a little jewelry store off Pitkin Avenue. I believe the owner gave me a good price." He gave me directions to the store.

I took Annette to the store. We found the small place, and were let in via a buzzer. A little old Jewish man sat in the back, and appeared to be repairing a watch.

"How can I help you?"

"A few months ago my friend Martin Sohn bought an engagement ring from you. Now we're looking for one."

The storekeeper looked at us above the glasses he wore

at the tip of his nose. "First, I want you to concentrate on a couple of beautiful diamonds. Don't worry about the rings, I know what you want." He then showed us two rings with beautiful settings. One had a larger diamond than the other.

"Do you like them?" I asked Annette as we studied them.

"Oh, yes," she said excitedly.

"Which one do you prefer?"

"They're both beautiful," she answered, while she kept the ring with the larger stone on her finger.

I was also inclined to buy the ring with the larger stone, figuring that it would have to last her for a long time. I was well aware Annette liked that one better; however, I also knew I didn't have the money to pay for the larger diamond. After a while, the little old man saw my hesitation, so he moved closer to me.

"Take the larger ring with you, have it appraised, and show it to your fiancée's parents. I'm sure everybody'll love it. Go!"

"Don't you need some money, my name, and address?"

"*Gey gesund!* I'm not worried."

"How can you let me out of your store with a diamond ring without knowing who I am?" I was shocked.

"*Gey, Gey,*" he repeated.

I left the tiny jewelry store with the diamond ring without even giving him my name. I was astonished. The old man trusted a perfect stranger with a valuable ring without even knowing his name. We took the ring and showed it to Annette's parents. Delighted, her mother hugged and kissed me, and her father shook my hand.

"I knew you were a fine young man," he said, tears welling in his eyes. "We wish you both a lifetime of happiness."

"Thank you." I didn't know what else to say. I felt strange.

Annette absolutely loved the ring, and since I could not pay in full for it, her parents offered to help. The price of the

ring was $1200, and I believe that Annette's parents gave me
$400. I also had the two-carat ring appraised. A day or two
later, I returned to the store and paid for the ring.

"How come you let me out of the store without knowing
who I was?" I asked the little old man.

"I knew that you were an honest young man. I saw it in
your face. I have never yet been wrong about an individual." To
justify and further explain his behavior, he asked me, "Do you
think I do that with everybody who walks into my store?"

By September, we became officially engaged. We had no
formal engagement party except Annette's parents took us out
for dinner in Manhattan, to a chic and romantic French restaurant. The waiters wore white gloves and violins played at the
table. I picked the restaurant, "Chez Vito's".

Annette's father bought me a *"tallit,"* a prayer shawl and
a Borsellino felt hat. He said, "A Jewish man about to get
married must have these two things."

"I thank you for the nice gifts and your thoughtfulness."
Then, I explained to him my feelings about religion. "I really
have no use for a *tallit* or a hat, because I have not been to a
Synagogue since the Soviets came to Beltz in 1940. It's been
about seventeen years. I was nine years old, and I'm now
twenty-six. I was angry with God for letting these terrible
things happen to the Jewish people. Besides, I don't know the
Hebrew prayers. I was never a *Bar Mitzvah*. When I was thirteen, I was a refugee in Stalinabad, Tajikistan. Mundane things
such as food and surviving the war preoccupied my mind, not a
celebration. My religious beliefs systematically eroded and fell
victim first to the war then the Soviet Union where religious
practice was forbidden. There was no way to study Torah and
prepare for *Bar Mitzvah*. Additionally, no one wanted to flaunt
his Jewish-ness and further feed the flames of anti-Semitism.
Yet, on my thirteenth birthday, my mother with tears in her
eyes reminded me that under normal circumstances I would

have celebrated my *Bar Mitzvah*. She told me the whole family would have been very happy, for such an occasion happens only once in a lifetime. When I asked her how she could think about it under our circumstances, she replied, 'because we are Jews.' Mother's statement brought a pang of guilt and sorrow to my heart. Before I turned thirteen I had to drop out of school and was glad to get a full-time job instead of studying *Torah*." My heart skipped a beat or two and my voice cracked, as for the first time I lay bare my soul and my deeply pent up inner feelings, which I tried to hide for so long. At the same time, I was afraid of being misunderstood, and misinterpreted as a pessimist glorifying my suffering. I felt I had to walk a fine line between not saying anything and revealing it all. Yet, after my discourse, I felt uncomfortable. That was the first time I opened up and disclosed some of the deeply buried rage in my heart.

Annette's father listened attentively to my discourse. From his facial expression, I could tell that he was more disappointed than sympathetic. I believe he realized he was dealing with a person who carried a heavy psychological burden on his shoulders. He must have also been concerned of the negative impact that this might have on our marriage and his daughter's happiness. I immediately felt I shouldn't have opened up to that extent. I wondered if I'd made a mistake.

"You'll learn to pray as time will pass," he said optimistically, trying to encourage me. "I also would like you to be called to the *Torah* in the Synagogue, as it is the custom before a wedding. It is considered a *mitzvah,* a good deed."

"I must decline, because I would feel hypocritical and very uncomfortable doing it."

I know now how much I hurt him. As time passed, I felt regret for having denied Annette's father the honor and pleasure of seeing me read the blessings in front of the *Torah* in a Synagogue on the day before my wedding to his only daughter. Several years later, Annette and I decided that our first-born son, Bruce, should attend religious school. We joined a Temple, and I relearned some of the prayers. I'm still not reading the Hebrew prayers well enough to keep pace with the congregation. After we joined the Synagogue, I apologized to my father-in-law.

"I am truly sorry for having caused you grief by refusing to partake in the *Torah* blessing on the day before our wedding." I took and held his hands in both of mine. "I know that I caused you pain, but I hope you understand my mental anguish at the time. One day, I hope you'll forgive me."

"I already have forgiven you, seeing that you have returned to our religion."

Even before we were engaged, all my friends and I celebrated the New Year in the basement of Annette's house. The basement was large, had a long, elaborate wet bar with a beer tap and a beautiful miniature sailing boat in a display. It also had a built-in long padded bench along one wall, upholstered in wine colored vinyl, and a TV. Annette lived in a predominantly Italian neighborhood. Her father told me the house originally belonged to a member of the Mafia, because several lived in the area. Annette's father used to say, "Only the Mafia could build such an elaborate bar." Everyone chipped in to purchase alcoholic drinks and sodas and we invited the girls to a New Year's party. We bought the liquor at a discount, courtesy of my friend Moritz who worked in a liquor store. Everybody had a good time during our parties, which became a ritual for several years.

Little time passed between our engagement and our wedding. Before we married, I needed to convince Annette to stay in college and get her degree, because when we became engaged, she declared, "Now I can drop my studies. All I really wanted was a Mrs. Degree."

"I'm not going to marry you," I threatened, "if you don't complete your studies and get your engineering degree. I think that it is an indication of a serious flaw in character, a lack of commitment and determination that you would abandon your studies. I don't want to spend the rest of my life with a woman who gives up on her goals, no matter how much I love you."

"Okay, if it means that much to you, I'll finish."

"I want you to desire to finish your school, not because I wish it. You mean to say that after all the years of hard work you're willing to give it up? I must have misjudged your character." I replied angrily.

"I understand and agree with you that it does not make sense to quit now. I wasn't really serious. I'm just tired of school," Annette said apologetically. We made up quickly and sealed the deal with a prolonged kiss.

"I know why you insisted I get my degree," she teased me later in life. "You wanted to make sure I worked all my life."

Saturday evening, on 2 February 1957, we married. Our beautiful wedding was held in a wedding hall called Casa del Rey in Brooklyn. We had close to one hundred guests. A terrific snowstorm came down during the day of the wedding, and we were concerned that our guests could arrive safely. We picked the date to coincide with the college winter recess, because I was attending Columbia University, and Annette was still finishing her studies at CCNY. She had only to complete Atomic Physics to obtain her Bachelor degree in mechanical engineering. Our best man was Paul Katz and the matron of honor was Shelley Felson, Annette's closest friend.

We spent a week at the Nevele Hotel in the Catskills, upstate New York for our honeymoon. The hotel was popular at the time with honeymooners. In addition to three meals a day, it had entertainment and activities designed especially with newlyweds in mind. The afternoons were referred to as the "sock washing time," and not a single person was seen on the premises during those hours. During that week, we also managed to ice skate and ski nearby at the well-known Grossinger's Hotel. Years later, whenever we met people from

New York who'd been married during the same timeframe, they all told us that they'd also honeymooned at the Nevele.

Bergenfield, located in Bergen County, Northern New Jersey, was not far from the George Washington Bridge. That's where we rented an apartment consisting of two bedrooms, a living room, a kitchen, and one bathroom. It was located in a two-story building with two apartments per building, called garden apartment, because the buildings were spread apart and separated by generous green belts.

All the buildings looked alike. Our apartment was on the second floor. We carpeted it with a gray wool Berber. Annette's parents gave us our bedroom furniture as a wedding present. They took us to an upscale furniture store called Sloan's where we picked out a set and asked for some modifications. We wanted them to insert cane facing into all the doors of the dresser and nightstands. We bought a large curved sectional sofa and a round walnut coffee table. The tabletop had several walnut tangential circles with ceramic inlays. We still use that table.

We also bought a desk and chair, and installed bookshelves to turn the second bedroom into a library. All the furniture was made of solid walnut. Our son Bruce still uses the old desk. We also bought hi-fi components and a single record of Tchaikovsky's "Violin Concerto." We played that record so much, our neighbors complained.

Both Annette and I earned good salaries straight out of college, and yet at the end of the first year of our marriage we had less then $100 in the bank. We'd spent all our earnings on furnishings for our apartment and a new Plymouth Belvedere. At the time, Annette worked at Curtis Wright Aeronautical Division in Ridgewood, New Jersey, while I worked at Curtis Wright Electronic Division in Carlstadt, New Jersey.

After work, we both attended college. At times, I took the old Desoto given to us by Annette's parents, and I'd drop off Annette at her office and proceed to my job. Other times

Annette used the car, and I carpooled with a co-worker. The two evenings every week that I went to Columbia University, I took the car.

Later after Annette graduated, she worked for Westinghouse International, at 40 Wall Street, in lower Manhattan. She dealt with foreign countries, designing the lighting for the Jakarta, Indonesia airport. Her position was considered a quasi-sales job. She took a bus to work. While there was ground transportation from New Jersey to New York, which Annette used, there was very little within New Jersey. Snow removal was also inadequate in New Jersey.

One winter day our offices closed early due to a strong snowstorm. The distance from my office to our apartment was seven miles, yet it took me seven hours to reach home by car. As I drove, I worried about Annette getting home from Manhattan. I was pleasantly surprised to find her there when I arrived.

One evening, while returning home from Columbia, it rained cats and dogs. At the entrance to the George Washington Bridge from the Westside Highway, the old Desoto went through a large puddle and stalled. Since I had stopped traffic, the driver of the car behind me offered to push my car all the way across the bridge. Luckily, Annette was in the car with me. After paying the toll at the New Jersey side of the bridge, I had to push my car to the nearest gasoline station a few hundred feet, but nonetheless I got soaked. I wore a suit and tie at the time. Upon opening the hood, the mechanic found the distributor box full of water.

"I expected to find some fish in all that water," he laughed.

He wiped the cables and blow-dried the carburetor. We paid him five dollars and were on our way home. After that episode, we decided to buy a new car.

We enjoyed our life in Bergenfield. Other than work each day and two nights of school, we had no other obligations. We delighted spending some of our free time shopping to furnish and embellish the apartment. The rest, we spent with friends. We were free to do whatever we pleased. We liked living in the country compared to New York. It was less crowded, green, and cooler in the summer; however, the mosquitoes had a field day toward the evening.

Practically every Friday evening, we went to the movies at the Queen Anne Theater in nearby Englewood, where they ran mostly foreign films. We considered foreign films more sophisticated. I believed they were more thought provoking, had an agenda I could associate with and were in vogue with so-called intellectuals. The movies considered art films, realistically depicted life during and after the war. I liked going to the movies, whereas Annette did not. This led to our major arguments.

"Let's go to the movies tonight," I would say.

"We went to the movies last week," Annette protested. "Not the movies again."

"But there's a good movie playing, and it's so easy and convenient. No planning or advanced tickets required. Come on, let's go. I'll drive."

Annette usually gave in. If there were two films featured, she'd threatened me, "I'll snooze."

"That's alright, as long as you don't snore."

The process has reversed in our senior years. Now, Annette likes going to the movies, whereas I can take it or leave it.

After spending two years at Curtis Wright, I accepted a salary increase and a position at Emerson Radio and Phonograph in Jersey City, New Jersey. My experience in flight simulators prompted Emerson to hire me. They had a contract to design and build a simulator for training radar operators for the MG13 Fire Control on the F101 Fighter. I was hired as a senior engineer to perform system analysis and design. When I arrived on the scene, I realized Emerson had accomplished very little during the year they'd had the contract. There hadn't even developed specifications or a set of requirements to initiate a design. I needed that information to do my job. Since Hughes Aircraft Company designed and built the MG13 Fire Control System, I flew to Hughes in Culver City, California to obtain information, specifications, and user documents, as well as to learn about the system. That was in the middle of the winter, and while it was snowing in New Jersey, California was sunny and warm.

I knew an engineer from Curtis Wright who lived in San Diego and worked at General Dynamics Astronautics at the time, so I called him from Los Angeles.

"Hi, Arthur, this is Bob ..."

Before I could finish my sentence, he asked, "Where are you calling from?"

"I'm in LA. I'm on a business trip to Hughes."

"How long are you staying? How about coming to San Diego to see us? Rosalie and I would be delighted."

"I'll see you on Saturday." We agreed upon the details.

Early on Saturday I took a bus from Los Angeles to San Diego. Arthur met me at the terminal and took me to his house. Both Arthur and Rosalie were very happy to see me. Their boy, Bobby, was about one year old. After lunch, Arthur showed me around the city, taking me to La Jolla Coves where I saw teenagers clad in shorts tossing a football on the grass. In that moment I decided that, as soon as I obtained my master's degree, we would move to San Diego. He also showed me Mission Bay and took me to Tijuana.

"What do you think of San Diego?" he asked.

"I like it a lot," I answered.

"Would you consider moving and living here? I'm sure you'd have no trouble getting a job."

"Right after I get my master's I'll be ready. I know that Annette would love it here. I have no reason to live in the cold and snow of winter and the humidity of summer. Besides everything looks so new, and there are plenty of open spaces."

"We'd love to have you here," he responded warmly.

"Arthur, you'll never guess what made me decide to move to San Diego."

"What?"

"Those teenagers throwing the football in La Jolla Cove, while everybody is freezing in New Jersey," I laughed.

While working at Emerson, I flew to Cleveland, Ohio to discuss subcontracting operational amplifiers to Thompson Products. I had a nice reception from a Thompson Products manager who met me at the airport, took me to dinner in a fine restaurant, and then to a baseball game. It must have been in late August or early September. I wore a suit and tie, and was uncomfortably cold at the stadium by the lake, where people sat wrapped in blankets.

At Emerson, I met other engineers somewhat older, married and with small children. I joined a carpool with two men and a woman clerk, who was in her early forties. During the carpool rides, the men always talked about their children, how wonderful they were, and how much pleasure they derived from watching them grow and all the little things they did. None of that meant much to me. I just listened to their conversations and figured that some day I might talk like them.

"When are you going to have children?" one engineer asked, one morning on the way to work.

"We don't want any children for several more years," I replied.

"Why is that? Do you think you're too young to have children?" he queried laughingly.

"We're still young, we want to enjoy our life, freedom and save some money before we decide to have children."

"Listen very carefully to what I have to say to you!" The woman in the car interrupted, sounding angry. "My husband and I had the same idea, and for several years after our marriage we abstained from having children. Later, when we decided to have them, we couldn't. We tried for years, sought medical help, prayed in church, but nothing helped. Let me assure you, you'll be sorry and it'll serve you right. When you'll want to have children you won't be able because you're abusing God's gift!"

I returned home feeling upset and somewhat scared. I told Annette what had happened. It did not take us long to decide the woman might be right, and that we should forego our freedom and financial ambitions and have a baby. A couple of months later, Annette and I happily learned that she was pregnant. Our parents were jubilant. They could not wait to become grandparents, especially Mama.

Happiness mixed with concern, uncertainty, anxiety, and impatience describes my emotions when I found out Annette was pregnant. Will the baby be alright? Will I be a good father? I assume that all couples are worried and anxious when they first find out that they are expecting a child. We were no exception. Questions nagged at us: will the baby properly develop, physically and mentally? Will we have some unforeseen problems? Will he or she be normal in every respect?" An additional concern was Annette's RH negative blood type, while mine was positive.

Natural childbirth being in vogue at the time, I started going with Annette to Lamaze classes and exercises. At one of the exercise classes, we met Paul and Rachelle Erman. They lived in Fort Lee, New Jersey, the first town west of the George Washington Bridge. Paul and I had worked at Freed Transformer Company, losing touch after I left the company. Rachelle was pregnant with Simone at the time. We renewed our acquaintance and became friends. Annette and Rachelle were able to compare notes regarding their pregnancies.

Later in Annette's pregnancy, the obstetrician took X-rays and was concerned the baby's head might be too large for Annette to have a natural birth, in which case a Cesarean section would be required.

Annette quit her job a few months before her due date. We

also timed several dry runs from our apartment to the hospital in Englewood. Railroad tracks between our apartment and the hospital concerned me if a train interfered with our trip during the most critical time.

When the time came, everything worked out fine. The size of the baby's head and the RH negative blood type were not factors. October 23, 1959 Annette gave birth to a perfectly healthy, beautiful baby boy. We named him Bruce Geoffrey after Annette's Grandma Bella Gitel.

CHAPTER 29

COLUMBIA UNIVERSITY

ETTING my master's degree at Columbia was no
picnic. I no longer had the problems that plagued me
during my undergraduate years. My monetary situation, my English, and my self-esteem were vastly improved,
even though I was still very aware of my accent. I was proud
to be a graduate student at a fine institution like Columbia
University, even though it was not as famous for engineering
as MIT. At times, I questioned if I'd made the right choice by
not accepting MIT's offer. Of course, I'll never know, but our
lives worked out well and I have no regrets.

I no longer felt like a foreigner, an outsider. I believed I'd
crossed the last frontier in my life, becoming a respectable U.S.
citizen. My difficulties at Columbia were more on par with
those of other normal American students who attended night
school while maintaining a full-time day job.

Most of the classes were interesting but difficult. Each
professor assigned homework as though the student had
no other responsibilities. They did not seem concerned that
students had other classes as well as a full-time job. Each
professor, well known and highly respected in his field, treated
us as if we were going for our PhD, and not merely for a
master's. In many subjects, the theory pushed the state of the
art. We were told that a particular theory ended at a point,
and we were expected to develop or invent it from there on.

Inspiring and admirable, it wasn't realistic because we didn't possess the advanced technical background.

That concept of pushing the state of the art during a master's program, instead of a less ambitious intent, supported the fact that the professors were tops in their field. It also enhanced the university's reputation. Thus, school ideology made our studies more difficult and frustrating. What we really needed was more instruction in basic theory to augment what we'd learned in undergraduate school.

One of the most notorious professors I had at Columbia was Dr. John R. Ragazzini. His expertise and reputation was in all aspects of Feedback Control Theory. As the subject was of great interest to me, I took all of the courses offered by him in that field. Consequently, it became my major. His class on Sampled-Data and Z-Transforms, offered for the first time, provided the latest analysis techniques and methods. He and Dr. Gene F. Franklin authored a textbook titled, *Sampled-Data Control Systems*. At the time of book's publication in 1958, Dr. Ragazzini was Dean of the College of Engineering at New York University, and Dr. Franklin was an assistant professor of electrical engineering at Stanford University. Professor Ragazzini, a good teacher and writer, was a rarity, because most individuals with a high reputation in the technical field did not know how or care to teach. They would lecture at a level over the students' heads without concern for the student's understanding of the topic. I believe that those professors were absent-minded and wrapped up in the science. They did not consider the students, or they didn't believe that something so logical and simple to them would be difficult to comprehend. Other professors used this method of teaching to showcase their knowledge and superiority, while underlining the students' lack of understanding.

One such instructor was Mr. Rudy Kalman. A young man in his mid-twenties, he'd already established his reputation in the technical field by having invented the Kalman filter. This was not a physical filter, but a highly sophisticated mathematical theory designed to extract and predict parameters out of little information, or noisy data. I took a course called Non-linear Control Systems taught by Rudy Kalman while he was still a PhD student at Columbia.

The course was very difficult, and Rudy did not know how to teach. He came to class without notes and wrote equations on the blackboard for the duration of the lesson. When someone interrupted and asked for an explanation, he said that what he was writing was obvious. Later he gave a quiz that no one in the class could solve. When we asked to show us how to solve the problem, he wrote the answer on the board, stating the obviousness of it, and then, proceeded to work backward to derive the statement of the problem.

Dr. Franklin, a professor in electrical engineering at Columbia at the time, sat in on the class taught by Rudy to learn the Kalman filter theory, which used the non-linear control systems as its basis. After missing a few class sessions due to minor throat surgery, Professor Franklin came to class prior to Rudy's arrival. He asked us if we had class notes for the previous lectures.

"Surely, Professor Franklin, you can ask Mr. Kalman for his notes," with great surprise we answered.

"I asked Rudy, and he said, 'you know I don't teach from notes'," Professor Franklin replied with a broad smile.

Prior to obtaining my master's degree, I inquired about employment in San Diego. Before long, I received a job offer from Ryan Electronics. Both Annette and I really wanted to live in San Diego, so we discussed it with our parents. Even though my parents were not overjoyed about our moving to California, they said they would follow us. Annette's parents, on the other hand, approved of the idea. Her mother's entire family lived in the Los Angeles area. They felt it was about time to sell their store and move to California.

I received my Master of Science in Electrical Engineering

degree in June 1960. I accepted the offer from Ryan, gave appropriate notice to Emerson, and at the end of the July 4th weekend, so as not to travel during the holiday traffic, we departed for San Diego. Ryan's offer provided me with a nice raise in salary and paid for all our moving expenses.

The movers packed our furniture, loaded it on a truck, and departed to San Diego. We packed enough clothes for a couple of weeks, with plenty of diapers and food for nine-month old Bruce, and departed New Jersey in our 1957 Plymouth Belvedere.

CHAPTER 30

SAN DIEGO

W E looked forward to our cross-country trip with
a bit of apprehension about traveling with a nine-
month-old baby. We traveled along Route 66,
trying to make the trip in the shortest possible time, while also
enjoying the country sights and the grandeur and diversity of
America.

I loved the rural feeling, tranquility, green fields, and old
trees covered in moss spreading over meandering streams as
we traveled through the Carolinas. I'd never seen those kind of
trees before. By contrast, Gallup, New Mexico left me with a
negative impression. For the first time I saw a U.S. city predominantly populated by Native Americans. We broke Bruce's car
bottle warmer, so we went to a general store to purchase a
new one. The customers were mainly Indians who purchased
their foodstuffs and other items of necessity by using company
coupons instead of money. It seemed to me they worked solely
for their food and very little else.

On the streets, their stone-faced expressions made me
wonder if they were drunk or on drugs, although I doubted
they had the resources to purchase alcohol or drugs, since their
pay was in coupons. The police constantly patrolled the streets.
Police cars running up and down the streets with their sirens
blasting kept me from sleeping the one night we stayed there.
I felt like I was in some sort of a foreign police state.

It brought back some bad memories. I drew some parallels

with life in the Soviet Union during the war. People depended on rations and coupons to purchase daily bread, meager food-stuffs, and, if they were lucky, very little clothing from time to time, while the NKVD (later the KGB), kept tight reins on its citizenry. When we lived in DP camps, we depended on handouts for our daily meals and clothing. We were grateful to the organizations running the camps and to the host country, but that was not freedom. While they allowed us to walk the streets in the local communities, we were strangers in a foreign country. On the other hand, the Native Americans were displaced, despite their birthright.

The tremendous heat we endured while traveling through the desert was the worst part of our cross-country trip. With no air conditioning, we drove with open windows as the tempera-ture soared to well above 100 degrees Fahrenheit. The hot air blowing inside the car was not of much help.

Our infant son paid the highest price in terms of pure phys-ical discomfort. His face and body turned red from the heat, and he wouldn't stop crying. Afraid of a heatstroke or even something worse, we had to stop the car in the middle of the desert. We took him out, carried him in our arms, and tried to pacify him. After some time we managed to get him to stop crying, and we proceeded with our trip.

When we arrived in Needles, California, the temperature was above 120 degrees. We stopped early in the afternoon and stayed over night. The motel had a swimming pool, and the room's air conditioning was very cold. As soon as we checked in, the three of us got into the pool. Later we had dinner in a restaurant. Bruce started crying as soon as dinner arrived. We could not make him stop, and because we were embarrassed and felt uncomfortable annoying the rest of the people in the restaurant, we left in the middle of our meal. We all caught colds in Needles, because of the big difference in temperature between the extreme heat outdoors and the cold room.

The large saguaro trees and cacti in the high desert were

magnificent. We looked at them in awe. That was the first time we had ever seen them. They looked unreal, like some strange guards from a different planet. The haze dispersing the sun early in the morning around San Bernardino created various hues and looked alien to me. The mountains appeared as dark silhouettes in the distance, like unrealistically painted images.

Finally, we arrived in San Diego and stopped at the Vagabond Motel, off Interstate 8 in Mission Valley on Hotel Circle. I called Art Gelernter to let him know we were at the motel. I believe it was a weekend, because Arthur was home. He came immediately to take us over to his nearby house. Bobby was not three years old yet, and Sandra was an infant in her crib. Arthur and Rosalie gave us a warm welcome, making us feel very much at home. Annette and Bruce stayed with Rosalie, while Arthur took me to see some apartments in the area. Within less than a week, we found one very close to my new job and to our friends, the Gelernters.

The apartment was in a new building and had a living room, kitchen and bath downstairs, and two bedrooms and a second bath upstairs. It also had a swimming pool in front of the building and a fenced patio in the back. The complex, called Cabrillo Palisades, was in the Kearny Mesa area adjacent to Sharp Memorial Hospital.

We lived within one stop light of my office, which allowed me to come home for lunch. Since we had no family in San Diego, and the Gelernters were very warm to us, we became the best of friends. At times, we believed we were one family. We spent practically every weekend with them.

On my new job at Ryan, I was assigned to perform analysis of an altimeter. The altitude information was a key parameter in the control system of unmanned aircraft. I was using the feedback control theory, which I'd learned both at CCNY and at Columbia University. From the very beginning, I didn't like the provincial atmosphere at Ryan. The entire product line consisted only of the one component, the altimeter, as opposed to large entities such as an aircraft or another entire system. The work entailed sitting behind the desk, doing analysis without interfacing with any people.

Thus far, in my career, I had associated with total systems, not single components. To add to my unhappiness at Ryan, I did not get along with my supervisor, who micromanaged the employees, including me. I felt too constricted; I might as well have been a computer, or a robot. It was my worst experience yet, and I knew I wouldn't stay long at Ryan.

After about six months, I gave my resume to Arthur Gelernter to hand in at General Dynamics Astronautics. After an interview, I received a job offer at Astronautics, located across the street from Ryan. I was glad to give my notice and accept the job at GDA.

The environment at GDA was completely different from Ryan, and so was my job. I started as a senior engineer in the Advanced Systems Group of the Guidance and Trajectory Analysis Department. Dr. Leger, the department head, was responsible for all the guidance and trajectory analysis for the Atlas and the Centaur missiles, while the Advanced Systems Group performed all the studies for future projects and new business.

GDA was among the first in space activities due to their Atlas missile and launch vehicle. This provided me the opportunity to learn and become involved in the space business. At GDA, I first learned the new and exciting field of trajectory analysis, and guidance and control. I started coordinating and managing a small study. The Air Force Systems Command issued three parallel study contracts: one on Lunar Vehicle Guidance to GDA, a second on Rendezvous Guidance to MIT Instrumentation Laboratories, and a third to ITT Laboratories on Earth Terminal Guidance and Lunar Landing.

My assignment was to participate in and manage the study at GDA. We developed and investigated trajectories for manned circumlunar flights, manned moon-to-earth flights and guidance concepts, launch from the lunar surface, and midcourse corrections. We were the first to examine the feasibility of going out to the moon in one trajectory plane, and returning in a different trajectory plane This could be useful in cases of an emergency, which required a different landing site. The study of liftoff guidance and trajectory from the lunar surface was another first, because the industry was focused on liftoff schemes from the earth. Unlike the earth, the lunar surface isn't enveloped in an atmosphere and has a weaker gravitational force. That implies, we could devise more efficient schemes for launch from its surface, because there are no restrictions due to drag and heat, like in the earth's atmosphere.

Guidance and control at the time was the new science of guiding a vehicle or spacecraft to its ultimate objective. It commands and controls the start and end of engine burns and the spacecraft attitude as a function of time. Errors occur during the burn, or thrust phase. The engine alignment is not perfect, and the thrust produced by these devices is not absolutely accurate or measured precisely. Due to those errors the spacecraft achieves a somewhat different trajectory than the one desired. If left unchecked, the errors propagate with time and the spacecraft would miss its target. Prior to making an orbit correction, the actual orbit obtained by the spacecraft must be determined. That requires navigational measurements. Again, each measurement is not perfect and introduces random errors.

The orbit determination process uses highly complex calculations and statistical methods to reduce these errors and to define the actual orbit as accurately as possible. The midcourse or orbit correction is the energy required to make up for the difference between the desired and the actual orbits. The orbit correction is considered mathematically a vector hence it has magnitude and direction. Therefore, to perform the correction, the direction, or attitude of the spacecraft, the time to initiate and the duration of the burn are specified. The preceding is a summary of the basics for the space enthusiast. It is important to note that no textbooks or real life experiences existed to guide the engineers and scientists in these endeavors, other than their knowledge of basic physics and astronomy.

The study included periodic meetings with members of the other study groups. I traveled to MIT for one conference, and MIT people visited us. During this small study contract, we performed original work, pushing the state of the art in lunar travel. It was very timely, in vogue, and in high demand. The study results were published in a report sent to the government library in March 1962. My name appeared on the cover of that report.

At the same time, the Apollo Program, with the objective of putting a man on the moon started. Therefore, companies that had or anticipated receiving contracts associated with Apollo were staffing up. Engineers and scientists with any knowledge in this area were in demand. Someone at North American Aviation, later known as Rockwell International, saw my study report, called me, and offered me employment. In truth, they made me an offer I couldn't refuse.

I was fortunate to have been involved in the field of lunar trajectories, guidance, and control early in the space program. I was also fortunate to have been associated with knowledge-able people in the field, among them some famous German engineers and scientists from Peenemünde German rocket base who'd developed the V1, V2 rockets in World War II. My boss, Dr. Robert Leger, reported to one, and Dr. Kraft Ericke headed the Centaur missile program, for which our department generated all the trajectories.

I found myself in the right place at the right time, working diligently in a glamorous field. We implemented trial-and-error techniques, derivation, and invention since there were no books on the subject. Quite literally, we all flew by the seats of our pants.

GDA sent me to UCLA for a one-week symposium on

guidance and control, which was being offered for the first time. The material presented was a compilation of technical papers on various aspects of guidance and control. There I met Dr. Richard Chang from Hughes Aircraft Company. He wrote the guidance and control equations for the soft lunar landing sequence for the Surveyor unmanned spacecraft, developed at the time. I had the opportunity to have worked with Dick Chang at Curtis Wright, where he'd spent summers while pursuing his PhD at Purdue University.

Even though the aerospace industry was large, one often crossed paths with coworkers from previous employment. Individual reputation preceded each of us, which became an important asset in networking and advancing profession- ally. Dick Chang became instrumental in one of my career changes.

Our life in San Diego was exciting, too. Everything was new for us. A new environment, a new apartment, a new job, and for the first time, we were far away from our parents and friends. Our friends the Gelernters were old-time San Diego residents. They'd lived in San Diego for two years, owned their own home, and knew everything about the town. We often spent time in their company. Bruce played with Bobby, who was about two years older. On weekends, we visited Mission Bay, La Jolla Cove, La Jolla Shores, or Balboa Park. We also traveled on the Del Dios Highway, marveling at the barren brown hills, which we'd not seen back east.

"These mountains look different, bordering on ugly," remarked Annette. "I'm used to green mountains, full of pine trees in the summer and white snow in the winter."

"I agree, but I remember the mountains in Tajikistan were awesome. They looked even more naked, made of gray stone, granite, I believe. Everything about the West Coast is different. Most of it I like."

"Especially the palm trees, new buildings, and relatively light traffic," commented Annette.

One winter day we bundled up Bruce and visited the Palomar Observatory. The city was rather small at that time. UCSD did not exist. In its place was a eucalyptus forest. Miramar Road was a two-lane road, bordering what is now the Marine Corps Air Station at Miramar.

During the time we lived in San Diego, we missed our parents and hoped they'd join us soon. We also house-hunted. There were houses built on a hill overlooking Mission Bay, and we almost bought one in the development called 'Pacifica.' We drove there several times and dreamed of owning a home with a magnificent view of the bay. In retrospect, we did well by not buying. In 1962, the aerospace industry started laying off engineers, and few were able to obtain other jobs in San Diego. Many left town without selling their houses. About a year earlier, builders had started developing University City. Many engineers had bought homes there, only to abandon them within a year.

Our Plymouth had various mechanical problems and we decided to trade it for a new car.

"I sure would love to get a Porsche. I wish I could afford even a used one," I kept saying every time the subject of buying a car came up. In fact, there wasn't even a Porsche dealer in San Diego.

"Would you settle for a Karman Ghia?" Annette asked as we passed a VW dealer displaying a Karman Ghia convertible.

"We'll have to call it our Porsche," I said.

I was not very practical and Annette went along. She was pregnant with Steven at the time. Even though Bruce was about eighteen months old, and Annette had difficulties entering and exiting the car, we managed and enjoyed cruising with the top down. A bright purple color, everybody could see us coming and going.

Several months before our move to Los Angeles, Annette gave birth to our second son, Steven Reid. We named him after my Uncle Zioma and Grandpa Rubin. It is a tradition among Jewish people of European origin to name their children after deceased relatives. This honors the relative, serves to perpetuate the name, and remembers the deceased. To give the child an American name, one uses the first letter of the Hebrew or Yiddish name.

During Annette's pregnancy with Steven, we were again concerned about her RH negative factor. I made a promise that I'd give up smoking if both mother and child were alright. We were delighted to see he was a healthy baby. He was born in Sharp Hospital, one block from our apartment. At the time, the maternity ward was located in a single story building, which displayed a stork on the street. On my way home from the hospital, I kept my promise and threw out my last pack of cigarettes. I haven't smoked since. We were proud parents of two boys, and I wanted to have more children, as I'd been an only child.

Mama had moved to Los Angeles about one year after we came to San Diego. She flew from New York, while Papa drove to bring over his car and some additional belongings. They settled in Los Angeles, in a small apartment on Corcoran Street in the Fairfax area. A short time later, they separated. Years later Mama obtained a formal divorce.

When Mama decided to leave Papa, she sat me down.

"I have a very serious decision to discuss with you. I want your concurrence because, for many years now, I don't make any important decisions without your consent. You know your father and I haven't had a decent marriage for a long time, but I put up with it. I've now reached a stage in my life where I must protect the few dollars that I've saved so that I don't become a financial burden to the State or to you and your family. I know, and I believe you're also aware, that if I stay with your father, he will spend it in no time. Therefore, I've decided to separate and get a divorce. You may think it unfair or even cruel, but I must do it for my self-preservation. I want your concurrence. I can't do it without you telling me that it's alright."

"That is quite a story." I said, "I must say that I'm not shocked, because you have talked about it for some time, but why now?"

"I cannot delay it any further. I am getting older, my savings are dwindling, and it does not look like your father will ever start making a living and stop spending," she cried.

It was very sad, but it seemed like she was right. She had been very frugal all her life, whereas Papa spent money much easier than he earned and with little thought of the consequences.

"I know and sympathize, but I don't think I should be involved in your decision regarding your marriage and a divorce. You're my parents." I felt deep regret for them both. "Please, don't cry."

"You are involved," Mama answered, "and your opinion is very important to me."

"Mama, you know I share your feelings and point of view, but I feel terrible to go against Papa. Please stop crying." I put my arms around her and gave her a kiss. "Yes, I understand and it's okay."

"I wanted to hear you say that you approve, and thank you." She hugged me for a long time, then, murmured, "You and your family are all I have."

Tears ran down my face, and we cried for a while. I felt bad, but I was also somewhat relieved. I knew she had been agonizing about this for a long time. I thought that now that she had made the decision, her suffering would subside. Even though I knew I should not be involved in the decision, I also knew my special and close relationship with Mama required that I support her choice. I understood she could not decide by herself, no matter how she felt. That scene will remain etched in my brain as one of the most painful moments of my life.

After their separation, Papa struggled financially. The money he earned selling real estate was not sufficient to live on. Gullible and unrealistic, he spent money unwisely on chemicals. He turned those into detergents, which he could not sell.

He developed a good product, but could not afford to have it packaged professionally. His products looked homemade and no one bought them.

Papa basically, could not make a living due to his ego and the lack of opportunities for someone with his antiquated skills, even though he had a fair command of the English language. I helped as much as I could, but I also struggled to support my family. Annette and I visited him and invited him to our house. We made sure that he attended all of our family functions and celebrations. After a lifelong of smoking, he developed emphysema. He died June 15, 1981. I've carried a lot of guilt for not having been able to get along better with him. He was my father, and God knows I tried. I also believe that he never forgave me for supporting Mama in her decision to separate from him and end their marriage.

Annette's parents were happy to have an excuse to move to California and be close to us and to my mother-in-law's sisters, brothers, and their families. A few years after we relocated to California, they liquidated their business and moved to Los Angeles. They found a nice two-bedroom apartment in L.A. near Santa Barbara Avenue.

Annette's father obtained a job at the May Company department store, and her mother worked at the Broadway store. They started as sales people. Later, her father advanced to become manager of the furniture department and her mother became manager of the children's department. Some time later, they moved to another apartment near Venice Avenue.

CHAPTER 31

LOS ANGELES

I accepted North American's offer even though Annette and I hated leaving San Diego. A medium-sized community with only a few engineering companies, San Diego didn't offer the variety of employment and growth opportunities for a young, ambitious engineer seeking professional advancement. Los Angeles, on the other hand, was home to numerous aerospace companies, which convinced me that the offer from North American Aviation made sense. My salary would increase, and I felt it provided me with the prospect of growth in a new, rapidly expanding industry. Lunar exploration in general and the Apollo Program in particular promised advancement to those with an early foothold in the aerospace field.

I took Annette to Downey, and we looked for an area in which to settle. At first sight of the town, she started crying.

"I don't want to leave beautiful San Diego, and I certainly don't want to live in the hot and smoggy Los Angeles."

"Neither do I, but this move is best for us as a family."

"I know, but I still don't like it," she insisted.

"Look at it this way," I reasoned, "I'd much rather live in L.A. than in New York or New Jersey. Besides, I promise you that we'll return to San Diego." I certainly did not know at the time that twenty-seven years would pass before I fulfilled that promise.

I wanted to live close to my work. Since we had no

knowledge of the area, we found a temporary apartment in South Gate. The small apartment with no other children in the building was in an undesirable neighborhood. However, we did not intend to move out within six weeks of our arrival. It didn't take us long to realize that we were not welcome in the apartment building. Neighbors banged on our wall every time Steven cried or made noise.

"Your boy (referring to Bruce) is not allowed to ride his tricycle in the little front yard. He's noisy, and the neighbors are complaining," the manager declared.

"But he's only a child. Besides, you can't expect him to play in the street," complained Annette.

"I'm sorry, but I can't lose my tenants because of you."

"You've got to get me out of here," Annette announced when I came home from work. "I can't stand it. You're not here all day long with the children. I feel like I'm living in a prison."

"I don't like it here, either," I replied.

A few weeks later, we searched for another place to live.

While working in San Diego, I'd heard engineers refer to Palos Verdes, near Los Angeles, as a nice area to live, so we began to look for a home there. A hilly peninsula in the southwest corner of Los Angeles county, it had beautiful ocean vistas, a sea breeze and no smog. We found a house in a development called "Seaview," in the Portuguese Bend area of Palos Verdes. No one had ever lived in the one-year-old house. The development consisted of about one hundred rather nice, well built, houses, which ranged in size from around sixteen hundred to twenty-two hundred square feet.

While building Seaview, a landslide occurred a mile west of the development. It didn't effect the houses in Seaview, but people stopped buying them for fear of hidden or eventual structural damage. Consequently, the builder reduced the prices to sell the remaining houses.

I concluded that the houses were structurally sound. They

had stood for more than a year without any sign of damage. Besides, we could hardly afford to look for a more expensive house. We bought the smallest, least expensive house, without an ocean view, while the houses across the street enjoyed unobstructed ocean views, but for a few thousand dollars more.

Located two blocks north of Palos Verdes Drive South, our street was called Exultant Drive. Our new home had three bedrooms, two baths, a nice living room with an impressive floor-to-ceiling stone fireplace, and a non-eat-in kitchen with a small family room that could also serve as a dining room. The entire house had hardwood floors, a slate entry, and a crawl space under the house, considered a plus because most houses in Southern California are on cement slab floors.

Our sizable backyard ended in a slope up a large hill. The house on top of that hill enjoyed an unobstructed ocean view. This was our first home, and we were very proud owners. Except of the concrete patio and a small retaining wall against the hill in the back built by a contractor, I single handedly installed sprinklers, seeded grass in the backyard, planted shrubs and a couple of trees. Instead of a lawn, I created a fish out of colored crushed rock on the elevated narrow front. That saved water and mowing the front. It also allowed me some artistic freedom of expression.

After a few years, the house became too small for us. In 1963, my wife and I had our third child. She was also our first girl. We named her Laurel Sue, but we always called her Laurie. After two boys, we were extremely happy to have a daughter with all the expected frills only a girl could bring. She had blond curly hair, was beautiful and easier to handle than the boys. Bruce, our oldest, was a tough kid. Prone to get into all kinds of small problems, it seemed like every time we took photographs he had a scraped nose.

In August 1966, we were blessed with another beautiful girl, Valerie Lynn. Annette and I decided that two boys and two girls made a perfect family. Besides, who could handle more responsibility? I had always wanted a large family, because I'd missed having brothers and sisters as a boy. Annette stayed home and took care of our children. My mother also moved in with us and helped with the children.

THE APOLLO PROGRAM

At North American Aviation (NAA), I was hired to work in Advance Systems on proposals for new studies and contracts in the area of spacecraft and missiles guidance and control. One of those studies involved developing guidance equations for a mobile ballistic missile. After a short time, the Apollo organization at NAA initiated a call for bids for building the Apollo Mission Simulator (AMS).

The purpose for the AMS was to train astronauts to perform the various tasks needed to fly the Apollo mission. To provide meaningful training for the astronauts, the AMS needed to simulate the Apollo space capsule in all aspects; to be an exact replica of the spacecraft itself. With the exception of simulating the zero gravity effects, it had to have complete fidelity. Large digital computers were required to perform calculations and realistically drive all spacecraft instruments, including the onboard computer. The AMS also had to allow instructors to introduce all kind of situations, problems, malfunctions, and errors to train the astronauts to recognize them and take appropriate corrective actions. Consequently, an astronaut's wife could often ask the question at the dinner table, "Honey, how was your day?"

"Fine, I only crashed once, but I'm okay and I've learned something new. And what exciting thing did you do today?"

North American sent requests for proposals to which seven contractors responded. It was understood that whoever won the competition and became the AMS contractor would likely remain the only company in the spacecraft simulator business. It would also become the strongest company in the airplane simulator business by virtue of the high technology knowledge obtained from the space business experience. Therefore, all the companies in the airplane simulator business responded with proposals.

Since the AMS was worth several million dollars, NAA's policies and procedures required an organization outside the Apollo project to perform an independent evaluation of the various proposals and select the recommended contractor for award.

When NAA management looked for candidates to carry out this evaluation, they realized I had experience in flight simulators and selected me. I spent several months evaluating all the proposals and traveling to the various companies to evaluate their capabilities, facilities, and management for the job. Curtis Wright Electronics was among the bidders. I knew from personal experience that they were the best technical candidate for the job. However, their poorly prepared proposal failed to showcase their expertise. It expressed high confidence they would do a good job because of their technical knowledge and experience in flight simulators. Our evaluation team concluded that Link Aviation's proposal came in first with a superior proposal. With the facilities of all major bidders similar, the proposals counted highly in the competition.

NAA assigned an individual to be the main interface with the astronauts. George Smith, a former test pilot at NAA, was the natural choice to understand the astronauts' needs and speak their language. He was also a medical miracle, a living experiment, a guinea pig. On a weekend in February 1955, George flew a test plane at supersonic speed without a pressure suit and crashed into Santa Monica Bay. Fortunately, a dentist fishing at the time picked him up. Because he ejected at supersonic speed without a pressurized suit, many of his blood vessels burst. He swelled up like a balloon. To my understanding, he's the only man to have survived that kind of an accident, and he became a symbol of great interest to medical science. For the rest of his life, physicians checked him out every several months. Because of my assignment to the AMS, I had frequent contact with him.

Ed Link, the founder of Link Aviation, met us in a restaurant for dinner during our first visit to Binghamton, New York. That evening, I discovered that George could consume an exorbitant amount of alcohol. The next morning Link personnel gave a presentation in their main conference room. The room, long and somewhat narrow, was located in an old brick building. The tables were set up to form the letter U. The NAA people sat at the head of the table and a tripod with flip charts stood at the far end at the opening of the U. It was a very important briefing for Link. The room was quiet enough to hear a pin drop. As soon as the Link presenter began to speak, George Smith, in a loud but muffled voice interrupted. "Would you speak louder, I can't hear a thing. I also can't see the small print on your charts very well. Last night's booze isn't helping either."

Dead silence ensued. George had stumped the briefer. No one knew where the voice had come from, until George removed his two hands from his face and lifted his head. "I meant that. I have a hell of a hangover."

Somewhat embarrassed, we all smiled. The silence and the stiff and serious atmosphere in the room dissipated. The presenter moved the easel closer to us, and the presentation continued without a hitch.

Having finished my assignment as an evaluator, I was transferred to the Apollo organization and promoted. As head of the AMS technical management, I was responsible for establishing the specifications and requirements, monitoring the subcontractor's analysis and design implementation, and coordinating with NASA and with the ultimate users, the astronauts assigned to the AMS.

I found the job very interesting, challenging, and frustrating. For the AMS to simulate the Apollo spacecraft with high fidelity, it needed the Apollo technical details and characteristics not fully available. While the spacecraft design started before the simulator, it had not matured enough to establish all its characteristics. The plans called for the designing and building the spacecraft and simulator at the same time. The AMS completion date was based on the need for adequate astronaut training time. The desire to reach the moon as soon as possible drove the whole Apollo program into nonrealistic schedules.

This was quite the catch twenty-two. It became obvious that the schedules for designing and building the simulator and training the astronauts were incompatible with those needed for the spacecraft design and building. We also insisted on and developed a realistic detailed schedule for analyzing, designing, and building the simulator at Link. That document served as a double-edged sword. On one hand, it helped me prove to the Apollo management at NAA that the information was needed as the schedule indicated. On the other hand, it prevented Link from arbitrarily asking for data before it was required, then using the lack of data as an excuse to slip schedule and incur additional cost. After some time, management realized that the AMS was pacing the whole Apollo program. It became a window into the progress of the spacecraft design.

The AMS was also required to provide realistic instruments and out-of-the-window displays for the astronauts. The astronauts needed to be able to look out the command module window and see realistic locations and relative positions as a function of time, of the moon, sun, stars, planets and earth with appropriate day-night shading. Accurate displays of navigational stars, landmarks, and landmass-water interfaces were needed to train the astronauts to perform orbit determination and midcourse corrections. The astronauts would use the sexton and telescope to take angle measurements to the various celestial objects, input them into the onboard computer, which would output orbit determination data. It would also calculate the orbit correction based on the newly computed actual orbit versus the desired. The astronauts would then train to perform the thrusters' burns and resulting orbit maneuvers. The AMS had to allow training for periodic spacecraft attitude maneuvers and positioning the spacecraft attitude with respect to the sun and the antennas to the earth was required.

Everything, including the scenery, was computer-driven, yet no one knew what the astronauts should realistically see when looking out at the earth from the window of the spacecraft cabin. Therefore, we couldn't write a realistic specification for the out-of-window displays for the AMS. The scenery changed and depended on the mission phase. A Mercator projection of a geo-sphere was used and painted in various shades of green, brown, white and blue to represent rivers, ocean, and so on. We didn't know if the colors were realistic or accurate. We met with astronaut Gordon Cooper in Houston. He had flown an earlier mission around the earth and had claimed to have seen minute details like moving trains and other objects. We showed him some conceptual paintings of the earth, which he corrected based on what he thought he had seen. I certainly thought it was not a technical description when he said, "This here should be a little greener, whereas the Great Lakes should be a little bluer, and the area around the Florida peninsula should be of a lighter blue color." However, that was the best information we had. I believe that at that time, Gordon Cooper was the only astronaut who had flown in earth orbit and claimed to have had such good visibility.

The Apollo was to be launched from Cape Canaveral, Florida. The entity that separated from the Launch Vehicle or booster (Saturn-4) consisted of the spacecraft Command Module (CM) and Service Module (SM) with the lunar Landing Module (LM) attached to it. The three astronauts stayed in the CM until they reached the lunar orbit. There, two entered the LM, separated from the CM/SM, descended, and soft-landed on the lunar surface. One astronaut remained in lunar orbit where he monitored and communicated with the earth and the moon until LM returned from the moon and rendezvoused with the CM. The two astronauts from the LM reentered the CM. The three astronauts in the CM/SM separated and dumped the LM, then returned to earth where the CM separated from the SM and reentered and splashed down in the ocean.

All the astronauts on the Apollo program were required to know all systems. However, one or more astronauts had to follow and be fully knowledgeable with one specific major subsystem. Astronauts Charley Bassett and Neil Armstrong were assigned to the AMS. One tragic day, Charley Bassett was killed in an accident while flying during a training exercise over St. Louis. That left Neil Armstrong as the only astronaut following the AMS. We had numerous meetings, reviews, and arguments with Neil, some conducted in my office. The most vivid was about the astronaut's seats.

Inside the simulator cabin were the three seats or benches, realistically located, which would have the astronauts lying on their backs with their legs higher than their heads. That was fine when they were in a zero gravity environment, but in the simulator on earth it would be tough on their backs. We suggested two modifications to the seats, which he objected to for fear they would compromise the realism of the module. The first was to add some padding to ease the discomfort on the back when lying on them in earth's gravity. The second, was to cut off the leg rest and reconnect it with a hinge so that it could drop down when not in use, providing additional room in the crowded module. Neil changed his mind after he tripped during a walk-through of the module.

The AMS preliminary design review at the link facility in Binghamton, New York took about four weeks, during which time the price of the AMS doubled due to modifications requested by NASA. A major improvement was to design and use a ten-digit pushbutton panel to replace a slew of manual switches on the instructor's console. The new device, named Malfunction Insertion Unit (MIU) provided the means for instructors to insert specific glitches by pressing a button on the MIU. The astronaut had to recognize the specific problems and take appropriate action. The consoles designed to accommodate the instructors training the astronauts were located outside the Apollo cabin or CM.

NASA originally specified the color of the instructor's consoles as Air Force blue. After several requests for changes, Link painted them brown. It so happened, purely coincidentally I'm sure that just prior to deciding on the color brown, one of NASA's young lieutenants just bought a new Pontiac of the same color.

"Good choice," I said as I smiled, "I also like your new Pontiac."

With a big grin on his face, he answered, "I thought so."

Later in the program, many AMS requirements had to be reduced, because the tasks were extremely complex and nonrealistic for Link Aviation to implement. During a review with NASA, Joe Shea, the NASA Administrator, referred to them as "the missing link" on the Apollo program. The complex tasks at Link improved with time.

We also had Neil Armstrong go to Link Aviation and shake hands with the workers in a morale-building effort. At the time, we hadn't expected him to go down in history as the first man to walk on the moon, only because he was among the youngest astronauts. Extremely intelligent and dedicated, Neil certainly did a great job. He made America proud.

I worked in various management capacities on the Apollo program. At the beginning, I was a supervisor in charge of about twenty engineers. When upper management realized the difficulties in obtaining design data in order to develop requirements for the simulator, management elevated that activity to a higher level. They created a Director for Project Management reporting directly to the Apollo Program Manager and Vice President. Initially, the Apollo Program Manager was John Pope. Later, Dale Meyers replaced him. Reporting to the director were several project managers, one for each major activity that required management attention at the director level.

A reorganization followed with my promotion to AMS Project Manager, reporting to the Project Management Director. In that capacity, and with the help of an assistant project manager, I identified the various problems of missing data and the dates by which they were required, and assigned action items for the various directors. To persuade the directors at higher levels to accept and commit to the assigned action items, I presented these action items weekly on closed circuit TV. The vice president and each director had a TV monitor and interactive communications (an open microphone) in their offices, so for each action item that I presented, the VP would obtain a commitment, or a reason why not, from the appropriate director, on the spot, in real time and in front of all other directors.

A politically difficult job, it required finesse. In addition to having stage fright about making presentations on TV, it put me in a sensitive position and required a certain amount of diplomacy to have to assign action items to people of a higher rank without seriously offending them and making them my enemies. After some six months, we identified all the action items together with a schedule to implement them. Having accomplished that task, Apollo management dissolved that organization and assigned about twenty engineers to me to manage and resolve all those action items. That scheme worked, although it felt ironic. I worked diligently and did not leave a stone unturned, identifying and obtaining commitments for design data from various Apollo design organizations. In the end, I still had to follow up and obtain that data.

Reorganizations like the ones previously mentioned were frequent and necessary. Everyone, including the Apollo management, encountered problems and took corrective actions as we went along. Nobody had ever before tackled such a technically complex and challenging undertaking under such stringent schedules.

My job required that I organize and attend monthly coordination meetings with Link. The meetings alternated between NAA and Link. Every other month, I traveled to Link in Binghamton, New York. Similarly, I traveled every two months to the NASA Manned Space Flight Center (MSFC) in Houston, Texas, or to the Johnson Flight Center (JFC) as it was later known.

After the AMS was designed, I was ready for a new professional challenge. The most interesting phase of the program had been completed, and I wasn't interested in following the hardware built by Link. My new assignment was to direct the activities of developing timelines for each specific Apollo mission. It entailed identifying in detail each task, its duration, and the appropriate sequence that each astronaut had to perform during a specific Apollo mission. To develop the timelines, my engineers had to know every detail and the interdependencies of all actions and the systems reactions.

While establishing the timelines, one of the engineers reporting to me wrote a memo that identified a scenario in which a fire could occur on board the Command Module with disastrous consequences because the crew compartment would be filled with oxygen instead of a combination of air and other less flammable or inert gases. A spark resulting from a faulty switch could ignite and explode the compartment with the astronauts inside. Nobody paid attention to that memo at the time. Some time later, that exact scenario unfortunately occurred and three astronauts perished on the launch pad. I assume that the tight schedules, coupled with incurring additional large expenditures of money, were among the reasons management ignored that possibility. Of course, after the accident, a design change was implemented, and pure oxygen was no longer used in the crew compartment.

Working and being part of the team during the Apollo period was exciting. Those were challenging times. Because of the Soviet Sputnik, President Kennedy had made it a national priority to put an American on the moon within a decade. We felt we had worked on a glamorous project with high visibility and a lot of hype. It felt like an adventure – mission impossible – going where only a couple of years earlier it wasn't even in the realm of serious human thought. We attempted to do a technically complex job that had never been done before. It was exciting to meet and work with the extremely dedicated and hard-working astronauts. Our work had made us space pioneers.

No money was spared. Funding did not seem to be a problem. During contract negotiations between North American Aviation and NASA in Houston, NASA would ring a cowbell to announce the start of the next session.

"What is the significance of ringing the cowbell?" we asked.

"Come and milk us dry," the NASA representatives replied. "You're getting all our money."

Prior to NASA's explanation for using the cowbell, I thought it was some sort of Texas cowboy thing.

Houston, home of the NASA Center, and Clearlake, where the astronauts lived and worked had a radio station that used the slogan, "Look out moon! Here comes Houston!" It was repeated frequently every day.

At various times while at NASA Huston for meetings, we ate lunch in their cafeteria. On one such occasion, I met astronaut John Glenn. Outgoing, friendly, and talkative, he preceded me in the food line and we chatted.

"I see you're wearing a visitor's badge. Who are you with?"

"North American Aviation," I answered.

"Oh, great, we need you to do a good job. We intend to fly this thing one of these days."

"We're all trying hard," I said as I smiled.

"My name is John Glenn." He extended his hand.

"I know. I'm pleased to meet you."

My reason for my writing about Apollo is to provide a true picture from an insider's point of view without any intent of criticizing or harming anyone. An interesting part of my life, it provided me with invaluable experience and served as a stepping-stone in my career.

That timeframe in space exploration was, and remains a piece of history. I felt privileged to be a part of it. I never lost sight of my own history. I am very proud to say that, because a ten-year-old boy from Beltz escaped the bombs and bullets of the Blitzkrieg he grew up to become an integral part of the Apollo program, and contributed to the first successful American walk on the moon. Never in my wildest dreams did I imagine becoming a part of the U.S. space program. I did my very best during all of my assignments on the Apollo program. I was dedicated, fair, and worked hard. That kind of behavior was in my blood, my upbringing, and due to my father's influence. Additionally, the war experience and the school of hard knocks had taught me that just to survive was not enough. I needed to strive, to overcome any hardship, to excel, to grow, and to make up for lost time. Always compelled to prove myself, I lived by that principle in both my personal and professional lives. At times, my drive was to my own detriment. At golf, I would swing too hard. When exercising, I would overdo it to a point of hurting myself. I also had to live with and learn to overcome the difficulties of corporate politics that exist in every company, particularly in the large ones. I did not like them, found them tough to live with, considered them unfair and many times felt inadequate in that environment.

Surveyor Lunar Lander

After the Apollo design was practically completed, I wanted to become involved in other space activities. I saw on television that Hughes Aircraft Company (HAC) had successfully landed an unmanned spacecraft, Surveyor I, on the lunar surface. I remembered that Dr. Richard Chang worked at HAC. He had devised the guidance scheme and equations for the soft landing of the Surveyor. I decided to contact him.

"Dick, this is Bob Frimtzis. I hope you remember me from Curtis Wright. We also spoke during the Guidance and Control of Aerospace Vehicles course at UCLA that was coordinated by Dr. Leondes."

"Oh yes, how are you Bob?"

"I'm fine. Congratulations on your success with Surveyor's perfect landing. You guys must be very happy," I said.

"Thank you very much. We are. What's new with you? Are you still at Astronautics in San Diego?"

"No, I've been on the Apollo program for the past four and a half years. Most of the analysis and design is completed, and I'm getting itchy. Do you think there might be something of interest at Hughes for me?" I then told him briefly about the work I had done at North American.

"Why don't you send me a resume?" he suggested. "I'm pretty sure we could find something interesting for you to do."

Shortly thereafter, Hughes invited me for an interview. After talking with Jim Cloud, Dick's boss and the Manager of System Engineering for the Surveyor, Jim offered me a position as Assistant Manager of the Guidance and Trajectory Department on the Surveyor Program, which I accepted. My new title and responsibilities came with a nice increase in salary. He told me that although Hughes was laying off some engineers at the time, they could always use people with my experience. That flattered me. This was in 1966.

After eight years of caring for little ones, Annette had had enough. She decided to go back to work.

"If I can't get out of the house, I'll go crazy," she would often say.

We both knew that she'd been out of her field for a long time and would have to start from scratch. Furthermore, she could not apply at a company without good references. I called Dr. Kazarian, a colleague with whom I had shared an office at North American Aviation. At NAA, we had both worked on guidance and control analyses prior to my transfer to the Apollo program. Kazar had been hired by NAA because of his reputation in the field of guidance equations at the Aerospace Corporation. Rumor had it that because of a simple error of not recognizing a vector symbol in the guidance equations, which he checked, a missile launch had crashed. Employed by Logicon in San Pedro at the time, I called him.

"Kazar, this is your old lost buddy, Bob Frimtzis."

"How are you Bob, long time no see."

"How about having lunch?" I asked. While at NAA, we had lunch together several times a week. When we met, I told him that Annette wanted to go back to work and asked if he would take her resume into Logicon. I also explained that as a mechanical engineer, she had no trajectory experience. He told me not to worry.

Annette went to work at Logicon, where she started at the bottom. The technology had changed, and she began to learn about software and trajectories. Thus, she initiated her second career. We employed a series of housekeepers and nannies to care for our children.

During my eleven years' employment at Hughes Aircraft Company, I was involved in a variety of activities. On the Surveyor Program, in addition to being the Assistant Department Manager, I headed up a small project called "The Lift-off and Translation Experiment," also known as the "Hopper." It entailed developing a small trajectory program, which accepted the initial conditions of the Surveyor spacecraft after it landed on a particular surface on the moon. The spacecraft attitude or inclination, as well as the immediate surrounding area, dictated the direction we could lift and translate the spacecraft.

The spacecraft, not designed to re-ignite its engines after it landed, provided us with no technical reason to prevent a second ignition. There was some uncertainty about blowing a hole in the lunar surface directly beneath the ignited engines. The direction of the hop was determined by the initial inclination of the spacecraft after landing, and the height of the hop depended upon the duration of the burn. There was also the concern and a very small probability of hitting a rock upon landing, which could tip over the spacecraft. The primary mission of the Surveyor was to photograph the surface and the rocks, and send the TV pictures back to earth, as well as to scratch the surface and analyze its composition.

After each Surveyor landing, we would develop a hopper trajectory, and then brief the Jet Propulsion Laboratory (JPL), our customer. They acted for NASA, who controlled the project. They directed the mission and Surveyor operations on the lunar surface, based on the requests of the science group, who were geologists. The science people always wanted more lunar samples and to photograph more lunar surface. After enough pictures and surface samples were taken, it was my responsibility to convince JPL to allow us to hop the spacecraft. We presented the proposed trajectory, quoted probabilities of success, and indicated the benefit of translating the spacecraft a few feet to a new location where new rocks could be studied. JPL and the science group responsible for the experiments always refused our requests. Finally, on Surveyor D, the fourth successfully landed spacecraft we received permission to hop. The experiment was very successful, and we drew great applause from the Hughes and JPL people in the control room. Hughes built and launched seven Surveyor Spacecraft, five of which were extremely successful. I believe Surveyor D was launched on July 14, 1967.

The Surveyor, launched by the Atlas/Centaur launch vehicle from Cape Kennedy, was the first unmanned spacecraft to ever soft-land on the lunar surface. The flight from launch to landing is nominally 62 hours. The missions were to demonstrate the feasibility of soft-landing an unmanned spacecraft with scientific instruments on the lunar surface in order to expand man's knowledge of the moon. Surveyor paved the way for soft-landing a manned vehicle on the lunar surface. It selected the Apollo corridor, an area where Apollo could land. In fact, one of the Apollo vehicles landed in close proximity to a Surveyor. An astronaut dismantled and brought back to earth the Surveyor TV camera for evaluation after it spent several lunar nights on the moon. Engineers at Hughes Aircraft Company examined the camera and found it was in good shape after the cold lunar nights even though it was not designed to survive that environment. This experiment occurred after I'd written a memo to Dick Chang, in which I suggested that such an experiment would be of scientific value and further connect the Surveyor and Apollo programs.

Toward the end of the Surveyor program, Jim Cloud moved into another area at Hughes. All the other engineers and I knew he was involved in some sort of classified activities. One day I received a phone call from Jim.

"Bob, I would like you to fill out this large security questionnaire. I want to submit you for a special clearance."

"You know that I was born in Russia?" I asked.

"Affirmative!" he answered and hung up the phone.

When the questionnaire arrived by company mail, I put it aside. I considered it was a waste of my time. After a few weeks, Jim called again.

"Hey Bob, I haven't received your completed questionnaire."

"Jim, please spare me the effort and the embarrassment to follow," I replied.

"Independent of what you think, would you please fill out the papers?"

"Yes, sir, I will."

I hung up the phone, feeling badly for not following a direct order. I filled out the documents and sent them to him. After several months, I received a call from the head of security, who asked me to attend a briefing in another building. I'd obviously gotten the clearance. Then Jim called me into his office,

"Congratulations! I realized you thought it was impossible to get you cleared. I guess you didn't know it was easier for you to get clearance than the average American."

"How come?" I asked.

"They (the FBI) have a detailed dossier on you because you were an immigrant from Russia."

"I apologize, Jim, I didn't know. Otherwise I wouldn't have delayed it a single day." I felt somewhat embarrassed.

"I know." Jim smiled. "You're forgiven."

Defense Satellites

I discovered a new world behind the closed doors of the classified program. Once briefed and introduced to the program, it became obvious that the technical activities conducted there pushed the state-of-the-art of the technology. The work was technically very interesting and extremely challenging. Jim asked me to manage the Spacecraft and Software Analysis Department in the System Engineering Laboratory.

My department was responsible for all the analysis of the spacecraft subsystems, and the development of all the equations, algorithms, and software to control and maintain it on orbit.

That included such complex functions as orbit determination, attitude control and pointing, and electrical power management. I had a group of highly qualified analysts and PhDs, who'd worked closely with software specialists to develop these computer programs.

Additionally, I was responsible for trajectory verification for the launch vehicle integration. That entailed the verification of guidance equations and constants used by the launch vehicle contractor, Lockheed, and coordination with Air Force personnel. The work was very exciting and demanding, and I was very happy. After a couple of years, I was promoted to Assistant Laboratory Manager for the Systems Engineering Laboratory.

On my first job, I realized that engineering is probably the only profession where one is paid for a job, which one does not know how to do. Later in my career, when I was a manager, supervised projects, and assigned tasks to engineers, I often made that comment to engineers who complained to me that they no longer wanted to perform a task because they already knew how to do it. They wanted something more challenging, that is, something they had not done before. This is especially true when dealing with PhDs in the area of analysis.

The spacecraft was launched successfully, and its performance exceeded its requirements. After the work became less interesting, I asked for new assignments and received several assignments to manage proposals for various upgrades to our system, as well as other new business. All the activities were of classified nature, therefore I cannot write about them.

Professional politics existed at Hughes, but Jim Cloud managed to keep them to a minimum. I felt somewhat protected thanks to my reputation and the many years I'd worked there. Nevertheless, incidences of insults and personal put-downs occurred on the job. One episode stands out in my mind. During a large technical review meeting with my program manager Frank and Tony, the vice president of engineering,

Tony made a statement regarding a technical issue in the area of my responsibility, to which I replied, "I believe that can't be done."

"We'll get somebody who can," he responded without giving it much thought. While Tony was very intelligent, he was also known for his quick temper, sharp tongue, and occasional insults.

"Why don't you?" I replied

My program manager, who sat beside me, signaled me to keep quiet and stay in my seat. Immediately after the meeting, he dropped by my office and apologized for the VP's behavior.

"Bob, you know Tony. He says things he does not mean."

That evening I came home, took a stiff shot of scotch, and slept badly, reliving that episode. Next morning, Tony passed me in the corridor. He smiled, and said, "Hi, Bob," as if nothing had happened less than twenty four-hours ago. These and similar incidents as well as the behind the scenes politics among management bothered me at times.

At Hughes, I traveled a fair amount. Most of it was to Aurora, Colorado, east of Denver. Our program built a new facility at Buckley Air Reserve Base, which we later staffed with our engineers. I flew out there once per month for a few years. Several times, I flew in the company plane from the Hughes airstrip in Culver City directly to Buckley.

Often I was the only passenger in the company plane. As an incentive to fly in that small airplane, it was stocked with liquor of my choice. I didn't like flying in it, because the turbulence over the Rockies could be severe.

The company plane was very useful when an emergency meeting needed to be held. It saved time and effort to get tickets, drive to LAX, wait for an available scheduled plane, rent a car upon arrival at Stapleton airport in Denver, and finally drive to Buckley. On one flight, the pilot swooped down over the Grand Canyon and presented us with a magnificent view.

In my capacity as manager of launch vehicle integration,

guidance, and trajectory verification, I often flew to San Jose, California for meetings with Lockheed in Mountain View. They'd built the launch vehicle. At times, I traveled to Vandenberg Air Force Base in support of an upcoming launch.

A few times, I visited the Pentagon to present unsolicited proposals to upgrade our program in a cost effective manner. At the Pentagon, I spoke to an Air Force Lt. Colonel who'd previously been in charge of our program. I dealt with him when he asked me to make a decision concerning the method I proposed to ease the development of the orbit determination program. He backed and supported my decision. I liked him. He was intelligent, hard working, and a reasonable customer. After the Lt. Col. received a much deserved promotion to work at the Pentagon, my management asked me to approach him, because he respected my opinion and knew I wouldn't conduct a sales pitch unless I believed my remarks and proposal were beneficial to our program. I smiled during one particular conversation when he said, "What our country needs..."

"I'm impressed," I said. "You used to say, 'what our program needs,' now you are concerned with our country's needs."

He understood my reference to his promotion and increased responsibilities, and we had a good laugh.

I also flew to Huntsville, Alabama, and Albuquerque, New Mexico for meetings regarding the Burst Detection and Reporting study, which I headed.

One summer, I was asked to go to Boeing Aircraft Company in Seattle. They were preparing a proposal for a large classified program. The Hughes Vice President, Bob Sears, called. "Bob, I need you in Washington as soon as possible."

"What for, what do you want me to do there?" I asked thinking the situation urgent and mysterious.

"Please go over to Jim's office. He'll explain. I cannot talk on the phone."

"Bob Sears called," I told Jim, "and said he wants me in Washington as soon as possible. What's up?"

Jim realized my confusion, "He wants you to go to Boeing in Seattle, Washington."

"I'm glad it is not Washington, D.C. in the middle of the summer heat. What do you want me to do at Boeing?"

"Boeing is preparing a major classified proposal," Jim explained, "and they have problems in the area of spacecraft control software. Another Hughes division is interested in providing them with a large ground antenna if Boeing wins the proposal. I want you to quickly assess their situation."

"Jim, I was planning a vacation with my family."

"Try to postpone it. This is important."

"I'm on my way," I answered.

"Thanks Bob, we'll make it up to you. Good luck."

"Please, get me a ticket to Seattle as soon as possible, and call me at home with the details," I told my secretary. Then I called home, "Annette, our vacation is postponed for a while. I'm on my way home, and I'll explain everything."

I spent a week at Boeing, and met with their management and the technical person in charge of the spacecraft software control. I came to the conclusion that they were in such bad shape, no one could help them.

"In my opinion, Boeing's proposal design does not stand a chance to win the contract." I described it as too little, too late. I briefed my management of my finding upon my return to Los Angeles.

"Go back and do whatever you can," they replied.

I spent the better part of the summer in Seattle. I even managed to include Annette, Bruce, Steven, and Laurie. We left Valerie at home, because she was too young. They spent close to two weeks there with me, while I worked at Boeing from early morning until late at night.

We stayed at the SeaTac Airport Hotel near the Seattle-Tacoma Airport. Each morning, Annette would drop me off at

Boeing. She and the children would then have the rented car a whole day. In the evening, I'd call her to be picked up. The children had a lot of fun. Before flying home, I took a few days vacation. In fact, as I was checking out of the hotel, I bumped into our VP, Bob Sears as he checked into the hotel.

"Hello! I thought you're working hard here."

"You didn't see me when I worked very hard. But now, I'm taking a couple days off to be with my family," I replied, smiling.

He smiled back at me, "Have fun. I guess you deserve it."

That was a typical comment from Bob. He was not a warm man, at least not to me.

We visited Victoria and Vancouver, British Columbia, enjoying the short vacation. The greeters at the entrance to our hotel in Vancouver wore Beefeater red uniforms trimmed in gold and black. After we returned home, I discovered that Howard Hughes occupied the entire upper floor of our hotel during our stay.

On my return trip to Seattle, I took my assistant with me. He had a PhD in computer science and was our data processing expert. The weather in Seattle that summer was perfect.

At Boeing, I interfaced with a smart young man whom I tried to hire. He wanted to join Hughes Aircraft Company. His wife, however, refused to leave Seattle. They were Seattle natives. During the next couple of years, he called me every time he was in Los Angeles on company business. He even visited us at home in Palos Verdes. Years later, I read he became a program manager and a vice president at Boeing.

I directed a nine months' study contract we won after I headed the proposal entitled Survivable Burst Reporting System. It entailed a conceptual design of a system, which could detect bursts, determine if they were of a nuclear nature, and identify them by magnitude or size. It also had a requirement to predict an approximate impact point. The latter accuracy was not very good. During the study, we came up with a conceptual design for an electro-optical sensor for that purpose.

While the work was always interesting and technically challenging, after eleven years at Hughes and most of my time spent in the classified arena, I grew weary of work I could not talk about. I wanted to be utilized in some other area of Hughes. Every time I made a request to management, they assigned me to a new activity, only to pull me back into the classified area if problems occurred. I decided to seek alternate employment outside the company. When I mentioned to some of my colleagues my intentions to leave Hughes, they thought it unwise and risky to make a career change at the age of forty-eight.

"You have all the security at Hughes," one manager reasoned, "and you'd retire with a decent pension." He continued, "If I had to sweep floors here, I would not leave until my retirement."

"That is exactly my reason for wanting to leave," I answered. "I hope I never reach your opinion and fear to try something new."

I admit, it was a risky proposition, but I had enough confidence in my abilities and was willing to take a chance. I felt driven to achieve. On one hand, I was happy with my achievements. On the other hand, I felt that I could and must do better.

On Sunday July 20, 1969, the television had been on since early morning. Around 1:20 in the afternoon we heard the long awaited announcement, "The Eagle has landed!"

"Watch children," I said, as Annette and I sat glued to the TV in our family room. "We are watching the most historic accomplishment by human beings."

Around eight in the evening, the Lunar Module camera provided live coverage of Neil Armstrong descending the ladder to the lunar surface. Everybody remembers the historic words he then pronounced, "One small step for man; one giant leap for mankind."

"We really made it!" I jumped off the couch, threw up my hands, and yelled at the top of my lungs.

"Wow! That's so exciting," with a loud laugh Annette stood up and we embraced without taking our eyes off the TV.

"You really worked with Neil Armstrong?" my nine year-old Bruce asked, while Steve, seven, Laurie, five, and two year-old Valerie looked on. They were all visibly proud.

"Yes I did, we even had meetings in my office," I replied.

"You've seen the signed photos of the Mercury, Gemini, and early Apollo astronauts, Dad's brought home from work," Annette reminded the children. "Dad's met a few of them. Tell the children, Bob."

"Dad, I thought you're working at Hughes on the Surveyor. Did Hughes build the Apollo?" Bruce inquired with a puzzled look.

"Before I came to Hughes, I worked at North American," I explained, "on the Apollo Program. I managed the work on the Apollo Mission Simulator, a device designed to train the astronauts to fly to the moon. Neil Armstrong was the astronaut whom NASA assigned to follow the simulator. Therefore, I met him often during design and progress reviews of the simulator."

That night I could not fall asleep due to the excitement of the day. I felt gratified. I reminded myself how far I've come, from the ten-year-old boy running from the bombs and bullets to the mud hut in Tajikistan, to contributing to the Apollo program. What came to mind was Neil Armstrong walked on the moon, in part because I survived the Blitzkrieg and imminent starvation, and because I crossed every border I encountered in life.

All work and no play would make life dull. In addition to work and family obligations, I needed some recreation. I had played nine holes of golf every Sunday at Los Verdes. Because it was a public course, it was practically impossible to get a starting time for eighteen holes of golf. One of the foursome had to begin calling the starter at Los Verdes at five in the morning on Sunday, a week in advance of the Sunday we intended to play, to get a starting time for the back nine. The starter could only start nine foursomes on the tenth hole.

We would have loved to have played eighteen holes. With activities like Indian Guides, little league, and soccer, as well as building walls in the backyard and gardening, golf was relegated to a few hours on Sundays. Our golf group called ourselves the Fearsome Foursome. We bet a quarter or fifty cents, and deposited all our winnings in a savings account in the name of the Fearsome Foursome. Evie, Billy's wife, took care of our bank account.

The original foursome consisted of Billy, Milt, Dick, and me. Dick and I lived on the same street whereas Milt lived one street below us. After Bill immigrated (*aliyah* in Hebrew) to Israel, Sherman took his place in the Fearsome Foursome. Once a year we supplemented the money in the bank account and took our wives to a resort for a weekend to play golf. We played golf at Singing Hills and at La Costa. One evening we dined at Mister A's restaurant. We all enjoyed a white-glove, elegantly served delicious dinner and fine wine in a private room.

Dick, who had a PhD in physics, worked at TRW, whereas Milt and I were at Hughes. Dick and I frequently exchanged information about our respective jobs. When I decided to change jobs, I gave my resume to Dick to pass it to TRW Management. Shortly after, I got a call from Dr. Al Sabroff, inviting me to come in for an interview. He was the Director of System Engineering at the Space Division of TRW. After a brief conversation with him, he introduced me to the Division Manager and Vice President, Bob Walquist.

The interview went very well. It became apparent that they

knew about the activities that I was involved in at Hughes. In a few days, Sabroff called and made me a verbal offer to come work for him as an Assistant to the Director, with a nice increase in salary including participation in the management incentive plan, an annual bonus program.

I accepted Sabroff's offer and submitted a letter of resignation to the vice president and division manager of my area at Hughes. He immediately called me into his office.

"What is this all about?"

"After eleven years at Hughes," I told him, "including the last eight in the classified arena, I am ready to leave. I've asked various times for other assignments without much success."

He picked up the phone and called Jim Cloud, who only a few months earlier was promoted to a group VP, which included several divisions.

"Bob Frimtzis is in my office threatening to leave Hughes." Don told Jim.

I took the phone, and I heard Jim say, "Bob, please wait till the end of the day. We'll talk."

"Sure thing," I responded.

Jim's new office was in Culver City, whereas mine was in El Segundo.

"What's going on?" he asked as soon as he walked into my office.

"Jim, I feel like a fixture in my current position, and I want out."

"Come work for me," he said, then handed me a folded sheet of paper from his breast pocket. "Here is a list of all the projects that are now my new responsibility. I am not familiar with all of them in detail because I'm new to my job." He pointed at two projects noted on the paper. "You can have a responsible position in any of these operations if you come with me."

"Jim, if you had offered me this one week ago I would have

kissed your feet, but it's too late now. I've already accepted an offer from TRW."

"You'll be back," he replied.

"Would you take me back?" I asked. "I certainly don't want to burn any bridges with Hughes."

"Definitely! Any time," he answered.

"Thank you for your offer, Jim. I enjoyed working for you all these years. It's good to know that should things not work out at TRW, you would take me back and I would have a place in your organization."

We shook hands, and he departed.

GAMMA RAY OBSERVATORY

At TRW, I spent several years supporting numerous new business activities. Then I was asked to be the program manager for the Gamma Ray Observatory (GRO) proposal. The proposal I managed won, and we received a study contract to design the spacecraft and to integrate the various gamma ray detection instruments. The customer was the NASA Goddard Center in Maryland. The scientific instruments were developed by various agencies in the US, including one by Max Plank Institute outside of Munich, Germany, which provided me with the only opportunity to travel to Europe on company business.

That was my first trip to Germany. While I traveled in style, stayed at the Four Seasons Hotel, and met with highly respected German scientists, I felt very uncomfortable. I kept thinking, how can they treat me so nicely? Do they not know that I am a Jew? Would they still consider me an *Untermensch*, a subhuman, if they knew I was Jewish? I hope not.

The first night in my hotel room, I watched television. When the program ended at 10 p.m., the German anthem was played. It contained the same melody as *"Deutschland, Deutschland über alles."* It might have been the same anthem that was sung during World War II. I didn't sleep that night, and I wondered what would have happened to me if I had worn a large sign saying, *"Ich bin ein Jude,"* on the streets, in the restaurant, or the hotel lobby, as well as during my meetings with the German scientists.

On that trip, I took along another TRW employee who reported to me and was responsible for the integration of the scientific instruments into our spacecraft. He was of German origin, and he expressed his happiness to visit the land of his ancestry.

"I feel great seeing the country where my folks were born," he said.

How could I tell him how I felt without making him uncomfortable? I didn't say anything. During the weekend, we drove to a beautiful resort town in the Tyrolienne Alps called Garmisch-Partenkirchen, where Hitler had vacationed.

Years later, after my Cousin Bronia and her daughter Zina, moved to Germany, Annette and I visited them many times. Even though we enjoyed seeing them and visiting beautiful towns and villages, I always felt a sense of discomfort. I could not forget that I was in the same Germany that had committed atrocities in Europe, created havoc in my life, killed eleven members of my family, and murdered six million innocent Jews. Yet I learned to live with the memories and the reality. Annette and I even drive German cars.

I realize that, with Mama gone, Cousin Bronia and I were the only two left of our generation. It feels lonely in that regard. Bronia moved to Cologne, Germany, with her daughter Zina and granddaughter Isabelle. After some forty-three years separation, when I had not known if she was alive, she calls me practically every Sunday. We talk about our children and grandchildren and their successes, which is uplifting. We also reminisce about the old days. I make it my business to visit them whenever we are in Europe. Now that Isabelle is seven years old and more able to travel, Zina has promised to visit us.

In 1989, Bronia and Zina visited us in Los Angeles. I advised them to remain in the US and told them I would try to get an immigration lawyer to take care of the visa extension. She refused because she was committed to return to Beltz to install a memorial headstone on the grave of her husband who died in 1988. Later I tried to get an affidavit for her and Zina but without success. The US immigration law at the time allowed only immediate relatives like brothers, sisters, mothers, fathers, sons, or daughters. I also wrote to Washington, but to no avail.

Bronia and Zina decided to immigrate to Germany. Their decision shocked me but as it turned out, the German government was good to them, providing my cousin with a free apartment and a monthly pension. Both Bronia and Zina were physicians in Beltz. Of course, Bronia cannot work. She is retired and in poor health. Germany recognized Zina's Soviet diploma, although she had to renew her studies before being permitted to work as a physician.

As the name of the project implies, the GRO would detect gamma rays. Even though gamma rays are the most energetic rays, they are fortunately absorbed into the earth's atmosphere. Otherwise, there would be no life on earth. At least not the kind of life we know. To detect gamma rays, the instruments or detectors must be placed on an earth orbiting spacecraft well above the earth's atmosphere. The scientific instruments needed to detect the gamma rays are rather large and heavy, some the size of a Volkswagen car, and they require a very large spacecraft that can be put into earth orbit only by the shuttle.

The scientific reasoning for the generation or birth of the gamma rays was interesting. Since the gamma rays are very energetic, they came into being by a terrific explosion like the creation of the universe. Furthermore, since it takes million of light years for the rays to arrive at the earth, it would be reasonable to consider that the gamma rays the GRO would be detecting are those generated during the Big Bang. In other words, by collecting the gamma rays, we are witnessing the creation of the universe. It's a pretty neat concept – to sit on earth and watch the earth being born. This is where science surpasses science fiction.

As the GRO Project Manager, I had to travel often to meet with NASA GRO management. I also briefed congressional staffers in Washington, D.C. on the importance of GRO to provide them with appropriate understanding and interest in keeping the GRO funding in the budget.

During a major presentation to NASA held at Goddard Space Flight Center, I created an embarrassing situation for myself. I gave my presentation at a podium on stage in the main conference auditorium at Goddard. In the filled room sat my TRW vice president. At the end of my presentation, he made a comment reinforcing my statements and providing NASA, our customer, assurances at a higher management level of TRW's commitment to the GRO Program.

"I couldn't agree with you less," I replied, assuredly.

The auditorium turned momentarily silent, with the audience expressing a collective expression of astonishment. I immediately realized my mistake and corrected my statement.

"I'm sorry, I meant to say I couldn't agree with you more." I smiled and blushed.

With a sigh of relief, the audience smiled. Even though I spoke English well at the time, I tripped up thinking *I couldn't agree with you less,* a statement with two negatives implied affirmation. I never made that mistake again. I sometimes wondered if my boss really forgave me for this mistake.

When the study ended, NASA awarded a hardware contract to TRW, a definite feather in my cap. After that, I was responsible for successfully negotiating a one hundred million dollar contract for building the GRO spacecraft. The gamma ray detection instruments were provided as Government Furnished Equipment, GFE.

Once I completed contract negotiations, vice president Bob Walquist invited me into his office. Over a cup of coffee, he said, "I want to congratulate you for your achievement! Well done, Bob. Seeing you've done a great job for the company on GRO, I have even a tougher project for you to tackle." He explained. "The laser crosslink on the Defense Satellite Program (DSP) is in trouble, and I want to ask you to manage it. You know how important DSP is for the company and our country."

"Why not let me manage the hardware phase of the GRO, which I have truly earned?" I asked unhappily.

He took a sip of coffee. "You have not been long enough with the company, and I'm afraid that you don't know the TRW culture yet."

"I'm disappointed," I told him.

"The laser crosslink is a bigger management challenge, and I believe you're the man for the job."

It was disheartening that after all my efforts during the study phase and winning a hardware contract, I wouldn't be managing it. It was a shock to my ego. Walquist thought I could not manage the job, or more likely, he was playing politics to appease other more senior people. Without telling him, I decided right then to leave TRW as soon as I could take early retirement at 55.

Years later, our daughter Laurie worked at Rockwell, formerly North American Aviation, on the space shuttle project. She was in the payload integration department and her assignment was to integrate the GRO into the shuttle for launch. Hence, another member of my family contributed to the success of GRO. When she first met GRO engineers from TRW assigned to interface with her, a few of them recognized her last name.

"Say, are you by any chance related to Bob Frimtzis ?" they asked.

"Yes, he is my father," she replied smiling.

"We knew your father when he was the program manager of the GRO."

THE LASER CROSSLINK

The laser crosslink turned out to be a technical and management nightmare. The objective of the crosslink was to enable one satellite to communicate with another. From a mission point of view, the laser crosslink would provide a very serious improvement in security. It would allow each satellite to communicate and dump data to the other without involving the earth station. If there were two satellites in space and one didn't have visibility of the ground station, it could send the data to the other, which could communicate with the ground. The satellite with the appropriate visibility of the ground station could then relay this data to the station. Without the laser crosslink, some data had to be transmitted to a ground station located on foreign soil, if it had visibility of the satellite. Fog or rain at the ground station attenuates the laser signal, which is the main disadvantage of any laser. The great advantage of the laser is its narrow beam, hence a small footprint, which makes it practically impossible to intercept by the enemy. It provides excellent security compared to antenna footprints. The security advantage for the defense satellite used to detect missile launches and relay the information to the Department of Defense as part of an early warning system is of tremendous importance.

Before this phase of the program, the Air Force ran a competitive technology study between Hughes and McDonnell. At the end of the study, Hughes admitted that their laser technology was not ready. McDonnell on the other hand received a subcontract from TRW to develop the laser crosslink for the defense satellite on a weak argument that some hardware they'd developed for testing on an airplane was similar enough to the hardware needed for the crosslink.

No laser had been used for that purpose before. It was an extremely difficult task and the technology was not ready. As McDonnell Douglas (the current corporate name) developed the new hardware and started testing it, various parts failed prior to the completion of the test. It was the responsibility of my group to check on their progress, review their results, make suggestions, apply pressure to improve their performance, and maintain schedules. I spent a lot of time in technical reviews and discussions with McDonnell management in Saint Louis, Missouri. During one such review, they discussed problems associated with cutting wafers without contamination. They had tried several techniques without much success.

"Have you tried a *moil?*" (a man who performs Jewish religious circumcisions on eight day old boys) I whispered jokingly under my breath, hoping nobody heard it.

"Ha, ha, ha, a *moil!*" Steve Mc Namara, my subcontract manager who sat next to me at the large table in the conference room full of people, laughed loudly. "A great idea."

His remarks drew a few smiles and puzzled glances from others. Steve, a practicing Catholic with a Jewish mother who'd renounced her religion after surviving the Holocaust, knew some Yiddish.

"I just tried to break the gloomy atmosphere," I commented somewhat sheepishly.

Politics came into play. Since McDonnell Douglas was a larger company than TRW, they were able to work around us. One time their high level corporate management asked our management to reduce the pressure on them. In other words, call off your dogs, because we intend to do business with you in the future in other areas. I had to walk a fine line. No, a tight rope.

Understandably, the Air Force wanted the laser to become operational as soon as possible. Therefore, TRW did not want to disappoint the customer, the Air Force, and perhaps lose the contract if it admitted the laser was not ready for production and integration into the defense satellite. As the project manager of the laser crosslink, I managed the subcontractor and kept the Air Force informed on the status of the project. The Aerospace Corporation, the technical arm of the Air Force, also monitored the activities at McDonnell and at TRW.

Since it was my job to brief the Air Force, I was asked to stand before them and convince them that the hardware was ready to go into the production phase. I told TRW management that I would not do that. I would avoid telling them that it was not ready, and let them draw their own conclusions from the poor and incomplete test results, but I refused to mislead them. Then my manager, and program manager of the defense satellite program, persuaded the Air Force to fund the next phase as a production contract.

Following that, TRW agreed to sign a cost-plus-fee contract with McDonnell Douglas for the production phase, because McDonnell refused to sign a fix-price contract. McDonnell knew very well that the hardware was not ready for production and would not risk committing to a fix-price contract.

TRW on the other hand had to accept a fix-price contract with the Air Force, because they'd convinced the Air Force that the laser was ready for production. I subsequently resigned from my assignment informing management that I could no longer accept responsibility for the project under the current conditions. I refused to manage a cost-plus contract with my subcontractor, which would run up the cost, while my company had to perform on a fixed price basis. It was a situation destined for problems. This was not an easy decision for me to make. I wanted to be a team player and support the company's decisions and strategies (or politics) to whatever extent possible, but I also needed to maintain my honesty and integrity.

I requested another assignment, deciding to stick it out at TRW for one more year when I'd be eligible for early retirement. Company politics had played a large part in most of my jobs. I bent with the wind whenever possible, aware because I'd graduated from the school of hard knocks and survived impossible odds, that one needed to be flexible at times. I could only bend so much without breaking, thanks to my personal honor and professional pride. I wished I had a thicker skin. My jobs and progress in management drained me at times. I paid a price. It was a constant load on my mind and self-esteem. I always wished I was better at politics. Now and then I still dream, that I have to make a delicate decision, a presentation, or conduct a meeting where I must express opinions contrary to my true beliefs.

At TRW I had to prove myself many times over because I was the new kid on the block, considered a relatively recent hire compared to those who'd spent many years with the company. I also found out that advancement and promotions often depended on whom you knew, not just what you knew.

CHAPTER 32

TRIPS TO ISRAEL
AND EUROPE

A S a young boy in 1946, I tried to immigrate illegally to
Palestine before the creation of a Jewish state.
Some thirty years later, in April 1976, the first opportunity to visit Israel availed itself. While living in Palos Verdes,
the rabbi of our congregation in San Pedro organized and led
a two-week trip to Israel. Mama, Annette, and I joined the
tour. Mama wanted to see her brother Tolia who'd immigrated
to Israel.

Our trip to Israel was a great experience. I felt tremendous pride in being in the only country in the world where the
policeman in the street, the fireman, the soldier, the judge, the
president as well as the thief and prostitute were Jewish. The
Jews had a country of their own.

No longer stateless and vulnerable to the tyrants of the
world, the existence of the State of Israel placed the Jewish
people on a par with other people in the world. Despite the
fact that this Jew lived in America and was a proud citizen of
that country, Israel became the symbol of my heritage, just
as Ireland is to the Irish-American, and Italy is to the Italian-
Americans. I was proud that Israel is a democracy with a
formidable defense force and was built by the refugees and
survivors of the Holocaust. My heart warmed when I saw the

street names and businesses, everything written in Hebrew, even though I didn't understand the language.

As tourists, we visited all the Jewish, Christian, and Arab sites. I felt as though I walked among the antiquities of religion and history. It was all real. The country is very small, and we explored most of it except Eilat on the Red Sea at the end of the Negev desert.

In Jerusalem, I prayed at the Western Wall, visited the Knesset, the Mount of Olives, the Dead Sea Scrolls Museum, the Dome of the Rock, the University, and *Yad Vashem* (the Holocaust Memorial). I spent less than five minutes inside the memorial. I could not breathe. I ran outside and broke down crying. During our stay in Jerusalem, we took rooms at the King David Hotel, where I saw Shimon Perez walking with a large entourage. He was not the Prime Minister at the time.

In Haifa, I visited the *Technion,* Israel's equivalent to MIT, and the glittering Bahai Temple. We were guests at a Bar Mitzvah on top of *Masada,* the old mountain fortress where the Jewish defenders fought the Romans, then committed mass suicide instead of surrendering to the Roman legions. We swam in the Dead Sea. We visited the Churches of the Nativity and of the Holy Sepulcher. In Hebron, I saw Abraham and Sarah's burial places. It was most poignant to see an Israeli soldier and a few Arabs praying in two different corners, while three nuns passed through the same room in the building that housed Abraham's grave. It served as a perfect illustration that Israel is the cradle to all three religions. It also demonstrated that the three religions could coexist, if only for a brief moment.

Annette and I encouraged each of our children to visit Israel on vacation during high school summer breaks. We wanted them to see the beautiful country and feel a special connection to the Jewish state. Three of our children accepted our offer, each one traveling with the group called Young Judea when they were sixteen years old. Our son Bruce did not go. Laurie went to Israel a second time when she graduated from high school. She spent a school year studying at Jerusalem University, lived in a kibbutz, and with a family in a *moshav* (a cooperative).

In the summer of 1982, to coincide with the end of Laurie's course in Israel, Annette and I spent a week with her. Afterwards, we planned to take her to see Europe. I intended to show my wife and daughter where I'd lived in Italy and Switzerland while waiting to immigrate to America.

My former golfing body, Billy Byer, who lived in Israel at the time, rented a furnished apartment for us in Hertzelia. He lived close by and drove a Volvo.

"Did I tell you about my taking possession of my Volvo in Israel?" Billy asked.

"No," I answered.

"You know I purchased my Volvo in Los Angeles before we immigrated to Israel? I must have also told you that the car was supposed to be delivered in Israel."

"Yes, you did."

"When the car arrived in Tell Aviv, the dealer called me. He said, 'Your car has arrived, we've serviced it, and it's ready to be picked up.' That happened on a Friday before noon," Billy continued. "By the time I came to pick it up it was near closing time, because in Israel, everything shuts down on Friday afternoon to celebrate the Sabbath. As I was ready to drive away, the dealer mentioned that the car was low on gas. By the time I found the first gasoline station, the car had stalled for lack of gas. The gas station owner did me a big favor and filled up my car as he was shutting down for Sabbath." Billy smiled. "That's not the end of the story. When I got home, I realized that the seatbelt lights didn't work. On Monday, I took the car back to the dealer and informed him of the problem. The dealer responded self-righteously, 'Of course, they don't work. We disconnect the lights as part of servicing the new cars after we pick them up at the port.' Why would you do that? I asked. 'So they will not annoy you. Nobody uses seatbelts in

Israel,' answered the surprised dealer, 'Didn't you know that?' A laughing Billy finished: "The moral of the story is, don't have a car delivered in Israel. If you do, never pick it up on a Friday and, above all, if a dealer tells you that your car has little gas, he means that there are only gas vapors in the tank."

Laurie, Billy, and his wife Evie were our guides for the week. Annette and I felt like natives. We lived in our own apartment, shopped in the local grocery store, visited places of interest, and went to the beach to swim.

Annette was invited by IEEE (International Electrical and Electronic Engineers society) to make a presentation on Software Quality Assurance in Israel. The day Annette made her technical presentation at IAI (Israeli Aircraft Industry), Billy and I enjoyed a game of golf at Caesarea, the only golf course in Israel.

"Bob, I believe you understand now the pride and sense of well-being I get from living in Israel," Billy said while playing golf. "I traded some of the comforts of living in America for the emotional gratification I get from living in a Jewish country."

"Yes, I know exactly how you feel. I also give you credit for your courage and decision to uproot your family and move here." I continued, "I could not follow your example. I had a very tough life during World War II, and worked hard in America to reach my current standard of living. I also could not leave the United States out of obligation and gratitude because it has provided me a safe haven and the unique opportunities to reach my full potential."

"On a lighter note," Billy said as he smiled, "you realize that the one and only golf course in Israel does not even have electric carts to ride in. Now, there is a sacrifice I can live with. Walking provides me with additional exercise."

"Look at it this way, Billy. Where else in the whole world could you play golf while being serenaded by all these Jewish birds?" I laughed and pointed to a flock of birds chirping melodiously in the trees around us.

The week went by very quickly, and we all had a wonderful time. I felt very much at home in Israel. From there, Annette, Laurie, and I flew to Rome and rented a car. At the Rome airport, I engaged one of the men in uniform sitting behind a desk.

"*Signore,*" I asked in Italian, "I'm looking for a centrally located *pensione* (a bed-and-breakfast). I haven't been in Rome for thirty years. Could you perhaps have any suggestions?"

"*Certamente, Signore.* I have an aunt who has a very nice and clean *pensione* in a very good location. Let me give you the address and directions to get there. If you're interested, I'll call and tell her to expect you."

"*Grazie tanto,*" I answered.

The directions the official gave me were very good, and we stayed there our first night in Rome.

We drove all over Italy. We hadn't made hotel reservations in any of the towns we visited. Toward the end of each day, I'd look around for a place to spend the night. At times, searching for a *pensione* was nerve racking. If we were lucky, we liked the first one we saw. Other times, it would take an hour or longer. In Milan, I spent close to two hours looking. We didn't like any of them, so I decided to drive on to Como where we found a beautiful small hotel on the lake. We spent two nights there and enjoyed it tremendously. One day we spent driving and visiting the tranquil and picturesque city of Lugano in Switzerland. Later in our trip, we returned to Milan and had no problem finding a place to stay.

The trip was interesting for Annette and Laurie and of special significance to me, a bittersweet stroll down memory lane. Only the building in Milan on Via Unioni 5 was the same as I remembered it from thirty-five years earlier. Nothing had changed in that area of Milan. In fact, we took the subway and emerged at Piazza Duomo. From there we walked to within one block of Via Unioni, at which point I asked for directions. The building at Via Unioni 5 housed law enforcement offices.

In Italian, I addressed the police officer at the gate, *"Agente,* some thirty years ago I lived here. This place housed a DP camp at the time. I have come all the way from America. Is it possible to see the place?"

He gave me a puzzled look. "No," he replied.

"But officer, I slept for a week on these cobblestones in the yard. Could I at least step on these stones again?"

"The answer is still no!" He was not in the least sympathetic.

"May I take a picture of the yard?" I asked.

He looked annoyed. "You may not! Please move on!"

I moved a couple of feet from the gate and asked Annette to take a photo of me under the sign "number 5."

In Cremona, I made inquiries wherever I saw a few local elderly men gathered in front of a bar having an espresso. I asked only older people, because I figured the youth in these locations would have no reason to know anything about 30 year-old-camps.

"Scusi, some thirty years ago I lived here in the DP camp. Could you direct me to where the camp used to be?"

"It's no longer here," was their initial response.

"I know it is no longer here. But do any of you remember where it used to be?" I'd continue.

The men would argue until they all agreed where the camp once stood.

"Go straight until you reach Garibaldi Street, turn right until such and such street, and then left, and so on."

"Mille grazie," I would answer before departing.

After the first or second street, I forgot the name of the other streets and had to repeat the same process of inquiring of the next people I encountered. That became a ritual. In every city, I tried to find the location of a DP camp I'd once lived in.

I finally found the place. At the time, it was a parking lot covered in gravel. I drove in and parked the rental car. An elderly woman approached me to collect the parking fee.

I said in Italian, *"Signora,* I was told that this is where the DP Camp used to be, but I don't see it."

"Si, what's left of it is now a government protected site." She turned and pointed to a section of the building behind the parking lot.

"I used to live here when I was about seventeen years old."

"Come on out of the car and take a look. Inside, they still have all the bunk beds. It is being preserved as a monument," she said.

I looked around in the parking lot and recognized the round arches on the second floor of the building.

"That used to be the boys' *Kinderzimmer* where I slept. You see the identical arches kitty corner. Those belonged to the girls' room," I said to Annette and Laurie. "I can't believe how small the yard looks now. I used to play basketball here. It seemed to be much larger."

The caretaker, who followed us around, pointed to an old wooden door. "I'll show you a crack in the door where you can look inside and see the beds."

I followed her and then we each took a turn looking inside. Indeed, there were the bunk beds as I remembered them. I felt very strange as I looked into my past, like Alice peering through a looking glass. I shivered, transplanted back in time after some thirty-five years. I saw myself in that room, surrounded by those familiar beds. Nausea gripped me followed by beads of perspiration on my forehead. This moment justified our trip to Italy.

"From time to time, people come to see the place," the caretaker told me. "They also tell me they once lived here."

Before we left, I thanked her and offered to pay for the parking.

"I can't take money from you," she said. She cut a rose from one of the rosebushes that grew around the fence, handed it to Annette, and gave her a hug.

I managed to say, *"Grazie Signora, ed arrivederci,"* before I broke down with tears in my eyes. Obviously, my emotions ran high that day. The caretaker, who was an elderly woman, no doubt without an education, served as an example of how kind and humane the Italian people were to the poor refugees who had lived temporarily in their country. While in Cremona, we also decided to visit the Stradivarius Museum, which was located in a small, unimpressive building that contained and displayed various violins.

I next searched for the DP camp in Iesi, near Ancona on the Adriatic coast. I spent the better part of a day unsuccessfully looking for it. Very disappointed, I finally abandoned my search. I also could not find the camp in Barletta.

"We must be very close," I told Annette prior to getting off the *autostrada* to Barletta, "because I recognize these endless fields of olive trees and the hand laid stone walls fencing them in and running for miles." After exiting the *autostrada*, I pulled up to a gasoline station to fill up the car.

"Can you tell me where I could find a hotel?" I asked the gasoline station attendant.

"Make a left and go toward the sea. After you cross the railroad tracks, you'll see the hotel on the right." As soon as we left the gas station, I told Annette that I remembered a small park adjacent to the beach. As we crossed the railroad tracks, I saw the park.

"Look, Annette, to your left, there is the park. We must be close to the beach." Before we pulled up to the hotel by the sea, I recognized the beach.

I remembered my friends and I had crossed a lot of sand before we reached the water's edge at the beach in Barletta. My friends exaggerated and complained whenever we swam there. "We get tired crossing the 'Barletta desert' before we can jump into the sea."

"Be glad it's not the Sahara," was the response.

We checked into a large hotel with an unfilled pool in front. It had obviously once been a nice hotel, but it hadn't been maintained. The window air conditioner in our room didn't work, and it was as hot as it gets in Europe in the summer. We were in the south of Italy. Warm and tired we took showers before deciding to have supper at the hotel.

The hotel dining room was closed due to the heat, so the hotel served supper al fresco on the patio. The waiters wore tuxedo trousers and shirts with black bowties. We were the only Americans in the hotel. Ten to twelve local people appeared to be enjoying a feast at other table.

"What do you recommend?" I asked the waiter.

"We have beautiful, fresh fish. The fishermen just delivered them to the hotel."

"What kind of fish?"

"Un momento, Signore," he said before he rushed off.

He returned pushing a metal cart beautifully displaying various fish on ice. We selected three fish and ordered bottled water and wine. The service was elegant and the fish tasted delicious.

"We're from California," I told the waiter in Italian a while later. "More than thirty years ago, I lived in the DP camp in Barletta. I'm back to revisit the city and see if I can find anything that's left of the camp, which wasn't too far from the cement factory."

The waiter grimaced, implying he didn't know.

"I am too young to remember anything about it, but I'll inquire of the other older people. Perhaps one of them knows."

A few minutes after we started eating, the waiter brought us a couple of dishes of seafood and pointed to the occupants of the other table. "This is from our other guests with their complements."

Completely surprised, I looked over to that table where a few of the men lifted their glasses of wine. *"Salute!"*

I picked up my glass, turned to them, and responded, *"Salute e grazie a voi!"*

We truly enjoyed our dinner, especially after the hospitality displayed by the locals.

The next day, we looked around the town and inquired about the DP camp. No one knew anything. Except for the beach and the park, I didn't recognize much about Barletta. I was disappointed that aside from Milan I didn't recognize a single street or building in Cremona, Iesi, or Barletta. The towns had changed beyond recognition in the thirty-plus years since I had last seen them.

While in Genoa, I wanted to show Laurie and Annette the statue of Christopher Columbus. I knew that Columbus had been born there, and I remembered seeing the statue near the railroad station prior to my departure to the U.S. in 1950. We drove around within a few blocks of the railroad station, but we failed to find it. I stopped the car, rolled down the window, and asked two local women walking down the street carrying bags of groceries.

"Scusi Signora! Could you tell me where the statue of *Cristoforo Colombo* is?"

They looked at each other, puzzled.

"There is no such statue in Genoa," they answered.

"I remember seeing it somewhere near the station," I said.

"We were born and have lived here all of our lives," one woman commented. "We should know. We've never seen it."

I didn't give up. After driving around a few more blocks, I noticed the statue right in front of the railroad station. We took pictures of it, and as we started to drive away, I spotted the same two women about half a block from the statue. I stopped the car next to them and smiled broadly, "Ladies, for your information this here is the statue of *Cristoforo Colombo.*"

"We pass by here daily," they replied, obviously shocked and embarrassed, "and we never knew that this statue is of Christopher Columbus."

We all laughed. As I drove away I shouted, "Now you know!"

We had another interesting experience while in Turin. Annette, Laurie, and I walked in the center of town around six o'clock in the evening. We were hungry, and all the restaurants were closed. I stumbled upon a beautiful restaurant, its doors wide open, and no one inside. While Annette and Laurie waited, I entered the restaurant and asked a man behind the bar if we could have dinner.

"We're closed and will not open until eight," the man apologized.

I searched and found on a side street, a very small restaurant, the door open and strings of beads hanging in the entrance. We walked inside and observed six small tables covered with plaid tablecloths. A woman came out from the kitchen, yelling at a boy to stop playing with the TV control knobs in the corner of the room.

"I hope you're open, because we're all hungry."

"Please sit at any table you like," she replied.

We sat down, and the woman brought us a hand-written menu on single sheet of paper.

"I have fresh mushrooms that I can sauté, but they're not on the menu."

We ordered dinner from the menu and asked her to prepare some mushrooms for Annette. I also asked for a bottle of water and a liter of white wine. The meal was delicious and we enjoyed the homey atmosphere. When she brought us the bill, I pointed out to Annette a couple of interesting and unexpected facts. The most expensive item was the plate of sautéed mushrooms. The price of the bottle of water was 1500 liras, whereas the bottle of wine was 1000 liras.

"The wine is cheaper than the water, so we must be in Italy." I said. We laughed.

From Italy, we drove to Switzerland. After we slept over a night in Geneva, I called for a cab and asked him to take us to the village Anières-près-Genève. The taxi dropped us off in front of the open wrought-iron gate of the Central ORT Institute. On that warm cloudless day, the door to the guardhouse stood wide open. We walked through the gate, pausing at the guardhouse. The caretaker stepped out to meet us,

"*Bonjour Monsieur-Dame*, may I help you?"

"*Bonjour,* I went to school here during the inaugural year, and I would like to see the place again after about thirty three years. I live in America now, and I'm visiting with my wife and daughter."

"*Bienvenu,*" he said politely. "It is an honor to meet a student from the inaugural class. I'd be delighted to show you around."

He then accompanied us to the front door of the building. He walked slowly the thirty yards or so to the front entrance of the building, apparently realizing that I was trying to look around and take in all of the sights. Except for normal aging, the building and the surrounding area were the same as I'd left them in 1949.

"There is little change," I remarked. "I remember it well."

"The building has not changed," he explained, "but there are no more classes held here. It is now a dormitory for foreign students. The students study in various colleges in Geneva." He then continued, "Since you were in the inaugural class, you might remember *Monsieur* Vittorio Pavoncelli."

"I certainly do. We shared a room. There were three of us from Italy. How do you know his name? How is he?"

"Unfortunately, *Monsieur* Pavoncelli died," he stated sadly. "I know of him, because after his graduation he stayed on and worked at the institute. That was before I was hired. I don't remember the cause of his death, but I was sad to hear it. He must have died a young man."

We walked up the steps and entered the building. I immediately recognized the mosaic ORT insignia in the terrazzo floor in the entry hall. I looked around the empty building and saw a student descending the staircase. He explained he was from some country in Africa, and ORT was providing him with an education and room and board.

We left the ORT Institute and made our way to the French border. The booth at the border had changed to a modern, concrete structure. We walked into the little store near the border where I had once purchased cigarettes and razorblades. I immediately recognized the modernized store. I looked around and bought a chocolate bar.

We enjoyed the rest of our European travel, but it lacked the personal and emotional resonance of Israel, Italy, and Geneva. After touring Luxemburg, Belgium and France, we turned in our rental car at Orly Airport in Paris. We'd logged over five thousand kilometers on the car odometer during our journey.

CHAPTER 33

OUR OWN BUSINESS

I'D always dreamed of starting my own business and of being my own boss. I equated that with financial independence, a high priority throughout my adult life because of my early struggles. During my career, I'd selected employment and changed jobs with that objective in mind. I believe that most individuals can and must take responsibility for his or her economic and financial status. Annette and I raised our children to understand the importance of financial self-sufficiency. I also believe that our schools fail to offer enough information or instruction on the subject of economic independence.

One can argue that trade schools teach a trade and colleges teach a profession to enable the graduate to earn a living. One can even obtain a degree in finance, but the emphasis is on specific technical skills. Then there are colleges that focus on a liberal arts education, which aids us in the area of human enlightenment and enrichment.

I believe that the importance of making a living should be taught in our high schools.

During my tenure at Hughes, Annette and I often discussed our desire to start our own business. We knew that our dream would be difficult to achieve if the business was related to spacecraft. On the other hand, we thought it might actually be feasible to consider a business dealing with software, although we didn't know how to go about it. Despite our combined technical expertise, we needed to connect with potential clients who knew our reputations and would be willing to trust us with a contract. During this timeframe, Annette worked at TRW in the area of software quality assurance.

As she attended a symposium on software quality assurance, a man approached her.

"Are you by any chance related to Bob Frimtzis?" he asked after noticing her name tag.

"He is my husband," she replied.

"I'm Sam Goldstein." He pointed to his nametag. "I work at Hughes in the software area and know Bob well." Hughes needs a quality assurance plan for our project. Could you write such a document?"

"Certainly," she said. "In fact I'm currently doing this type of work at TRW."

The next day Sam spoke to me, and I reassured him that Annette was capable of doing the job. This resulted in our first contract for $12,000. Annette wrote that document while she worked full time at TRW. That was the beginning of RFA, which stood for R-*obert*, F-*rimtzis*, A-*nnette*.

While at TRW, Annette interfaced with an Air Force captain involved in software quality assurance (QA). When the captain retired from the Air Force, he joined a small, company called OAO. Designated 8A (minority owned), it allowed the company to obtain government contracts with little or no competition. When Annette was ready to leave TRW, she contacted the captain who referred her to a retired colonel named Pete, the head of the Los Angeles office of OAO. He offered her a job, which she accepted. Soon after Pete resigned from OAO and joined Rockwell International as a director of logistics. In his new position, he needed help with software, so he offered Annette a small contract to evaluate the software being developed for his group by another software organization within Rockwell.

The value of the original contract was $75,000. When the contract ended, I negotiated additional new contracts.

Eventually, the total value of the Rockwell contracts was on the order of $1.5 million. To execute the contractual obligations, Annette hired programmers.

I generated the proposals, establishing the hourly rates for the programmers, Annette and myself, and the overhead and fees. I had to establish a set of accounts required for government contracts. I felt uncomfortable negotiating contracts with Rockwell while I worked for TRW. I was particularly concerned that I might encounter some Air Force personnel whom I knew as an employee at TRW.

At the time, I was impatiently waiting to turn fifty-five so that I could retire from TRW and start working full time in our own business. I felt that we were losing out monetarily because I could not devote time to RFA. I took early retirement from TRW the moment I became eligible.

I rented office space on Hawthorne Boulevard in Torrance, designed our offices, and began construction. We hired a secretary as well as additional programmers and engineers. Annette took care of the technical issues at Rockwell, while I ran the business.

After the Rockwell contract was over, we proposed a new statement of work and negotiated a contract with Northrop Aviation. Annette knew an engineer in the logistics area at Northrop, whom she'd met at TRW. Assigned to the project office of a logistics software development activity, he approached Annette when his project ran into trouble and he needed a software subcontractor. Consequently, we bid on the project and received the subcontract.

I initially negotiated a $1 million contract. Later, we negotiated an additional $1.5 million contract. The software was associated with the Minuteman Missile Program. When the Minuteman Missile hardware got into trouble, the Air Force stopped payment to Northrop, who in turn stopped paying us. When I inquired about the non-payment, Northrop implied there were some irregularities with the time cards of our employees, and that our charges were in question.

Northrop owed us $365,000. It took us a lot of effort and haggling. Within about six months, they finally paid us the majority of the money owed us. While Northrop was not paying us, we had to meet our payroll of sixteen engineers and a secretary. It took an additional year and a letter from an attorney before Northrop paid us the remaining money.

As soon as I retired from TRW and could work full time at RFA, I bought a Porsche. During negotiations, I had difficulty justifying it as part of RFA overhead, although I did use the car for business. We worked very long hours, but Annette and I were extremely happy to have our own business.

After six months at Northrop, our employees informed us that the software design pursued by Northrop would not meet Government specification requirements. Annette pointed out that fact to Northrop program management. She was told to continue the development as directed by Northrop. Later, testing of the software revealed that it would not meet the requirement of running in real time.

Northrop created a special team of technical people, "a red team," to make quick modifications that would improve the software running time. Three RFA personnel were on the red team. After concentrated effort, they managed to reduce the running time from twenty-fours to three hours. The Air Force still refused to accept the software.

At that time, I prepared and presented an unsolicited proposal to redo from scratch the software for the test case in four weeks and for $50,000, knowing full well, that it would cost us more. If the RFA new test software worked and ran in real time, I told Northrop that for $1 million, RFA would provide them with a completely new software program. I received verbal approval to proceed from the Northrop program manager.

We hired a PhD, an expert in relational databases, to

assist us with the design. After four weeks, we ran our test case in fifteen minutes on a personal computer (pc). Northrop declined to witness the running of our program, so we invited engineers from the Aerospace Corporation to come to verify our success. Several months passed before RFA received the $50,000 promised from Northrop.

We learned that the Air Force planned to discard the Northrop software after having spent thirty million dollars. We approached the Air Force Colonel in charge of the Northrop program. I made a presentation, proposing that RFA build a new program for $1 million. The colonel passed, not willing to admit that a terrible mistake had happened on his watch. After that episode, we decided to develop our own logistics analysis program based on a MIL Spec (Military Specification) and sell it directly to the users.

To develop a program based on a government specification and to have it validated by the government proved to be a huge undertaking. We hired a software programmer and a friend of our daughter Laurie. Along with a few other programmers, we managed to accomplish the task in about a year.

Selling the program we called LISA for Logistics Interactive Support Analysis, was even harder. Despite no sales experience and no sales personnel, we sold several programs. LISA was a superior program compared to what the competition offered. However, the competing companies were well established. They had cornered the market.

Later the government changed the requirements specification for the Logistics Support Analysis (LSA) Program. The new spec required that the LSA use a relational database. We discarded LISA and started from scratch, designing and programming a new software entity. Even with our knowledge of the Informix relational database program, it took us another year to develop the new version of LISA, but our program didn't pass the government's validation process. After several attempts, we determined that the government's program used to validate contractors' programs contained an error. We pointed out their error. They agreed, apologized, and subsequently validated LISA.

CHAPTER 34

FINAL THOUGHTS AND PERSONAL REFLECTIONS

KOSOVO -I was horrified, as I watched on television the endless lines of refugees trying to escape their bomb ravaged villages and towns during the war in Kosovo in the late 1990s. The sight of these people in such dire circumstances brought back painful memories of the desperate days of our evacuation from Beltz.

Many years after my personal ordeal, the war in Kosovo reawakened the nightmares of my past, causing me many sleepless nights. The flames of World War II had left a smoldering coal deep in my soul, one that the passage of time would never fully extinguish. I was shocked that events in Kosovo affected me so profoundly.

I thought back to a time fifty years earlier, and I couldn't help but draw parallels with the refugees of Kosovo. I also noted the differences. Jewish refugees during World War II were refused admission to the countries of the world, causing millions of needless deaths. Regardless of the reasoning of these various countries, including the United States for several years, hindsight has provided us with a lesson about tolerance and intolerance – a lesson that, more than fifty years after the attempted annihilation of the Jewish people still must be learned, over and over again.

As a nation, we viewed the spectacle of war on our televisions in vivid Technicolor as events in Kosovo unfolded. The painful lessons learned from World War II and the Holocaust prompted a more humane and more sensitive response to the fleeing refugees of Kosovo.

NATO, the United Nations, British, and American armed forces came to the rescue of the afflicted and persecuted in Kosovo. Fortunately, the world did not wait for years after the war ended to accept the surviving refugees. The nations of the world did not stand idly by while millions perished.

Mama -The principles and standards I learned from Mama were primarily to be considerate toward others and to live within my means. The latter, an accounting principle, is a lesson that Papa, an accountant, should have taught me. Mama was often too considerate of others, at times to her own detriment.

Mama did not always agree with Papa's disciplinary actions. She suffered to see me punished or restricted. She was a much more forgiving person, and she considered Papa's disciplinary methods inappropriate, excessive, and sometimes cruel, which resulted in friction between her and my father. Being an only child, she was constantly protective of me and concerned with my health and safety. Her influence and Papa's coalesced to shape me into the man I became as I matured.

Thinking back, I realize that I was no angel as a boy. In fact, I was a tough, wild kid, hard to handle and discipline. I resented the restrictions imposed on me, and refused to obey them at times, resulting predictably in punishment. My misbehavior was proof of my rebelliousness and my tendency not to follow orders.

"I can't keep up with you and I'm worried you might get hurt," Mama used to plead with me. "Wait till Papa comes home!" she often threatened me and yet, many times she said nothing to him for fear that he would punish me. "I wish you should only have children like you," she would frequently say, implying that only then would I realize how bad I was and how tough I was to handle.

During the hungry war years, she shared her food with me. She was the most loving, wonderful and dedicated mother a son could have had. She devoted her life to me, and later to my family.

"Annette, I love you as if you were my own daughter," she often told my wife. "I cannot think of you as a daughter-in-law."

Perhaps it was because she did not have much of a life or love with my father that she lived vicariously through us. We were friends, not simply mother and son, and for that blessing, I will always be grateful.

She lived a long but a very difficult life, and she cared little about possessions. Annette and I had difficulties convincing her she needed nicer clothing. She often returned gifts that we bought for her.

"I don't need it," she would say. Actually, she said, "I don't need'em." She liked to be independent. Practically until the very end, she lived alone in her own apartment.

For a few years, she lived with us in Palos Verdes and helped take care of our children when they were very young. I believe that the only pleasure she had was related to my family and me. She died at the age of ninety-two on April 8, 1998. During the final decade of her life, she endured a lot of pain from arthritis, yet Mama's heart and blood pressure were normal and she took few medications.

Her death was a severe blow to me. I still miss her and often dream that we're together.

My Children -I love my children, and I'm very proud of them and their accomplishments. Three have earned the title "Dr." in front of their names, and the fourth is a mechanical engineer like her mother. Bruce, the oldest, and Valerie, the youngest, are optometrists. Steven is a dentist, and Laurie is the engineer.

Anyone who has raised children knows that it's no easy task. Annette and I stressed the importance of education to them, yet guided them to pursue and bring to fruition their own dreams and aspirations. When they were in college, we could not afford to pay the full tuition for each of them. At one time, we had two in undergraduate school and two in graduate school. We urged them to select the college of their choice, and we promised to pay half their tuition. I wanted to make sure they felt the need to get the education. In reality, Annette and I contributed to more than half their expenses.

We stressed the need to attend college to learn a profession and a stable living for themselves and their families. All four of my children knew how hard I had to work to get my college education. As parents, Annette and I derive great pleasure from their successful lives.

All four went to University of California in San Diego, UCSD. Each spent the first year in dormitories on campus.

Upon graduation from UCSD, Bruce enrolled and graduated four years later from Pacific University Optometry School in Forest Grove, Oregon. Steven graduated from Tufts University College of Dentistry in Boston, Massachusetts. Laurie transferred from UCSD to California State University, Long Beach, and graduated with a degree in mechanical engineering. After her bachelor's degree in biology from California State University, Long Beach, Valerie graduated from Southern California College of Optometry in Fullerton, California.

My wife and I also adore our grandchildren.

Boria -My father's mother had a sister who lived in Ataki on the River Dniester. She and her husband had five sons. Two lived in the United States, and one in France. Only Boria and Lazar lived in Ataki. Before the war in the 1930s, I recall hearing Mama saying that Boria was "sitting," which implied he "sat" in jail for communist activities outlawed under Romanian rule.

In the 1990s, Lazar, the youngest brother, finally managed to immigrate to America. He and Lena, their daughter, her husband, and their two children settled in Fair Lawn, New Jersey. On one occasion, I visited them. Matusia, who lived nearby in Wycoff, New Jersey, came to see me. He brought a video tape he'd received from his brother Boria who lived in Paris at the time.

He put the tape in the VCR, and we watched in amazement a parade celebrating the 50th anniversary of the liberation of Paris from the Nazis. Boria was the man of honor during the parade.

The procession included Mitterand, the President of France, and Chirac, the Mayor of Paris at the time and later the President of France. They all shook hands, embraced, and kissed Boria on both cheeks. After the video concluded, Lazar showed us a book written in French by Boria. Since then I purchased the book and read it. The title, *"Testament"- Apres 45 ans de silence, le chef militaire des FTP-MOI de Paris parle....* translates into English as, "Testament" – After 45 years of silence the military chief of the Resistance responsible for Paris speaks." It was published in 1989. He had changed his name to Boris Holban, since there was a price on his head. The book contains photos taken when he ran the Resistance while France was under the German occupation.

Boria described being released from jail in Romania and his departure to Spain to fight the Franco Nazi regime, but he never reached Spain. In Paris when Germany invaded France, he joined the French army to fight the German invaders. France fell three weeks later. He and his brother Liova became prisoners of war. Liova was freed toward the end of the war. Boria, on the other hand, escaped and joined the French Resistance. Several months later, Francois Mitterrand and Jacques Chirac escaped via the same route. The men were in prison together.

Responsible for Resistance activities in Paris, he details the various missions undertaken against the Nazis. The list of the combatants contains a large percentage of Jews, who fought with him in the Resistance. He also writes that all five brothers fought the Germans in various parts of the world, and they all survived. Mosia and Matusia served in the American Army, Liova and Boria in the French army, and Lazar in the Red Army.

After the liberation of Paris, Boria became a major in the French Army. He then returned to Romania, which was under the communist regime, and became a general in the Romanian Army. Years later, when Ciaushescu became president of Romania, Boria realized that as a Jew he had no future there. He left under the pretense of visiting his brothers in America. After seeing them, he made his way back to France. In Paris, the French government bestowed on him the highest medal of honor, the *Chevalier d'Honneur*. They also provided him an apartment, and a retirement salary. He lived there for many years. In 2004, he died at the age of about ninety-seven.

A few years earlier, he and Liova's son Jean Claude visited Matusia and Lazar in Fair Lawn. I was invited to join the reunion. I'd been amazed by Boria's vitality. At ninety-four, his mind remained as clear as that of a young man. Not only did he remember me, but he also brought two photos of me as a boy about six and eight. Those are the only pictures I have of myself at that age, since our family mementos were destroyed in the fire that claimed my family's home in Beltz when the Nazis invaded. The story of his life is utterly fascinating. I am glad he was a part of my life when I was a youngster, as well as the last time during the Thanksgiving weekend that we spent together, reminiscing about the old days, and singing Russian songs.

The 9/11 Attack -This terrorist attack on the United States left a terrible impression on me and brought back memories of World War II. I watched the horrifying scenes of death and destruction. The collapse of the buildings in New York and above all the masses of people running away from the smoke and fire made me relive the scenes of those unfortunates. It reminded me of the Beltz inferno when my family fled the bombs that destroyed our burning neighborhood when I was a ten-year-old boy, and of spending the night watching the fires from the town's outskirts. I remembered my terror, and I immediately shared the awful fear of the thousands of New Yorkers running, pursued by the smoke and soot shown on television.

Which other buildings and areas would be hit next – the White House? Is this a war on America? Yes, I concluded, we are at war. I immediately thought that this attack was worse than Pearl Harbor, because then, the attack had been perpetrated against the military and by a country intent on war. This time, the attack was against civilian population by an invisible enemy.

We're now fighting a war on our own territory where our innocent citizens are being killed. No longer is America a country that wages wars only overseas. That was a huge distinction between us, Europe, and the other nations of the world. We have lost that advantage, and with it our innocence.

From that moment on, our whole lifestyle has changed. I witnessed the kind of living that includes caution and fear in daily life when I visited Israel. We are worried that someone may want to hurt us in our streets, homes, airplanes, theaters, or businesses, when we least expect it. Like most Americans, I never expected to live with the threat of an attack. We've witnessed a profound change in our national circumstances. Even though I watched some of our embassies attacked in Beirut and Africa I never thought we would be attacked on our soil.

My Surgery -Soon after we moved back to San Diego I joined the Fairbanks Ranch Country Club and started playing golf fairly regularly. As long as we had the business, I managed to play a couple of times a week. When we closed RFA, I played at least three times a week and sometimes on Sundays with Annette.

On June 18, 1997, I went to play golf. I told my golfing partners that my heart was racing. I assumed the problem would go away soon. One of my golfing buddies was a physician, who insisted I not golf and see a doctor instead. It turned out I had an episode of atrial fibrillation requiring cardio version to stabilize my heartbeat. The cardiologists thought that the inhalers prescribed by my pulmonary doctor for asthma had induced my irregular pulse.

Meantime, I had an echocardiogram, which showed the start of stenosis of the aortic valve. The cardiologist told me the valve might require eventual replacement. By 2003, I experienced distress while exercising. Additional tests indicated that while there was no emergency, I should simply plan on surgery to replace the valve.

I contemplated this serious operation with a certain amount of anxiety. After all, not everyone survives open-heart surgery. My mental outlook was rather grim, but I realized I had no choice. I felt helpless and vulnerable. I had no control over the situation or its outcome. Yet I didn't want to give up hope. I looked back and reviewed my entire life and thought: I'm satisfied with my life, but not ready or willing to call it complete and say good-bye. I'd like to go on living. I decided to have it done.

On October 30, 2003, I successfully had surgery, and after five days in the hospital, I came home and started the recuperation period. My body and mind underwent a traumatic experience. I believe I now have a new lease on life. I'm pretty much back to normal. I play golf, exercise, and travel. This episode was the most serious and scary since the war.

Immigration –It will not surprise anyone, I suspect, that being an immigrant in America who lived through enormous difficulties and had to endanger my life to become eligible to apply for immigration, I possess strong opinions on the subject of immigration. I believe that immigration is necessary for America to remain strong, productive, inventive, and innovative in science, medicine and, technology, and a beacon of freedom throughout the world. Immigration also provides us with a rich social, moral, and religious mix, which leads to constitutionally guaranteed rights and liberties for all U.S. citizens.

The trend for the past several years, however, disturbs me. Too many people have entered and are still entering our country illegally, and the majority of them do not become Americans. Those who want to enter legally must wait for years.

Teaching the newly arrived in their native language encourages them not to learn English. I believe this policy generates and perpetuates low-echelon employment and no contributions to advances in any scientific endeavors. Many of these people live in America as foreigners, their allegiance to their native countries. America's history as an integrated melting pot, which is what it should remain, is instead a splintered society.

English is no longer the language of our land. I don't mean to imply that immigrants should forego their language and culture. That is what enriches us as a nation, but we now see large masses of people demonstrating under foreign flags. This is especially dangerous after 9/11, when we discovered just how many people wish to enter our country with the sole intent of doing us harm. Open borders pose a very real threat and make us easy prey for terrorists and drug traffickers. It does not make sense to search for terrorists in Afghanistan and Iraq at the expense of the lives of our young, courageous soldiers while leaving our borders open and unguarded.

Our government is responsible for our security. I urge our

legislators to take control of our borders and allow admission to our country only those legal immigrants who want to become citizens and integrate into our society, and who do not pose security risks to our citizens and institutions. Providing illegal inhabitants free schooling, medical care, and other social services when they do not pay taxes is unfair to the law-abiding taxpayer, bankrupts our coffers, and encourages a larger influx of illegal residents. Not giving them these services is morally wrong. In many locations across America, citizens and noncitizens with divided national and cultural loyalties constitute a danger to our society as we know it.

In Closing -In recent years, some of the most pleasurable times are when our family has gathered for holidays or family functions. It has been a tradition that the whole family, including Annette's brother Arthur, his wife Anita, their son Jason, his partner John, and sometimes friends, gather to celebrate the Passover Seder. Passover is a happy, historic holiday. It commemorates the exodus of the Jews from Egypt where they were slaves. Everyone in the family is nicely dressed and in a festive mood, ready to celebrate and partake of the special Passover foods and drinks. The brightly lit house focuses on the beautifully decorated Passover table with a white tablecloth, china, crystal, silverware, candles, Elijah's cup, and matzos. To accommodate everyone for the Passover *seder*, we add one and sometimes two long tables and additional chairs to our circular table, which normally seats ten people in our dining room.

After conversation, "noshes" (snacks) and drinks at the family room bar, we all sit down at the table where my two sons usually flank me. Even though we don't follow all the rituals, each of us in our seated order reads a passage from the *"Haggadah"* (the Passover Book), which reminds those gathered of the times when the Jews were in slavery, and how God saved them by punishing the Egyptians until Pharaoh permitted them to leave. Everybody has seen the movie about Moses.

Usually, Arthur, followed by Bruce and sometimes Steven, are impatient for the food and start kibitzing and joking before we finish reading.

"Knock it off guys! We're almost ready for the dinner," I often say in good humor.

"When are we going to finish? I'm starved," Arthur might respond, trying to look serious.

"You can't be hungry," I always remind him, "not after the noshing, all the chopped liver and drinks you just had at the bar."

"Grandma Rae ate most of the chopped liver," is the usual response from everyone in unison. She loved chopped liver.

"Okay, who is going to read the four questions? Who is the youngest?" I ask when we reach the page.

Jason used to be the youngest, and he would read them. Sometimes, he suggested that Valerie should be the reader. Now, we have our grandchildren, Hannah and Sarah, read the four questions.

It has been interesting as well as nostalgic for me to see the changes in our family with the passage of time. The changes are most obvious during Passover holiday, when we all sit around the table. Some have made me very happy, whereas others have made me sad. It doesn't seem that long ago when our children were not married, and my parents and Annette's joined us at the *seder* table. Then our fathers, first Annette's, then mine, passed away.

Our son Steve was the first to marry Mirta and adopt Danny, her son from a previous marriage. The family around the *seder* table grew after Steve and Mirta had Hannah and Sarah, which made me proud and happy. Unfortunately, my mother passed away in 1998, followed by Annette's mother in 2001.

In February 2000, our daughter Laurie married Mark. Our family and consequently the celebrants around the Passover table further enlarged after Laurie gave birth to twin girls, Sophie and Isabella. I'm happy to say that our family has further enlarged. On May 8, 2005, our youngest daughter Valerie married Michael. Our family and my happiness grew when Alexander was born to Valerie and Michael on September 15, 2007.

I'm a very happy man when I sit at the Passover table and count my blessings. I look with great satisfaction and pleasure at my family, our beautiful home, and the environment in which Annette and I live. I can truly say, "I have arrived. I have fulfilled my goals, and then some." Never in my wildest dreams did I think that I would achieve such happiness. I am blessed with a wonderful wife, remarkable children and grandchildren, loyal friends, and I play golf – too bad I don't play better!

I have come a long way from the boy, Buma, who fled Beltz, the same boy who endured the terrors of war, near starvation, persecution, and illegal border crossings in search of freedom and the American dream. Mine is a happy story, and it could have happened only in America.

I'm grateful to my parents for my upbringing. From a very young age, they instilled in me a proper moral code, the importance of education, and to do my very best in all of my endeavors. Anything less was not acceptable. I also appreciate their sacrifices, leading me, protecting me, and sharing their meager food with me during the war years. I'm also grateful to America for opening her doors to me and providing the opportunities to succeed.

I've learned from my own experience: "Persist and you shall succeed, do nothing and you shall lose." I don't know if it's a bona fide slogan, but it certainly worked for me. I also think, if I could do it with many strikes against me, anybody can.

Now, I wish success, good fortune, and happiness to my children and their children. As for my loving wife and myself, I wish us good health and a long life so that we can enjoy all our many blessings.

EPILOGUE

ON February 2, 2007, Annette and I celebrated our golden wedding anniversary by attending Mussorgsky's *Boris Godunov* as a commemoration of our first date at the Met in 1954.

The next evening we threw a black tie party at our country club for about eighty guests, including our children, grand-children, a few cousins, and many friends. To our delight, Annette's matron of honor, and my best man were also there. After cocktails and hors d'oeuvres, the guests were treated to a sit-down supper and dancing. Annette and I could not have been happier as we shared our celebration of fifty years of married life.

Not in my wildest dreams did I expect to reach this happy occasion in my life, considering my saga from the tender age of ten. Yet, here I am, a very happy person who against all odds reached happiness and the American dream.